WHAT THEY MIGHT HAVE SAID ABOUT DAVID CALDWELL

He spoke of his respect for the Covenant his people had with the King before Alamance, but he told those same people, that Covenant had been broken by the King after Lexington. Is there no honor? **GOVERNOR WILLIAM TRYON**

Men like Caldwell provided me with the friendly field at Guilford Court House. They were my eyes and ears and my rallying cry when battle was near. We would have been hard pressed if such men were Tories.
GENERAL NATHANAEL GREENE

I knew the source of sedition. I gave him fame when I put the price of £200 on his sanctimonious head. He did more damage to the King's cause in the South from his two pulpits than any General in Greene's command. **LORD CHARLES CORNWALLIS**

If I had spent more time within his influence as a young man, I might have heard the call to ministry that my mother thought she heard for me. Imagine "Old Hickory" in the pulpit.
GENERAL ANDREW JACKSON

When friendship is based on the interaction of ideas shared between persons who truly respect each other, it is like the mix of ambrosia. In our lives, politics and theology did mix as should faith and common responsibility.

GOVERNOR ALEXANDER MARTIN

My Southern Tour was intended to shape for the people the role of what a President should be just as, for over sixty years, his pastorate defined the place that a man of God must assume for a congregation.

PRESIDENT GEORGE WASHINGTON

I shared with him my approach to the afflictions of the body and of the mind. I was allowed to help ease the burden for him of the tragic loss of the brilliant minds of two of his children while advancing my study of the care and treatment of mental illnesses. His grasp of theological understanding guided me to the order of my own beliefs.

DR. BENJAMIN RUSH

He accepted me as a student after he had stopped operating his Academy. I enjoyed the full attention of the finest teacher of his age and I thank God that my nature was such that I was a fertile soil awaiting seed. All my life I was inspired to achieve because he had implanted so much of himself in me. **GOVERNOR JOHN MOTLEY MOREHEAD**

IF THE LORD IS WILLING AND THE CREEK STAYS LOW

NOVEL

Based on the Life and Influence of
Rev. David Caldwell and Rachel Craighead Caldwell

For Judy
Thanks for your information and interest
Charles Rodenbough

By CHARLES D. RODENBOUGH

Cover: Photographic copy of a portrait of Robert Caldwell, 1826, attributed to the Guilford limner, found in the Greensboro Historical Museum archives. The picture has been colored based on examination of three similar images in the GHM attributed to the same painter. Cover design by Kit Rodenbough @Design Archives, Greensboro, NC.

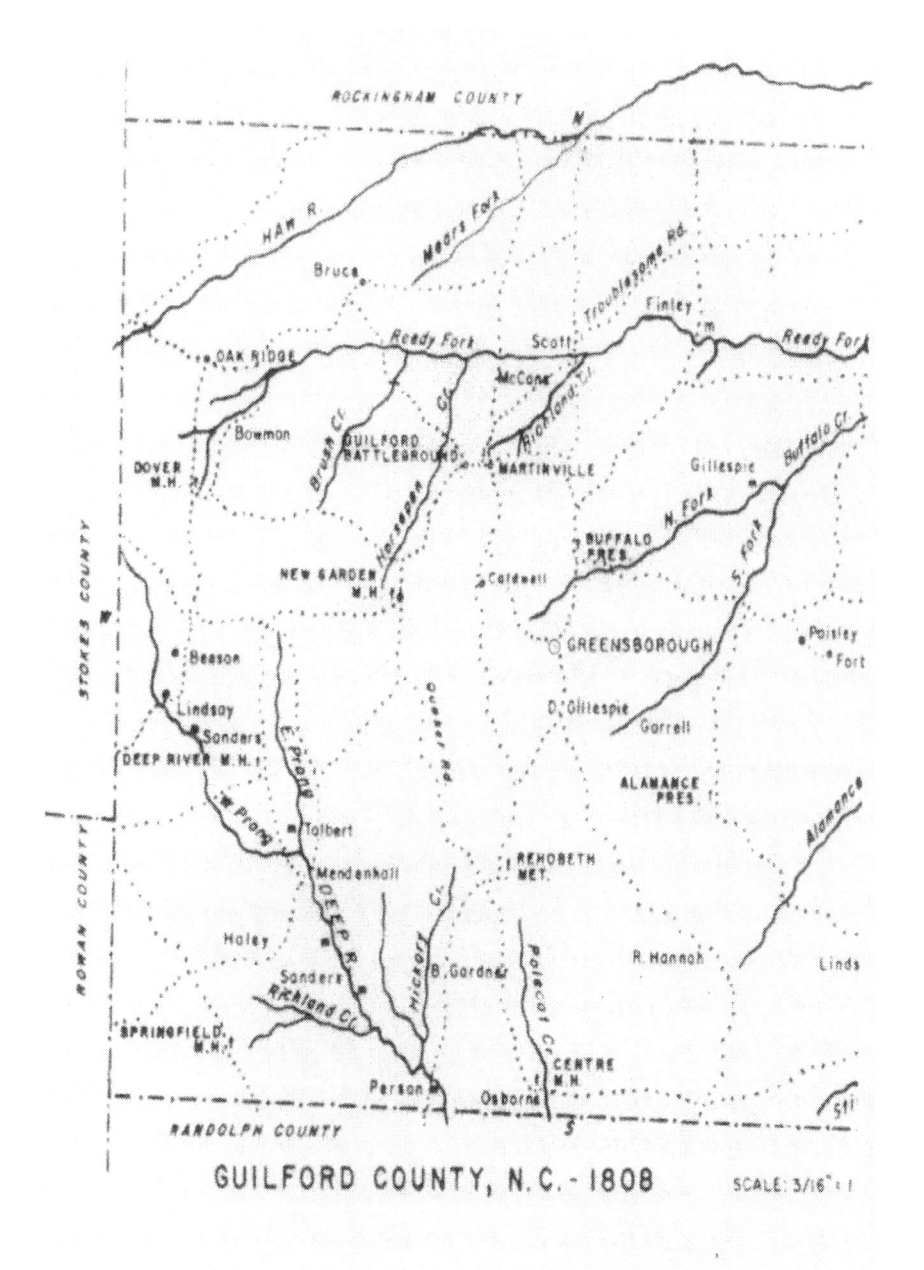

GUILFORD COUNTY, N.C. - 1808   SCALE: 3/16" : 1

This 1808 map shows Guilford County with Greensborough proposed. Note that "Caldwell" is in the center of the map and shows the relationship to the locations mentioned in this book.

To all the teachers who encouraged me to find joy in learning and in memory of my parents: Stanley Leigh and Katherine Boone Rodenbough

CONTENTS

PREFACE

David and Rachel Caldwell have been considered an important couple in the early history of Piedmont North Carolina. Within Presbyterian church history, they represent a popular testimony of the influence of that denomination in the early American story. Much of what continues to be retold about them comes from their first biographer, Rev. Eli W. Caruthers, who succeeded Caldwell at Buffalo and Alamance Presbyterian Churches. Caruthers was constructing his biography of David Caldwell at the same time he was preparing a record of the reminiscences of the remaining veterans of the Revolution. As time has passed, only bits and pieces of information have been discovered to place upon these biographic bones from Caruthers. There is no archival collection of letters or diaries that has yet come to light. While honored to this day, in the telling of their story, David and Rachel have lacked sufficient dimension.

I began by writing another academic Caldwell history only to discover I was similarly short of grasping the human emotion, the struggle of these lives, to be matched against their accomplishments. In order to capture their qualities, the many dimensions of their influence on other lives, the essence of their struggle which for nearly one hundred years were the lives of David and Rachel Caldwell, I decided I might gain perspective if I wrote the story as a historical novel. This century of the lives of David and Rachel Caldwell also incorporated the formative years of a new nation with an experimental

--

form of government. Some events known to have had deep impact on the couple's lives had never been examined. In spite of the remote world of the Carolina frontier, these people had important associations that were known but only marginally had been interpreted as influences.

Douglas Smith, in his preface to The Pearl, says that, "Biography is impossible without the life-giving breath of fiction."[1] He also quotes the literary biographer Richard Holmes, "That ordinariness, and that family intimacy, is the very thing that the biographer – as opposed to the novelist – cannot share or recreate."[2]

I believed that the lives of David and Rachel Caldwell lay like a matrix for the story of the frontier mid–Atlantic region. Their story had been limited to the ecclesiastical and educational influences of their lives to the exclusion of their influence in areas of medicine, creation of constitutional government, political evolution, the issue of slavery, even the debate over church-state relationships. How indeed had they gone from colonials loyal to a king, to revolution, to restoration of community out of chaos? How had their Scots-Irish roots influenced their progress through New Side/Old Side debates, judgment in war and compassion in peace, Deism, and the Great

---

[1]. Douglas Smith, *The Pearl, A True Tale of Forbidden Love in Catherine the Great's Russia* (New Haven: Yale University Press, 2008), 8.

[2]. Richard Holmes, *Footsteps: Adventures of a Romantic Biographer* (New York, 1985), 120.

Awakening?

I have used this novel to develop the evolution of their story, the polity and theology of their church, their contribution to education, their emersion in the application of medicine and how it came to dominate their family, and the debates on political thought through an interplay with fellow Princeton men, Alexander Martin and Benjamin Rush. I have attempted to let these threads play between the pages to more closely reflect the full-blown depth of these lives and their unmistakable impact on the forging of our national identity.

There are no school ledgers extant so the importance of the classical academy comes through the individual biographies of a few graduates. Caldwell's pre-Revolution sermons and papers were burned by Cornwallis, except for two sermons, and few of his later works survived, perhaps by choice of his family. His ministerial record must be drawn more from the results of his dynamic influence on people in time and place. We know there was an important relationship between the Caldwells and Dr. Benjamin Rush but the written record is not there. We have proof that David Caldwell and Alexander Martin had a very close relationship from their early years at Princeton but I had to take their stories and wrap them together in order to recreate their debates and the evolution of their thoughts.

As a form, it was the novel that gave me such a latitude to let ideas foment, facts color, human nature respond, and theology underline. I have attempted to avoid contradicting facts where they were available. In the absence of facts, I have looked at other lives, other recorded incidents, to reflect what might have been. I have not wanted to throw all the facts at hand on a page and then fill in the gaps with guesses. I have looked at the flow of the story and the interplay of sources to let David and Rachel tell their story, in the context of an infinite God working His purpose out with faithful Christians seeking to recognize, and be instruments of, that purpose.

Finally, I have an incumbent responsibility to mention individuals who contributed significantly to this novel. My wife, Rev. Dr. Jean Rodenbough, with her masters in English and doctorate in divinity was perhaps the best editor this book could have had. My son, Dr. John Rodenbough, a neuro-psychologist, was especially perceptive when I needed insight into early treatment for mental illness and brain damage. Rev. Charles Howell gave me instructive advice on points of historical theology. Gary Brown spent hours in a detailed analysis of facts related to the lives of the Caldwells. Bill Moore, past Director of the Greensboro Historical Museum, Adrienne Byrd, curator David Caldwell Museum, and Josh Howard, research historian at the North Carolina Office of Archives and History were kind enough to review my book and provide me valuable critiques.

May the reader enjoy the story and feel an appreciation of the struggle of life and the impact of lives well and faithfully lived in any time and place.

Charles D. Rodenbough

April 2010

PROLOGUE

The manse was called Poplar Springs and it was a house of relative elegance within the Waxhaw settlement of what the English clergyman, Rev. Charles Woodmason, called "the most lowest vilest Crew breathing-Scots Irish Presbyterians from the North of Ireland." The Rev. William Richardson and his wife, Agnes, had occupied the house since he was called in 1759 as minister at the Old Waxhaw Presbyterian Meeting. Educated at the University of Glascow, Richardson was exalted by his back country parishioners. His literary evenings in his well lit library mingled narrow-minded "Pennsylvania Irish," who had migrated down the Great Wagon Road, with Scots-Irish Calvinists, who had come inland from Charleston. At his newly established academy, he offered training in Latin and Greek.

In contrast to her austere husband, prone as he was to frequent periods of fasting and prayer, Agnes Richardson was vivacious and demonstrated social graces out of place on this unforgiving frontier. As he aged, Richardson developed a personality that was described as morose and melancholy that some attributed to his Spartan diet and work habits and others saw as the result of a bitter disappointment that his attractive wife did not bear him any children. He persuaded his older sister, Mary, and her husband, Archibald Davie, with their family, to immigrate from Scotland to the Waxhaws so that he might have the broader nucleus of a large family.

July 20, 1771.

"Elder Morton, how handsome you look this morning." Agnes Richardson's sprightly greeting typically tilted the rigid bearing of most Calvinists including this one who was newly arrived from Ulster. "I have advised my husband of your impending visit and he awaits you in his study."

The gawking Scot doffed his broad-brimmed hat as he clomped across the threshold.

"You are welcome to go in to him and I will see that you are not interrupted."

They turned from each other and Elder Morton knocked softly and opened the door to the study.

"God! God! God!" With the booming voice of a bailiff, the Elder appealed to His Maker. As he continued with his cries, maids, Agnes Richardson, Archibald and Mary Davie appeared in quick succession, rushing into the open study. Before them Richardson knelt motionless, hands upraised in supplication, a bridle wrapped around his neck, rigid in the rigors of death. A scene out of the Inferno of Dante, there was a moment of loud silence, then as if on direction, an hysteric tantrum. Agnes rushed to her husband who seemed to teeter toward her. She recoiled. Archibald stepped in to reach for a pulse in clinic calmness. It was unnecessary. Everyone recognized death but of such parody as to be beyond easy comprehension. Elder Morton had indeed declared the hand of God but by what human means.

Time lost pertinence, overcome by shock. The women entered into an aria of weeping. Elder Morton had been cast adrift. Archibald Davie found himself the comfort to which his wife and sister-in-law turned for support.

"Maggie, tell Sam to go notify John Medley and have him contact the others of the Session." The little maid, herself almost immobilized by fear, turned in response to a directive and began to run. Until the arrival of others that had not experienced the moment of emotional discovery, a babel was the only description that could be made of the words that bubbled in that room. They were disjointed, terrified, incoherent.

John Medley, the Clerk of the Session of the Waxhaw congregation, was the first to interrupt the discord and start the easing of the atmosphere. "Come away. All of you, come away," was his first direction. They all backed slowly into the entryway as more officers of the congregation entered the house. Together the new arrivals eased the undone into seats in the parlor. The uncontrolled chaotic pressure began a palpable relief.

Later in the hour, the widow described for the sheriff the events of the morning. "For three or four years he has complained of his sickly constitution. I had urged him to restrict his activity but he refused to be confined to his bed. Others found him equally depressed but disparaging of any suggestion that he reduce his work. For a time, I adjusted to his demeanor until I noticed signs that his mind was fading. He became nearly deaf and his preaching lacked the sharpness that people had been accustomed to over the years. Then, about three months ago, he withdrew to the house claiming to be more sickly than others perceived. In the early morning of the 20th, Elder Means visited him, and I later was advised, purposely led him into a heated discussion to try to animate his general lethargy. Afterwards he had retired to the study and that was where Elder Morton found him several hours later."

"Madame, I am befuddled," commented the sheriff. "It appears that he was at prayers when he died." Then turning to John Medley he continued. "Were I in any other place, I would make a first assumption that this man had been murdered with the harness. But here in this house, it surely cannot have been.

"I cannot explain the presence of the bridle wrapped as it was but it cannot have been a weapon," said Medley, in an attitude of certainty. "It seems clear that Brother Richardson was at his devotions when visited by death. It was God's will. The hand of God rests on this place as none other.

"I would leave it at that were not there marks of ligature upon the neck. Conversely, I see not a single evidence of a struggle nor of resistance to an act of strangulation." The sheriff retired again to the study but as he passed Medley, he motioned for him to follow.

In the study, standing before the victim, he wondered, "These are strange circumstances for either a murder or a natural death. We have no obvious suspect and the victim is the most admired person of the community." Speaking to Medley he asked, "Do you have any reason to suspect any of the servants?"

"None at all," replied the Clerk.

"What of the immediate family or even of the members of the church community?"

"Again, nothing."

Without motive or suspect of foul play, the sheriff left, and without any charges, the common practice in the community proceeded as friends and family prepared the body for the wake and final burial.

Suspicion was a slow process initiated by comments as members of the Waxhaw congregation became participants at this point. First, it was casual references to the strange position of the body – remarkably respectable as at prayer but with the strange bridle. "What could that be there for?" The marks that indicated that somehow the harness could have been an instrument of death. "Why else could it have been there?" Gossip interacted with fresh yeast and the suspicions gathered form.

As the days passed, the abnormal curiosity about the devotional position of Rev. William Richardson that the sheriff observed the first morning, had become seditious murmurs of an unforgiving Calvinist community. What they had resented in the spirited charm of Agnes Richardson had become suspicion of an ungodly woman who had surely dispatched her sainted husband who could never have committed suicide. His unnatural death had to be the act of another's evil and the widow was the suspect. Over time, suspicion advanced to a more sinister level of embellishment and exaggeration; then Mrs. Richardson, before the year was out, married George Dunlap, a man of some considerable worth. The community spoke openly of a prima fascia case of murder against the widow. Congregation suspicion became community resentment that developed into mob hysteria.

Agnes was hauled into the graveyard one evening, to the grave of her first husband whose body was publically exhumed. Exposed to full view, Agnes was forced to undergo the archaic ordeal of touching the forehead of the corpse, on the theory that blood would flow from her fingers if she indeed had been the murderess. When no blood appeared, Archibald Davie, her brother-in-law, manically forced her hand down on the head of her dead husband, but to no avail. So repulsed by their own action, the assembled community turned with ridicule on those who had been the main influences on this farce.

Subsequent versions of this tragedy sought to vindicate the actions of a Calvinist mob but none denied the melancholy nature of Rev. Richardson or the "vapoury disorders" he had experienced from his youth. Melancholia!

CHAPTER ONE May 1771 Alamance Creek

The flap of the large, square tent of the Governor stood open, the lights from many torches identifying it as the command point of this expedition. I stepped through the entrance at the direction of the Governor's aide. Behind his camp table, William Tryon rose courteously from his chair. He was a small man with an oblong head resting above a pear-shaped body. His eyes were wide-spaced above a strong nose and a rather pursed mouth. I bowed and greeted the Governor, "Your Excellency."

Tryon acknowledged the greeting, "Preacher Caldwell, I welcome your visit." I was wearing a black frock coat and knee britches with a clerical collar and white stockings and always wore a broad-brimmed hat. At the time I was fifty years old. My self-image was of a pleasantly imposing man just over six feet and I attempted always to contradict the common description of a "blue stocking" Presbyterian. The Governor offered me a seat on an uncomfortable folding stool that positioned me awkwardly low to the Governor's table.

"I was impressed when I received the letter that you and your Presbyterian colleagues addressed to me not two years back," Tryon began, "along with the petition that you had sent to other Presbyterians in this colony. Can I assume that your attitude of loyalty to the King, and toward my administration on his behalf for North Carolina, remains as it was in the correspondence?"

"Your excellency has my abiding loyalty," I responded, "and in that spirit I have taken the liberty of appearing before you. The same forces of disaffection are arrayed against you at this moment and we are both aware that some individuals among them are Presbyterians. Indeed, some are active members even in my two congregations at Buffalo and Alamance."

"That has not escaped my notice," replied the Governor with a touch of sarcasm. He was cautious, not willing to hear any artifice.

"I will speak plainly, Governor," I began. "We Presbyterians are a people of the Covenant, a people of the law. But for us, a colonial law can become distant in its administration and local administrators of the law can take advantage of their circumstances to the detriment of the governed. Sometimes then in ignorance, the yeoman blames God, or the King, or the Governor for the ills delivered by the local administrator. He has difficulty qualifying his rebellion against a grievance. Most of those who stand against you are in that category of the misdirected."

"Ignorance cannot be justification for rebellion, Pastor Caldwell. Let me remind you that those whom you call administrators, have been appointed to their positions by me or by the King. They operate as extensions of our governance."

"Quite so, your Excellency. Here, however, on the

frontier of the colony, they are less under the supervision of the Crown, and more to the point, these less informed, more isolated citizens do not believe that grievances are being heard by the Government."

"Is that why this rabble has taken to ridicule of my person in calling my home a "palace" paid for at their expense – the 'Governor's Palace'? "

"Surely you understand that is a political exaggeration advanced by only the most belligerent among them. Most of these people will never see the Governor's house and they take pride in a well-conducted government properly housed."

The Governor seemed not persuaded. "I am afraid that you play too much the peacemaker, Pastor, and too easily would forgive sedition. You and I both are aware that your congregation is rank with Regulator sympathizers, if not with active Regulators. You yourself have been known to express very favorable opinions of the Regulator cause in spite of the objectivity that you now express. I have many friends who report regularly from your neighborhood. As Governor, I must maintain the peace of this colony. I cannot even consider grievances as long as people stand armed against me. Under these circumstances, the inevitability of bloodshed cannot be a stay to my actions."

"Would your Excellency at least consider these grievances that I have been asked to present to you by citizens of this county?" I rose and stepped forward presenting Tryon with a very carefully prepared list of complaints.   "Will you deliberate upon them before taking to the field against loyal subjects?"

Raising his voice slightly as I placed the pages before him, he responded, "Loyal people do not rebel against their King, sir. Out of my respect for you, I will review this document and respond in the morning after council. I will in turn give you opportunity to make a fair effort to gain the acceptance by the rabble of my terms."

"You do me a great personal honor, Governor, and I retire with respect for you and faithful support for my King."

"Properly expressed, Preacher.   By the way, tell your lawyer friend, Alexander Martin, who I am informed travels with you, that I consider that he has a public trust to exercise his office with fairness and propriety.   If he and the members of the King's bench are charging excessive fees for services, they should admit their guilt and return their overcharges.   He had the audacity of negotiating on my behalf with the Regulators in Salisbury in April, and scheduled for me a negotiation of their grievances, when he and his ilk were in fact the object of much of their grievance against court officials.   I will not tolerate such duplicity.   I hear it said now that he really favors the Regulators in their complaints.   By my soul, Preacher, he can't have it both ways.   He can't be in the pudding and eating it at the same time."

I thought it better that I keep my counsel at this point. Nothing I would have said would have been received favorably, so I took my leave.

As I returned to the camp of the Regulators, I rode casually through the damp woods, feeling the atmosphere that surrounded me but not alert, my mind fixed on concerns. An occasional limb tipped lightly with rain, brushed against my coat. It took a solid slap of such a drooping swag to redirect me to my surroundings.

I was only marginally encouraged that my meeting with the Governor might somehow avert a battle the next day. I understood implicitly the position of Governor Tryon. He would not negotiate or even entertain consideration of grievances, as long as he faced an armed citizenry. I had the strong impression that the Governor embraced this confrontation as the ultimate opportunity to overwhelm the nagging Regulator unrest, whose existence was an embarrassment. If he had seriously considered negotiation, the Governor would no doubt have raised the issue of the capture that morning of militia captains Walker and Ashe by a Regulator gang. At least that would acknowledge that each side had points at issue. Tryon was not looking for grounds for negotiation.

As I approached the camp on Alamance Creek, the stillness of the May evening was smothered by rowdy camp sounds – loud music, cheering, arguments, and drunken revelry. I was immediately depressed. Without command, without any discipline, there could be no hope for these people in a battle with the Colonial military. I took no delight in their unbending stubbornness, their refusal to see that their hatred of government was misdirected. They were being manipulated by domestic politics, by demagogues, agitators who sought power by exploiting ignorance. From the pulpit I had reminded them that they were people of the Covenant. Law was the security of the wise. God's Covenant protected the weak from the tyranny of the wicked.

By the next morning the news of the provocative capture of two officers of the Colonial militia had spread and was enough to convince some of the wavering Regulators to abandon their challenge of Tryon. The Scots-Irish that I knew remained stubborn in their conviction to a cause.

Riding into the glow of the camp fire, I found Alexander Martin, who had accompanied me to Alamance Creek that day. "Alex, the Governor will show no flexibility. He sees this as his opportunity. He will tolerate no effort on our part to mediate between the two positions, as he sees no legitimacy in the Regulator cause. It is as you said, based on your experience in trying to similarly negotiate after the confrontation at Salisbury."

Martin seemed to appreciate my disappointment. "As a King's attorney, I know that we must have law and order within this colony. I fear that only a substantial confrontation can restore the government and the courts to uphold the law. I have told you, and said publicly, I acknowledge my culpability in demanding excessive fees for legal services. I stand ready to repay anyone who claims that I have overcharged. To the extent that I contributed to the outbreak of this Regulator business, I am ready to make restitution."

"You, my friend, are naive. None of your mea culpas will influence this confrontation. If you have wronged any of your neighbors, as a Christian, you must give back and ask forgiveness of God and neighbor for your sin. As to the Governor, he sees you as playing both ends. He had a clever metaphor for you, suggesting that you and the court officers were in large measure responsible for the disaffection of the Regulators."

I laid the chastisement before him and he commented, as if to himself, "Our friends are in rebellion but they are wrong to believe they can defeat the government with arms, and we must stand and watch."

I then advised Thomas McQuiston, William Mebane, William Rankin, and Robert Thompson and some others, "The Governor has your petition. Please be sure that John Gillespie hears about it and Gilmer, Forbis, and Montgomery." These were the key members of my congregations that I knew to be on the field. "I have no doubt that the Governor will read the petition and he will have an answer in the morning before any action is taken. I cannot do more."

"Preacher Caldwell, you are the only one to whom he would listen. The Governor is against us and he means to destroy us," claimed McQuiston.

"No, Thomas," I said, "you are incorrect! The Governor means to maintain order and I believe he will. You have been wronged, but not by Governor Tryon, nor the Council, nor Parliament, nor the King. You are the victims of dishonest courts and lawyers and tax collectors, but they won't be in the field against you tomorrow. You will be fighting against your own government, your lawful militia. They will kill you not because you are right or wrong but because you are in rebellion."

Thompson replied, "What about the Stamp Act and the curse of the Granville District? Are not these fair grievances against the King?"

"Yes they are, but the one is a valid grievance of the eastern men of commerce and the other is the result of mismanagement outside the governance of the King. You are no merchantman and the Granville District needs to be under the King's governance in order to be fairly administered. You don't have an applicable grievance in either matter but you have been convinced to carry the other man's fight."

There was a pause and these men of Buffalo and Alamance might have glimpsed the reality of my advice, but not with sufficient enough personal conviction to turn their backs on the others who called themselves Regulators. They began to drift away aimlessly. As they did, a man rode into our midst who looked vaguely familiar. When he dismounted someone welcomed him as "Herman" and I knew instantly it must be Herman Husband, the pamphleteer.

"Preacher Caldwell, I do not feel you and I need

introductions as I am certain we were at least near–acquainted in Pennsylvania," he began with a soft but easy manner. "Our paths were so close. We may have met at any of George Whitefield's preaching points. And we are products of nearby Presbyterian Log Colleges."

I judged the man to be near my age and I had heard his name as frequently as he now claimed to have heard my own. "I have just come, sir, from a consultation with Governor Tryon and it may be no surprise that your name did come up in our exchange."

" 'Come up,' I suppose to be a euphemism for a loathsome characterization if not damnable." He smiled and I acknowledged his insight with a slight nod of my head. "I too consider myself something of a preacher but my platform of late has been the printed word. I find men of means, such as the Governor, fear the printed word almost more that the preached word. At least it has brought me more attention than I ever sought to draw to myself."

I was skeptical of his claim. I had the distinct impression that he relished the attention given to his several pamphlets defining the Regulator cause. "I only recently have read your tract, what was it titled, 'Shew Yourselves to be Freemen,' I believe. It is a shame that you just missed Alexander Martin, one of those lawyers to whom you assigned such censure. He is my good friend but I too have personally criticized his actions, and those of his fellow lawyers and court officials, as to the extortion of the poor farmer.

I believe he has come to see his responsibility and he professes to be willing to redeem his involvement."

"Oh, I too saw Alexander this evening and I am inclined to accept the idea that he would willingly make amends for his contribution to the extortion of the poorest among us. The question is, can we really expect such restitution from the system generally? I would that the Governor could see where we really direct our rage and back away from this armed confrontation."

I spoke in the greatest earnestness. "Husband, you are asking Tryon to place too fine a point on insurrection. The government, the law, the magistrates, are all part of the same structure. On the one hand it presents itself as the source of order, but when confronted, it becomes self protective as a system of control. Threaten the one and you threaten the whole."

"You are very accurate, preacher."

"I just tried to separate the grievances in negotiating with Tryon himself and he would have none of it. 'I will not negotiate while men stand in arms against my authority,' were his very words," I told him. "What will come to pass tomorrow will surely be folly but preacher or pamphleteer, we will be helpless observers."

"You and I are lonely voices in such circumstances," confessed Husband. "We seek to serve a common good but we are faced with such mutual recalcitrance that we have no room to maneuver. My life seems to be a constant conflict to raise the better nature of people in the face of rigid doctrine. You may know that I was raised an Anglican and in connection with my schooling at East Nottingham, I became a Presbyterian. Then I became associated with the Quaker Meeting. Finding great value in their personal relationship with God I was drawn to their more peaceful faith in the universal brotherhood of man."

"Herman, you are another who tilts with the angels. In my case, I find that two congregations, disparate in their views, keeps me alert to my personal theology. I must be consciously sensitive to the guiding of my flock, protective of God's will for them. Being a servant of God is a constant struggle but I am certain you and I will persevere even in the face of these uncertain times."

I took my leave and rode the five miles back to the Alamance Presbyterian Church community to pass the night. Rachel was there to greet me with our children, including Andrew who was yet suckling.

"Rachel, I fear the die is cast," I told her. "We can but pray that God's will be done and that our people might be spared injury or death. In the morning I will be on the field at sunrise to receive the answer of Governor Tryon. Then I will make a last, and I fear inevitably futile, attempt to prevent bloodshed. After that I will retire to await the carnage." Andrew awoke at that moment, fretful and demanding. While I played with his tiny fingers to try to divert a baby's cares, I thought how all my efforts today had been directed at diversion with people too childish to understand my message, too resolute in their purpose to consider other possibilities.

Just a few hours later, in the early morning mist, I rode back into the Regulator camp. Those able had begun to stir; others sprawled limp around the camp ground. There was no one charged to rally them into combat units. Instead they gathered as Quakers, or Presbyterians: as men of Sandy Creek or men of Centre Meeting. As the sun rose, Tryon dispatched his reply to the Regulator petition with directions that it be delivered to me as the only man worthy of an official reply. The Governor demanded withdrawal, surrender of arms and our ringleaders, and submission to the leniency of the King's representatives. He recognized no other issues as relevant. The insurgents had one hour to accept the terms and return to their homes. If they remained arrayed against him at that time, he would commence firing.

I then entreated with the Regulator clusters, finding most excited and unrealistic. They were more interested in frolicking and wrestling like children without cares. Older men tried to form them into fighting units in preparation but they had little interest. I, along with Martin and with two of the Regulators from my congregation, William Thompson and Robert Mateer, made several passes between the armies, facing complete intransigence in each. Finally, I rode out in front of the Regulators once again and urged, "Those of you who are not too committed to this cause should desist and quietly return to your homes. Those of you who are liable for acts against the Crown should submit immediately, without further resistance, and I pledge that with others, I will work with all my energy to obtain for you the best terms possible. You all need to wait until a more favorable moment to press your complaints. This day the government has the means on the field to defeat you and the Governor means to use that power. Please, go home."

I was not alone in my entreaties. Herman Husband had a very similar message which he too pressed on his friends among the Regulators. Twice I passed him riding among them.

On the last approach of our party to the Governor's line, with the hour about to turn, I was dumbfounded when Tryon refused to let Thompson and Mateer return to the Regulator lines. Surely he was confused because he knew Thompson had appeared on the field only as an observer and not as a committed rebel, and the Governor knew Mateer as a man he had used as a messenger to Alexander Martin only two months earlier. I could not believe he would take such an arbitrary and provocative action. Then I was startled even more as I saw Thompson break free and run for the Regulator side. "Please God, no!" I screamed. On Tryon's command, he was shot down just 50 yards in front of me and in view of each army. There would be no further appeal.

The Governor's final demand for surrender was met with the challenge "fire and be damned" from a Regulator hothead and others danced and mocked the militia. An old Scotsman cried out to me to "get out of the way!" When Tryon gave the order to commence firing, there was a hesitation on the part of the colonials. Rising in his stirrups, Tryon demanded, "Fire! Fire on them or on me." I barely reached safety.

For two hours the military units, about a thousand men and artillery, from eight counties under the command of the Governor, laid down orderly fire and pressed forward with unrelenting discipline against twice as many randomly armed, marginally commanded, irate farmers, who styled themselves Regulators. The Governor's drums beat, colors, brilliant silks, floated in the breeze, and artillery boomed above the crack of rifles. At one point the frontiersmen, crouched behind field rocks and firing with inbred accuracy, drove away the artillery and captured one of the guns. The small victory was valueless when they realized no one knew how to fire the gun and they had taken no ammunition. But many of their fellows, never having seen battle, vanished from the field and returned to their nearby homes. Each side lost about a dozen dead, and five times that were wounded by the time the militia commanded the field. Fifteen of the Regulators were captured.

The battle did not end suddenly. Smoke from guns settled softly into low areas. At one moment a white flag was sent out from the Governor, appearing to the Regulators from behind a small ridge. I saw only the top of the flag when suddenly it dropped out of sight. I learned later that an ignorant farmer had shot down the unarmed man in an act for which there would be retribution. Single shots rang out crisp and distinct from the general cacophony of the battle. Shouts, cries of alarm and agony came from different directions. Militia commanders attempted to reassemble their units and to determine the impact of the fighting on their men. Regulators, who had not fled, wandered aimlessly, some searching for friends, others unaware of their next move. The only surgeons available, all assigned to the militia, treated the wounded of both sides.

I had observed the fighting from a safe distance, as had other neighbors who were not committed to either side of the conflict. Even these non-combatants understood that the day had transformed relationships within the colonial community. Herman Husband had left the field before the first shots, and aware of the treats of the Governor toward his person, had left his family and fled back to other family in Maryland. Tryon would be given other assignments by the King, but following these killings on an Alamance field, tomorrow Regulators and militia would be neighbors again, with a bitterness that had deepening roots. For hours, I did what I could for the wounded and attempted to identify the dead and dying. I felt helpless to assist medically, but emotionally and spiritually I also had a feeling of ineptitude. A minister contradicts all of what a battlefield is about. If I could not find the means to create peace, had I not failed? Was praying for dead and dying men a service of my calling or a substitute for my failure? In the afternoon, I found Henry Patillo, my Presbyterian counterpart at Hawfields Church, similarly walking the field.

Patillo's church was about as far to the east of the battlefield as mine was to the northwest.

"David, I too had people among the Regulators. Did you lose any in the fighting?"

"Regretfully, I watched the Governor's men shoot down William Thompson in cold blood. I am yet too conflicted to take stock of what I have seen here." Both of us continued to minister to the extent that we could. In the evening, as the descending sun cast shadows from the forests that enclosed the battlefield, bodies and equipment had been retrieved and only the crushed stubble and some exploded earth of the field testified to the struggle that had played out here within a few hours in May.

I returned to Alamance Church. I found that John Gillespie and several others had been late on the field but had escaped capture. They had fled toward the mountains. I tried to comfort those who feared that Tryon might take some vengeance on the community because of these men. I wondered if Gillespie had fled for fear of the retribution of the Governor or that of his neighbors. I recognized that trust had been sacrificed and would be difficult to recover.

I arrived home mud-spattered with the blood of other men upon my sleeves and waistcoat. At some point I had lost my hat. My hair was matted and I am certain my countenance was that of defeat and dejection. I spoke in confession to Rachel, "today I glimpsed a scene of Hell that I never expected to engage in this world and I failed to prevent it. I failed even to influence it. A representative of what I thought was God's will, and I proved helpless interference between two determined forces bent on destruction."

In a tone mixing directness and compassion, Rachel replied softly, "today God may not have needed you, David. He may be saving you for tomorrow. I have heard you say yourself that it is not for us to attribute to individual events the purpose of God, but to be prepared to be God's instrument when He calls. God moves in mysterious ways. Perhaps He has not put you here to mediate between armies but to administer to the wounded and to restore community among belligerent neighbors."

"Ah, my faithful and provident wife," I admitted, "can I not always depend on you to clarify my vision and to redirect me into the path of righteousness? But I am bold in the Lord and I cannot let neighbors come to blows, especially mortal blows, without expending all my energy to intervene."

"I understand that my dear, and I love you for it, but you need not then chastise yourself when your best efforts cannot prevent that which others are determined to do, even when it means killing one another. Today may have been just one of the first days of tribulation in this land. You are a teacher and a preacher and it may be that your purpose in this place will be to teach the truth in the face of ignorance and to preach love in the face of tyranny."

I folded her in an embrace. Without a word further, that embrace was meant to say to her, and remind me, that ours was a marriage of mind and heart. Together, we represented a single instrument called to faithful conviction.

The next day there was only a single army in the field. The Regulators became again what they had been, pockets of discontent on a scattered frontier. Tryon understood that he could not succeed to pacify in a single victory, however thorough. He had to restore respect for the authority of the King and he would use force and fear and terror as justifiable instruments.

To satisfy the bloodlust of some of the most intense of the militia, James Pugh, one of the Regulator prisoners, was hung that day. The Governor's camp said that action was "to appease the murmurings of the troops, who were importunate that public Justice should be immediately executed." Some claimed that Pugh's life was taken as reprisal for the killing of the man with the white flag. To balance the severe with compassion, a pardon was proclaimed for all who would come into camp and surrender their arms, swear an oath of fidelity to King George, and agree to pay their taxes and submit to the established law of the colony.

On Tuesday, the army relocated southwest to Sandy Creek, an area of Baptists, along with some Quaker settlement, that was known to have a particularly virulent concentration of Regulators. There the army burned the home and barns of James Hunter whom

Tryon had taken to calling the "General of the Regulators," intending a mocking insult to an army without real command.

"Plant the King's flag on this spot," the Governor had said. "This is the core of the rebellion. I expect nothing but disclaimers from these wretched people. You can be sure that every missing husband was at Alamance and he has fled to the woods, but here they assembled and here I will demonstrate the cost of rebellion against the King."

"Sir, there stands the farm of James Hunter," pointed Captain Waddell.

"I consider that to be the Regulator command post. Burn it!"

Hearing Tryon's command, neighbors rushed to Hunter's house and reported to his wife. Martha Hunter hurried out, baby in her arms, four tiny children following close behind. "You cannot, your Excellency. I am a poor woman alone with five little ones. Do not destroy our home. Please, do not put us out so cruelly."

Tryon said, "Madam, I have no claim against you or your little ones. Your husband took arms against the King five days past and he led others in this mutiny. Now he is an outlaw. He assembled his force here and I intend to burn his house. Were he here, I would hang him first!" He spoke with increasing force, and at this moment, his horse shied and circled as if to reinforce the message. "I will send my men first into your house to search your possessions for seditious material and arms. Then I will allow you an hour to remove your furniture and personal belongings before I torch the house. In the meantime, Captain, burn the barn and all the other farm buildings. Take possession of all the livestock."

The Governor's continued progress through the Piedmont carried with it the possibility of ravaging that accompanies all armies. On that same evening, other units took possession of Herman Husband's farm and they carried out similar destruction. Husband had already fled, on his way to Ft. Pitt, and left his children to rebuild his plantation. Each day, more neighbors came into the military camps and qualified to affirm and to gain a pardon. At Deep River and Camp Creek the militia requisitioned more provisions from the Quakers. At the Jersey Settlement along Abbott's Creek and the Yadkin River, it was the Germans who sought pardons, as many of their number had acted as Regulators. At the Moravian towns, Tryon knew there were no Regulators, but these Germans were the best provisioners on the frontier. In their case, the Governor was paying a courtesy visit to settlements that supported law and order as necessary to healthy commerce. The army turned east, crossing the Haw River and Big Troublesome Creek and driving the fleeing Regulators further toward Virginia. The governor came down High Rock Road where he was so close to us that we feared he intended to do harm to our people around Buffalo. We were relieved when he proceeded along the lower road to Hillsborough.

For a month, Tryon had marched through the counties of concentrated Regulator disaffection. Hundreds had come to his camp and sought pardon. The colonial troops had demonstrated order and legal restraint while they clearly held the capacity to destroy rebellion. Exactly a month after the Government had crushed the Regulator army at Alamance Creek, the Colonial Army of the King paraded smartly through Hillsborough. There Tryon held a public trial of his twelve prisoners. I attended, although only Mateer was from my congregations. I had hoped that I would be allowed to testify on behalf of the condemned, but that was refused. The Governor did permit me to help the captives to prepare for death. It was a sad and melancholy duty. After a month of being paraded around the state as if they were already convicted, they entertained no hope for this life and were much eased when I spoke to them of the next.

The next day, the Governor, after seeming to attend personally to all the details, marched down through town to the place of execution. He had formed the troops in a hollow, in an oblong square with the artillery forming the front and rear faces. The first line made up the right face and the second line, the left. The main guard marched in the center along with the sheriff and the prisoners. The light horse covered the outside of the flanks to control the crowd. At the field of execution, with the gallows in sight, Tryon announced the reprieve of six of the men, then proceeded with the hanging of the other six. It seemed to me as I watched this grizzly scene, intently observed by a vast crowd of the morbidly curious, that Tryon had acted out another calculated statement of the power and "compassion" of the King.

While Tryon, as a public testament, had marched his army in a circle around our two congregations, I had indeed given succor to the people in their homes and also comforted them from the pulpit. Each Sunday I had risen in Buffalo, and the next Sunday in Alamance, to find God's voice in the darkness.

"Can God be present in such a time as this?" I asked rhetorically, attempting to speak about their concerns and mine. "Can I give you absolution? Where is your guilt? These are unanswered questions with which you and I must struggle.

"A month ago," I continued, half to myself, "I watched William Thompson, a child of God and one of this flock, shot in the back by a soldier of the King. On Wednesday last, at Hillsborough, I watched Robert Mateer, my dear friend and a Christian of this congregation, hung with five others as rebels to their country. I am bereft! I have prayed over both their bodies and I have laid them to rest at this hallowed place. I have comforted their families. But who comforts me? I have gone to the well – the well of God's mercy. I have drunk deep but I am not yet filled. Grief is struggle, a process of illumination. It does not come in a rush of vision but slowly, as a sunrise enlightens the day. In the Bible, Paul says that we will know, but knowing now is partial. We see only puzzling reflections in a mirror, but it will be whole. I declare to you: it will be whole."

I understood that I had to perform the impossible task of clergy in times such as these. I could not process my grief, or fathom my anger, or interpret the will of God, then return to bestow those insights on my congregations. I wasn't Moses at Sinai. I was a shepherd with lost sheep in the darkness. My role was to restore their confidence without exposing my concerns. Connected to God in prayer, mine was the task of circumspection, all the time nurturing them as novices and leading them around to the comfort of prayerful insight. I wondered, was it just the magic that the magician was expected to be able to perform or was this the moment when the call of God required an inward testing?

They were being asked, they were being forced, to take an oath of allegiance to King and Parliament. It was a forced oath and as such, it was not a binding oath, so I told them they should take it without fear of commitment. But I did say that they must remember that they already were governed by this King and this Parliament and that a covenant existed to that effect which bound them. The Regulators had issued complaints, specific complaints, against the actions of local colonial government but no claim had been made that Royal Government had acted to break their covenant. They were bound to that covenant relationship unless they could establish specific actions on the part of the king that severed that relationship. Rachel warned me, "what you have spoken from the pulpit will be heard with friendly and unfriendly ears. It will be misquoted by every party."

"I understand," I said. "I cannot be ambivalent from the pulpit. These people expect my judgment. I have spoken truth, and for that I answer only to my congregation and my God. I am myself bewildered in these times but I can't let such feelings abrogate my responsibility. Criticism may be just the mildest risk I am taking, but I know of no other method of speaking the truth."

"Your words fill me with pride and the conviction that you are acting as God's messenger. As your wife, and possessing the frailty of a woman, I cannot but fear for your safety though, David. You surely can understand that. No one else has to make such public utterances when men are being hung for less. I married you as a minister, not as a martyr, and I do not think that confession too dramatic. Demonstrate your commitment to the growth of a peaceful community under your covenant, by attention to your academy. The children need your efforts. In my own home, I feel I am raising a covey of savages. Believe me when I tell you that brilliant minds, unattended, can create more trouble than an equal number of dullards and you, sir, have no dullards."

CHAPTER TWO **1763** The Craighead Influence

I came to North Carolina eight years before my disquieting experience as the mediator between Governor Tryon and the Regulators.   I was not a young man as missionaries go, but I was a novice as a minister, and in that capacity, New Brunswick Presbytery in New Jersey had sent me south.   My patrons in New Jersey had recommended me to the obstreperous Alexander Craighead, the minister at Sugaw Creek in Mecklenburg County.   It was a natural contact that I had determined to make myself as soon as I knew I was going to North Carolina. I had known the Craigheads when Alexander's father, Rev. Thomas Craighead, had been the minister at Pequa in Lancaster, a church near my home and the place of my early education.   As I rode south along the Valley Road from Pennsylvania, I had the frequent opportunity to anticipate a renewed acquaintance with the Craigheads, for they were not a household easily forgotten. No family had ·deeper roots in the institutions of the Scottish Presbyterian Church than Alexander Craighead. His father, Thomas, had been born in Scotland; his family was persecuted under the Stuarts. Thomas Craighead had studied medicine, but while a student, was called to follow a strong attachment to the ministry that had been served by his family for several generations.   Once ordained, Thomas went to Ireland as preacher for about a dozen years, then came to the colonies, settling first in New England, I believe.   He was a man of singular piety, so they say, and I have heard my father speak of him as "Father Craighead," so great was the veneration of the people of Pequa. I have to laugh as I consider this family history because we Presbyterians, tempered in the fire of persecution, did not emerge as chastened spirits. The story of Thomas Craighead was so often remembered among the faithful at Pequa that even now I can recite the details of the events of October 27, 1736.

On a Saturday night some months earlier, Rev. Craighead had broken the news to his wife that he had given permission to his son, John, and his family to move in with them. Margaret Craighead's reaction did not satisfy her husband and then next day he assumed the prerogative that lay with the church Session and forbade her to take communion. That was possible because he did not provide her with the token everyone must have that confirms their worthiness to partake. The other officers of his Session disagreed with their pastor but Rev. Thomas was adamant and unrepentant. The congregation was in an immediate furor, the extent of which was so dangerous to the peace and quiet within the Presbytery, that they terminated the pastoral relationship at Pequa and moved Thomas west to the Susquehanna River as the first full-time minister in that wilderness. That is where he died, three years later, in his pulpit preaching in full form and fury.

Is it any wonder that these actions divided this pious family and made martyrs on both sides. Such stories of persecution and judgment, the conviction of chosen souls destined to receive the blessings through the ordinance of God predetermined before birth, constituted the structure of my faith from the cradle.

That was not the lone influence I anticipated as I approached Sugaw Creek. The door that opened on my arrival at the Craighead home revealed a stranger, and perhaps I would not have been so taken back had she not been such a pleasant vision. There was a hesitation. My expectations, simple as they were, had been compromised and my whole body seemed to have to re-calibrate. "Oh, may I introduce myself? I had expected to see Rev. Craighead or his wife. I am sorry."

There was another pause. Then, with a sweet but entirely commanding voice, the girl in the door said, "I am waiting sir. You said you wanted to introduce yourself."

"Again forgive me. I am Reverend David Caldwell and I am a friend of the Craigheads from Pequa. I believe I am expected."

"Of course you are Reverend Caldwell. I am Rachel Craighead, one of the daughters of this house. I cannot be sure, but I suspect that we were once acquainted in Lancaster. Please come in." She was as composed and courteous as any well-born maiden. Surely I had known her but she must have been just a child.

I feared that I would soon begin to stammer and attempted an explanation. "I am struggling, Miss Rachel Craighead, to unravel in my mind which of the daughters you must be." I could feel the pressure of my blood easing slightly and struggled to recover some command of my senses. She signaled for me to come in. As I crossed the threshold I continued. "When in Lancaster I believe there were your mother, Agnes, and sister, Margaret. Then there was a whole "covey" of younger girls, Rachel and Jane, I remember by name, and others I can't name, and younger boys." I was feeling more serene and composed.

"Please sit down Reverend, and perhaps I will be able to bring you up to date on our family." It was a pleasant room hung with red velvet curtains, fringed, that extended just below the window. Beside the fireplace was a wooden bench with a high straight back, and cushioned. I remember two upholstered chairs such as I had not expected in Carolina. A round central table was covered by a rug of oriental weave. "My father is out at the moment, called to a near neighbor who has been very ill, and Father and one of the Elders have taken him communion. You see before you Rachel, whom you say you remember by name, but obviously I was lost in the 'covey.' Mother died after we left Pennsylvania, during our sojourn in Virginia."

"I am quite saddened to hear that, as I remember her as a very kind and caring woman."

"Oh, she was, and her death left Father grieving and overwhelmed with eight of us. He married almost at once but our stepmother died in a short time and he has since remained a widower. The result is that we girls have had to assume care of the household quite early and I fancy that we have served Father satisfactorily. At least he has not hastened to marry again to fill the opening as mistress of the manse." She chuckled. "I am sure you can appreciate that in a large congregation, there are many fair ladies anxious to oblige a widower minister with motherless children.

"Anyway, my sisters are indeed Margaret and Jane whom you remember by name; then there is Agnes, who is married to the Reverend William Richardson, whose congregation is at the Waxhaws just across the line in South Carolina. Jane is also married, to Patrick Calhoun, and they too live in the Waxhaws. Mary and Elizabeth, along with Robert and Thomas, are still young and at home here. There you have it, caught up to date with us." She rose purposefully. "You must give me a moment and I will have us some tea," she said as she went, over my protest, into an adjoining room.

Rachel and I spent a very pleasant hour together before we heard her father approaching. Our conversation I could attribute as comfortable, as if we had known each other for many years. Once Alexander Craighead entered the room, what had been an airy exchange darkened into a more earnest tone – somber even. The good reverend was not one to brighten the corner.

He was a man of medium height, sinewy, of olive complexion and with a sheaf of straight white hair wildly protruding. His greeting was warm and pleasurable for us both. "Only God could have ordained this, David. My young farmer–carpenter friend is now turned into a divine by the powers of those New Light scholars at Princeton, and now sent on a mission to the unchurched of this colony. Mysterious ways indeed."

"Believe me, Alexander, I have similarly marveled on more

than one occasion. Had it not been for my brothers, my father would have surely blocked my way to the pulpit. And I must add that my education, under the Craighead influence at Pequa Academy, planted a resilient seed that was determined to be fulfilled."

"God has given me just enough of such confirmations of my pastoral exertions that I have been able to persevere," he confessed. I had opened the door to an inevitable recitation that Rachel had obviously heard with laboring frequency.

"You do, of course, remember the inexcusable behavior of my father." I did remember that Thomas Craighead had so divided his family that when Presbytery placed him at one of his last assignments, Alexander had refused to take part in his installation.

"I am afraid," he went on, "that the Craighead name among Presbyterians generally is apt to divide opinions. I have no quarrel with that. Conviction and selection are not characteristics born in order to elicit friendships."

"Oh, Father," Rachel spoke up momentarily startling me. "You need not make all Craigheads martyrs to the spiteful acts of Grandfather. Even his Elders refused to support him in using Presbyterian polity to deny his wife communion."

The discussion was becoming awkward for me – something of a family matter debated before an outsider, but I was impressed with Rachel's balanced insight. She would not allow her father to paint her with a common brush only because she shared a name.

"You see, Brother Caldwell, my motherless daughters tend to

a strong degree of independent thought. It can be a bother, but it often is a source of great personal satisfaction."

Later in the evening, Alexander Craighead spoke casually of the circumstances that had brought him with his family to Mecklenburg. "I left Pennsylvania when my views on the truth of the Covenant that I preached became too warm for the colonial council. You may remember a small pamphlet that I authored that was denounced in New Jersey as fomenting rebellion. My inflaming action in Pennsylvania was to lead my congregation to renew the covenants, both the Solemn League and the National Covenant. Then they denounced George II, held their swords aloft and declared they would defend Christ's Gospel and the national liberty from all foes from within and without. In Virginia, in an even briefer length of time, I was at odds with the Governor's Council. It was their order that I cease preaching until I recanted my "treasonable principles," that arrived only a short time before the disastrous defeat of General Braddock loosed the Indians upon our frontier congregations. I must say I felt hard pressed for myself, my family, and my congregation. I experienced the metaphoric role of the shepherd when I led my entire flock here to Sugaw Creek. We say of ourselves that 'we passed out the rear door as the savages entered by the front.' So here we are. I will tell you that Presbyterian ministers are no more welcome in this colony than we were in either Virginia or Pennsylvania."

"That does not encourage my prospects, Alexander."

"Don't fear for your prospects. You will be welcomed

enthusiastically by the Presbyterians of Carolina. They suffer from being cut off from their church. They are not even given the option of the Anglican communion because there are few priests present on the frontier. Our Scottish brothers are in the majority in the Piedmont from Pennsylvania south, probably because they were so poor that the frontier was the only place they could hope to be able to afford the price of land. Many have nothing, but squat upon some virgin tract until men of worth buy their land and evict them and absorb the benefits of their labor. How many times must eviction be our lot in Scotland, then Ireland, and now in colony after colony? I preach from the roots of persecution. A hundred years ago, it was the Solemn League and Covenant by which the Scottish and English Parliaments pronounced Presbyterianism to be the true doctrine found in the Holy Scriptures. It was by the restoration of the Stuarts, and then their German cousins, that the Covenant was repudiated and the king became the 'Defender of the Faith,' the false and Popish Anglican doctrine. Even a Stuart, by any name a human, cannot abrogate a covenant made with God. It is a heinous act."

"Alexander, you preach to the converted. I am from Pequa, from Lancaster, where the covenant bound our belief. It is bred in my bones. But doctrine, tenaciously held, can become a stumbling block."

"Too little faith," he interrupted.

"No, no, hear me. This is a land of beginning again. It will not be won by the French, or the Germans, or the British or Spanish; indeed we Scots and Irish will not win it alone. So our faiths must find a way to flourish because only God's will can be done. I find Presbyterian doctrine to be well structured as to order, as it came through the covenant struggle of a hundred years ago. As such, it seems to me to be destined to have a disproportionately high prospect to influence the way law and government will evolve in the colonies. Our struggle must be to oppose any maneuver to impose, upon this land, that 'Popish Anglican doctrine.' We hold in the Covenant the obvious alternate doctrine by which we can eventually be ruled. We cannot agitate with such intensity as to become essentially treasonous. That is not a new struggle for Presbyterians but a continuation of our tradition."

"You are young, David, and you make a compelling argument to soften the rhetoric. There was no soft rhetoric in our Covenant. It must be defended, expounded, re-confirmed in all generations."

"I make no quarrel on that point, and I presume no advice to you, for your pulpit will always be a stronghold in defense of the faith. I would covet that my message may similarly be faithful. But I think the stage upon which we now find ourselves is vast, with many voices, and that too is our strength. God makes us a voice among many. It is not only we Presbyterians that He will use, if this land is to flourish. Ours must be a faithful influencing of the struggle, keeping before us the infinite will of God. At all costs, we must avoid rebellion. Can we not see what happens to us as colonists when we allow our land to be drawn into the meaningless wars of Europe? I believe that we Presbyterians can demonstrate to our fellow colonists the truth through the Covenant as a form of institutional government and as a confirmation of a binding charter between God and His people."

We came to agree that method was not as important as message, and we held together, steadfast in the message. I came to see our discussion, and many that followed over time, as a sifting of my impulses with the influence of wisdom.

With Sugaw Creek as my unofficial base, I moved into an itinerant ministry mostly in the Piedmont of North Carolina. I had been advised at New Brunswick of the particular settlements that had written requesting the service of a minister. Craighead had been similarly contacted from other settlements and he gave me that list. So scattered and primitive were some of these concentrations of cabins that they had not even taken a name. I found myself riding on roads so little traveled as to be hardly wide enough for my horse, and going for miles before I saw a cabin. Sometimes I stopped and found an eager believer who would insist I stay, and in a day or two had assembled people from a wide area to hear my message. Often there was an eagerness to have me baptize children born since a family had left their home church in Pennsylvania. Infant baptism may have been a divisive doctrinal issue, but where life was so fragile upon the frontier, families grieved over the frequent loss of children and tended to find special comfort in baptism.

One destination, near the Virginia border, was a settlement of families from Lancaster and Chester Counties who had come together to North Carolina about ten years earlier as the Nottingham Company. They had bought 21,000 acres on Buffalo and Reedy Fork Creeks from Lord Granville. On my arrival, I found that having formed one church at Buffalo Creek, they had within the last year begun a second on Alamance Creek. My initial assumption was that their mission had become so successful that they had been forced by the distance between stations to provide a second place of worship. That was only marginally correct and I discovered that the doctrinal differences that had flourished in the northern colonies as New Light and Old Light Presbyterians had invaded the Carolinas. Buffalo was Old Light and Alamance Presbyterian was New Light. My influence at Pequa had been New Light, and consequently I tended more toward a more aggressive missionary ministry. Old Light believers put more stock in the literal nature of the chosen of God, which made them exclusive in their approach to the wider community.

I found my reception in both groups to be enthusiastic and eager for the preached word. More than once I was reminded by a member that as a young man in Lancaster, I had known him or her. That fact, once established, they would remind me that they were still in Lancaster when I had been called to the ministry and had left for my seminary training at Princeton. "Do you also remember," they would say, "that I told you we were going to Carolina and wished that you would commit to come to us as our minister when you finished your education? Do you remember that?" they would press. I admitted I remembered such discussions, not in particular detail, but as general encouragement at the commitment we were both making. For them, however, I discovered that my arrival was the hoped for culmination of my religious calling. I was uneasy. I felt I had certainly not made a firm commitment and to have done so would have been foolish at the time. I could not ignore their plight. They had been ten years with their congregation organized but without a minister. They had prayed so long that God would send them a called preacher. I stayed with them for longer stretches of time than I did other communities, feeling a special affinity but unwilling to commit myself. I will admit that I had considerable concern that a single pastor would find it difficult to minister to two congregations, as close as they were geographically, if they held so fast to a doctrinal discipline that they could not toil in the field together.

Sugaw Creek was first my base because I found such energy and commitment in the ministry of Alexander Craighead. From my first visit, I also found an emotional attachment to Rachel that I did not understand was possible between people. I had seen good marriages. I had observed my young friends become hopelessly enamored of a young woman and I had seen my brothers similarly stung by what they called love. I tended to think of myself as more serious, more committed to a high calling that had claimed my life. Emotionally, I suppose I was immature.

Rachel and I had become such immediate friends that we found an intense interest in everything we did or said and we could not conclude decisions without the concurrence of the other. We had become inseparable before we had understood that we were in love. I longed for her when I was away and I found it increasingly more difficult to answer my missionary calling. I delayed departures for days, even for a few hours, because I could not tolerate separation. I do not know at what point her father first observed the bloom of our attachment, but he found it immediately acceptable. Her brothers and sisters were excited about the prospect of a marriage.

I knew that by mid-year 1765 I must return to New Jersey for my ordination, and the focus of this date framed our courtship. Just before the prior Christmas, I interrupted a rather esoteric debate on predestination by announcing to Rev. Craighead my intention to ask for Rachel's hand in marriage. His answer was to rise and embrace me most enthusiastically saying, "yes, yes my friend, by all means." A man of conspicuous words found that a few could seal the deal.

I proposed to Rachel in the parlor moments later. I suppose that I was more the clergyman than the romantic. She knew full well the style of life to which she was committing, but I believed myself honor-bound to chronicle a litany of the uncertainties which I proposed she accept in affirming this marriage. "I will be taking you away from your home and family, but I presume that is a prospect agreeable to most brides. I am a minister and you have lived your life in the restrictions that come with such a calling. I can offer you almost nothing of material comforts."

She listened with a smile then mercifully relieved my "litany of the inconsequential," as she called it, with the soft words, "I will have you and no other." We considered together the calling from the Nottingham people and agreed to make it our commitment.

Our wedding was at home, surrounded physically by her friends and family. I had reassuring messages of support from my family by letter. Rachel's sisters Nancy and Jane attended her, and her brother-in-law, William Richardson, came from the Waxhaws with his family and he performed the service.

It took more than a year to complete our home on the land I had been able to purchase on Buffalo Creek. I preached each week at one of my two congregations and Rachel remained in Mecklenburg with her family. On occasion she would ride with me to Buffalo and stay the week with a family in one congregation or other. By the fall such riding had to be ended because Rachel was pregnant with our first child. She felt guilt that she was not fulfilling her responsibilities as the wife of the minister but she was pleased to be among her siblings during her confinement.

In the spring of 1767, I was able to bring my wife and baby son, Samuel Craighead Caldwell, to their new home on the Buffalo. It was a typical frontier house, log construction, measuring 20 feet x 20 feet. There was a full basement with stone walls and a pounded earth floor. Stone walls on each side of the fireplace rose up through the first floor and out the loft to create an interior chimney with fireplaces to serve all the rooms. The basement was our kitchen and dining room. On the first floor we had a large room and smaller ones for my study and our bedroom. The loft was open at first but soon partitioned into two rooms. I was able to use my skills as a carpenter to produce a finely finished house that was the envy of our neighbors. As children arrived, we were quickly out of space, and on the west, we added another twenty-foot square log section on piers with a single room and loft. Our construction took the form common in Pennsylvania, square-faced logs with filled chinking.

After presenting me with a son in our first year, Rachel presented me with a second son that we named Alexander. Our third son, Andrew, arrived concurrent with the Regulator showdown in 1771.

Rachel, having been raised in the home of a highly educated minister, had been informally provided more of an education than any young girl of her time could expect. In our almost sixty years of marriage Rachel and I were literal partners, as it related to the commitment to education and informed participation in public affairs and doctrinal interpretation. By generations of tradition, I was the public expression of this partnership but she was equal to the task in every way and essential to the reputation that I earned in my lifetime.

All these responsibilities had their impact on my ministry in this time and they were superimposed on the rapidly maturing events of colonial frontier America. We took stock of our situation after the fight at Alamance Creek. I was forced to deal with violence and death in a civil conflict where roles were unclear.

I told Rachel, "Governor Tryon understands that he is the

agent of the King in our colony. It is clear and unequivocal for him. But for other civil officers, King's attorneys, judges, militia officers, even though they have taken responsible oaths to protect the interests of the King, they are themselves colonials. They have brothers, neighbors, church members, who are of the Regulator persuasion." I was trying to sort out, identify for Rachel and for myself, where the interests were in this conflict. How could I identify right, where there was conflict, if I could not understand motivation? I could not simply curse all authority through the prism of a Covenant. I represented too many Presbyterians who no longer appreciated the power that the Covenants represented to Scottish Presbyterians. I was also among Colonials who had been attracted to cross an ocean by the promise of religious liberty and were not Presbyterians.

Rachel knew her task was to inspire the progress of my reflection. "Should not God's hand be on the side of justice?" she asked.

"Yes, of course, but who are the just in such a struggle?"

"It seems to me that in such a case, your task is to identify what justice is before God. With that understanding clearly defined, others can then make their choices. It is not for you to sanctify the just, even though that is probably exactly what my father might have done."

"We depend on English law to defend our order. We have pledged by oath our allegiance to the English King. But we, Rachel, are people of the Covenant. The Lord knows that we lack that passion for tolerance that Jesus preached. We are strong-willed and harsh and opinionated, and we want to be left alone even in a world that can only be preserved through co-operation. In the struggle that is surely to come, we will be the most belligerent and it will always be difficult in such circumstances to be guided by justice and mercy. I minister to such intolerant people, Rachel, and God knows, I am one of them."

"Do you think that disturbs me? You and I are products of the same house of believers. We struggle in the face of who we are and God does know from whence we came. But we are also those who believe that knowledge is the channel to redemption. We have been called to a great work in this place, David, and I pledge to stand firm beside you in the task. We have a faith to preach and responsibility to teach in our home and in this community. I fear nothing because I know God, and I have faith in the message of Jesus Christ."

"Were it only possible that this Sunday, you and not I, could preach that message at Alamance. My Rachel," I added most sincerely, "you are my strength."

Against that facade, Rachel struggled to suppress the fears inside her body. She was terrified by a world around her that placed her family in the eye of a swirling tempest. Yes, it was her faith that folded her in assurance but she was stretched thin, laboring to create for me a sanctuary in our family. The public demand on me as pastor was critical and prodigious. She felt she must shield me from domestic demands in order to release my absolute capacity to minister.

I marveled at the clarity of perception that I could imagine when I could counsel with Rachel. There were astute leaders in my congregation. Within the small membership of clergy in the new Presbytery, I had a collegial relationship on which I could depend. But it was early evidence to me that Rachel was already my other dimension, my truest critic, my trusted counselor. I always turned to God in prayer seeking guidance, but more and more I saw Rachel as the wise insight to God's purpose.

CHAPTER THREE 1773 New Side – Old Side

On the road to Campbellton I passed through Stinking Quarter, across Deep River and Barbeque Creek. Stinking Quarter was the heart of the Quaker settlement and Sandy Creek was a community of Separate Baptists, both considered sources of Regulator agitations. From Barbeque south, I was in the Presbyterian region of Highland Scots. It was not possible to define these areas outside their religious affiliation.

Campbellton was named for a town on the Kintyre peninsula, in Argyleshire. Beginning in the late–1730s, the elimination of the "tacksman,"[1] low wages, high rents and unemployment transformed land tenancy in Argyleshire and adjacent Highland regions. That motivation for emigration was exacerbated after the defeat of the Scots at Culloden in 1745 The Highlanders who came at that time to the Cape Fear basin were Presbyterians, but no ministers accompanied the groups that typically left from Kintyre.

My friend, James Campbell, was born in Campbellton in Argyleshire, I guess about 1705. I know he was educated and ordained

---

[1] tacksman-one who holds a tack, a lease, of land from another

43

in Scotland before he came to Pennsylvania about 1730. He became disillusioned with ministry and his own calling but he told me he heard George Whitefield preach during his tour at the end of that decade and sought a personal meeting. He discussed with Whitefield his concerns about his calling and afterwards made a re-commitment to ministry. For a time he preached on the Coneweheog in Lancaster County, where I came to know him while I was a candidate for ministry. In 1757, Rev. Hugh McAden, who was serving as a Presbyterian missionary in North Carolina, made the connection between the Cape Fear Scots, many of whom had come from Argyleshire, with this preacher from Campbellton. For nearly a decade, the Argyll Colony had been petitioning the Scottish Presbytery of Inverary to send them a minister, but with no success. McAden convinced Campbell to accept a call to North Carolina eventually to preach at the three mother churches of the Scots: Old Bluff, Longstreet, and Barbeque. Thus he became the first called Presbyterian minister in the settlement. This was no mean accomplishment and perhaps was completed only because Campbell had unique qualifications. Most important, as a kinsman, he could speak English and Gaelic and this settlement demanded sermons in Gaelic. He qualified by always preaching two sermons each Sunday, one in English and one in Gaelic. Also, before he could preach as a Presbyterian, outside the established Church of England, he had to give and record an oath to the court "that I do believe that there is not any transubstantiation in the sacrament of the Lord's Supper, in the elements of bread and wine at or after the consecration thereof by any person whatsoever."[2]

As I rode south, I watched the subtle change in terrain from the hills of the Piedmont to the sand hills of the lower Cape Fear. Hardwood and pine forests became pine barrens with a different kind of long leaf pine. I wondered at the difference it must have seemed to Highland Scots, accustomed to their craggy, treeless mountains and lakes. Off the main road, I was directed to the bluff on the southwest side of the Cape Fear on the lands of Roger McNeill. I could see the log meeting house well ahead as I approached the McNeill house. There I found McNeill and Campbell, prepared for my anticipated afternoon arrival.

I rode up and was greeted with a warm salutation by Campbell. "David Caldwell! When we last shared each other's company, now perhaps five years ago, I never expected to greet you next in the Carolinas. How are you?" Campbell reached out his hand as I dismounted and approached them.

"James, my Christian brother, how I have looked forward to this meeting. And Brother McNeill, I have heard of you as a firm defender of the faith."

"Ah, yes, a defender once for certain but now just a laborer in

---

[2] Cumberland County Records, January session, 1759 (Recorders Office, Fayetteville, N.C.); Duane Meyer, *The Highland Scots of North Carolina, 1732-1776* (Chapel Hill: The University of North Carolina Press, 1957), 114-115.

the fields." They all chuckled at the reference to the "persecutions" in Scotland, never far from the memory of any of the Argyle men.

Inside, I was told that Mrs. McNeill was over with Mrs. Campbell at the latter's home preparing our evening meal, which we would all take together later. In the meantime, we would be left to talk of church matters. The house was open to the breezes of late spring. We sat down at the table and Campbell offered a prayer of thanks for my safe arrival.

As we sipped the cold cider that Rebecca McNeill had left for us, we rejoiced at the new energy of the Scots that their own minister had brought with him. Although I was as familiar with the litany of the "persecutions in Scotland" as any Presbyterian minister, McNeill felt compelled to be certain I knew from whence his highlander influences came.

"We are a hard-sufferin' people, friend Caldwell," began McNeill, almost apologetically. "We call ourselves Covenanters because we opposed the Book of Common Prayer that King Charles imposed on Scotland in 1637 and we established our Covenant over a period of harsh treatment. Our ministers were thrown out of their churches. We met to preach in the open air, barns, houses in 'coventicles' and for that we were persecuted. We held for our Stuart king in '45 and some of us even came here under pardon in '46 and '47. Many of our families were here well before, having been victims of the hard times in Scotland. We came because we were promised cheap land and ten years without taxes and we have succeeded in this new place. I say to you frankly, we have no regard for the Regulator cause up your way. We haven't suffered from high fees or bad courts but there is a further reason why we are of an unrebellious nature. We came to terms with the Hanoverians and we were given the chance to begin again under their law. Just as we adhere to the National Covenant, we are no longer Jacobites."

"Brother McNeill," I said, "let me assure you that I am not a Regulator and that only a few of my most aggrieved congregants follow that cause. Neither do I look on myself as a Scot in the terms that are common to you. For several generations, I and most of my flock come from those who suffered like your families at the hands of King Charles and were persecuted as Covenanters. For various reasons, they left Scotland or were transported by King James to the plantations in the north of Ireland to establish their homes. Most of us are also come from families of the lowlands of Scotland and the north of England. So, while our roots are the same, and we both hold to the Presbyterian Church as the faith of our fathers, the more recent influences on our attitudes differ widely. Now, James Campbell here does indeed bridge this gap."

Campbell looked up, somewhat unprepared that I had made him the common denominator between these two avenues of Presbyterian emigration. "I presume you both see me as an associate of the other but I find that a little awkward. David, if you would allow me, I think that my history more blends the experiences than bridges a gap. I was born in Argyleshire and ordained in Scotland, so I meet the demands of the Cape Fear Scots. But I came to Pennsylvania, was re-committed to the faith by Whitefield, served among the log college trained, so I meet the standards that might be acceptable to your Nottingham Colony. Of course I speak and think in English and Gaelic so that pleases you both. I see that as a blend because I see that as the way the Presbyterian Church in the Colonies will be blended into a more brotherly body with time."

"Your point is indeed well taken and it appeals to me for I have at my church at Buffalo a congregation more in line with the standards of McNeill's Presbyterians, those of the Covenanters; the congregation at Alamance is much in tune with those you have described in Pennsylvania. Now of course in the colonies we speak of those differences in terms of Old Side and New Side beliefs," I asserted. "James, I am not certain that when I knew you in Lancaster I was aware of your common roots with these Scots on the Cape Fear. It seems fortuitous that you were able to come here and serve your own people."

"Fortuitous!" exclaimed McNeill. "It was surely God's will."

"Ha!" replied Campbell. "I think of it more as, 'not my will God, but yours be done.' David, I came to the colonies at the same time the first boat loads of Highlanders left Campbellton. I was a minister but I knew that if I merely accompanied these determined Scots to their new home as their minister, I would be defined by their ways rather than by the new, liberated ways of the denomination, which I saw as occurring in Pennsylvania and in New England. I'm afraid that I observed most of that conflict in terms of the Covenanters, represented by your father-in-law, Alexander Craighead, and those influenced, as was I, more by Whitefield. I went to Pennsylvania to struggle with the faith, to be re-exposed, re-educated in the faith and, unbeknownst to me, that struggle approached the combat of Jacob and his angel. I was repeatedly referred to the needs of these Scots for a minister, as the certain call God meant for me, but I knew these people." He smiled and nodded at McNeill. "I already knew them to be stubborn, unbending, infallible Covenanters in their theology, and I frankly demurred. Then Hugh McAden came among them and later met with me, and he wrestled with my determination, and we prayed over the needs of these people, and ultimately I surrendered. I labor in a rocky field of intransigence and I understand that God does not intend to make it less. It is only the support of men like McNeill here, and there are others, I pledge you, that gives me the strength for the task and with that, I am content." He paused having made his confession. "Now, Rebecca has her moments of desperation." Then he laughed.

I said, "I consider myself prone to the Covenanters, under the influence of my late father-in-law. Many of my fundamental beliefs are rooted there. For example, I have little respect for distant governments. I have come to perceive , however, that the structure of government at the heart of the Covenants, may be too parochial to embrace the needs of our colonial circumstances. That does not quarrel with the truth of the Covenants but I confess that I have yet to conclude how to build a civil contract in this land."

"It is true, I am afraid. We are a contentious group," said McNeill. "Our struggles have led us to be suspicious of authority beyond ourselves. James has learned to preach truth in the face of that churlishness and let the Lord soften the hearts. Many who are here as a result of the defeat of Prince Charlie in '45 consider that the subsequent oath that they took to King George is a Covenant that they must respect. They may abhor central authority but I believe that they will support the Royal Standard if it is raised in their midst."

Shifting the subject, Campbell suggested, "tell me now, David, of the reports you receive from your presbytery in Philadelphia."

I told him that we are now a part of Hanover Presbytery centered in Virginia. "I know you have come here as part of the Presbytery of South Carolina. We will soon have enough who call themselves Presbyterians in North Carolina, that we can petition to form our own presbytery and you should plan to be included. As to other matters, I can advise that the missionary zeal of our friend Whitefield continues to energize preaching throughout the colonies. Of course McAden has had success in organizing congregations in Duplin, New Hanover, and Caswell. Henry Pattillo increases his congregations in Orange and Granville. The churches in Mecklenburg and Rowan are growing quickly. These men are all the products of Presbyterian education in Pennsylvania, although some were at least born in Ireland or Scotland. McNeill, there is where the growth of the faith among you Scots will be stunted. For now, the Presbyterian Church can hold to its tradition of an educated pastorate only if we accept the product of our academies and seminaries in America. If we restrict our calls only to men educated in Scotland, we cannot keep up with the demand. The tree of Presbyterianism will wither if it must depend on only Scottish fruit. That is a crude but true analogy."

We continued to examine in detail the separateness of these two ranges of Presbyterians, understanding that the different venues each supported a different cast. We would each have a different story. "God does not determine uniform experiences for the elect," was the way Roger McNeill put it.

The Scots of the Cape Fear saw themselves at this time as a reflection of Biblical Israel; after unspeakable tribulation, they were chosen of God, and delivered to a promised land, as God's elect. Comfort and conviction accompanied their transfer to the Cape Fear where they could virtually proof-text their story in Exodus. They were intent on believing that they could control their story by envisioning God in the Biblical confines so that they would be able to know God's will absolutely. For them God did not work in history; God fixed history in the Bible to be replicated.

Our ride over to the Campbell house gave McNeill a chance to display for me the success the Highlanders had in subduing their surroundings. "We still build with logs, I'm afraid. It is not the great stone walls of the high country. We have traded rocks for tar and timber but we got fertile fields in the bargain. The McAlister house yonder is our most ambitious to date. Alexander McAlister came with me in '39 with five gentlemen and ninety poor families. Some of his family went back, but Alexander is an Elder at Bluff Church along with Hector McNeill. It was my father, Neill McNeill, who gave the acre of land on which we built that first log church that you saw next to me on Tranthams Creek. We have meetings at the home of Archibald McKay on the Long Street and at John Dobbin's Ordinary on Barbecue Creek, and Preacher Campbell serves them in addition to Bluff." The Campbell house drew in sight.

We were greeted at our arrival by Rebecca Campbell. "Please come in Pastor Caldwell. Welcome to our home. This is Roger's wife, Suzanne, who has been helping me prepare our supper."

"I am pleased to meet you ladies," I responded. "I appreciate the time you have given for me to speak about church matters with your husbands this afternoon while you were busy preparing for our care and sustenance."

"Rebecca, we have agonized much over what makes us Scots such a fractious bunch," warned Campbell.

"You have, now what are your conclusions?" she asked.

"Oh, I liked the quote they attributed to Hector McNeill," I said with a little mischief. "I can hear him now. 'I hope they will agree because they know I am hard to turn.' That seems to get right to the essence of the character of the Scot to me." They all chuckled.

We sat down to a hearty banquet which, as a special treat,

included haggis. I was pleased. "Now here is a Scottish delight that may lose its appeal away from Highland sheep. You know my family made that short crossing of the Irish Sea from Kintyre to Ulster a hundred years back but they still had haggis on special occasions even though sheep were not such a staple of their diet any more. But here, I think that the dependence on the hog and the preparation of sausage will replace haggis in another generation. It is a rare commodity up in our region."

"Now can we make haggis a metaphor for Presbyterians, gentlemen?" asked Campbell to everyone's surprise.

"And I guess you would then make sausage the metaphor for Baptists, James," I shot back. A nervous but subdued laugh circulated. "With all seriousness, I see our denomination as far stronger than sheep's brains. We are a branch of the Reformed tradition of John Calvin. We believe that salvation is not just the result of our choices, fallible human choices, such as haggis or sausage, but also of God's acts which first extended the invitation and the opportunity to us to respond to His saving grace. God's free grace pours out on His elect. It is God's will that will be done. We whose religious roots are through the Scottish Church express that belief in our creed and in the acts of covenant by which we have given particular form to our chosen relationship. On this I hold the strongest conviction in the enduring capacity of the Presbyterian Church."

I am sure that James Campbell felt mildly chastised and regretted his too casual remark about metaphors in the face of serious debate. He became most profound. "Of course you state quite properly our common conviction." Then, in order to press beyond, he added, "I feel our American Presbyterian debate is the result of firm convictions transferred to new soil. In Scotland, even within the extent of the Isles, having defined our beliefs in creed and covenant, we could monitor and matriculate our beliefs through a centrally trained clergy. In the vastness of America, and the rapidness with which European settlement is coming to new frontiers, we must depend on colonial seminaries to train our clergy. That means that our orthodoxy will be difficult to sustain and will demand more latitude for interpretation."

"In that, have you not identified the rub, preacher?" asked McNeill.

I said, "I believe you have James," and I added, "I did not mean to sound like a chastising school master before. I did not intend to direct that epistle at you but as a general comment. Anyway, I think Presbyterians are bound to education as an integral element of our denomination, more perhaps than inspiration or perspiration. I believe I have seen in Pennsylvania and New Jersey, and indeed am a product of, the proper paragon for the integration of theology and education."

"I know your background, David, but I wish you would review it for McNeill and the ladies because I think we need to be exposed to your ideas," requested Campbell.

"I do this only at your request, sir," I began. I certainly did not want to put myself forward as the 'perfect paragon' I had just defined, of theologian and educator. I hesitated before speaking further. "I came to ministry late in life under the influence of the missionary message of George Whitefield. I had frequently attended Pequa Presbyterian Church so I began my preparation at the academy at Pequa. Many people have given that school and others started in that part of Pennsylvania, the fashion of 'Log Colleges.' They are in fact classical schools. Log College is the popular term but it is meant to indicate that these schools are preparing students for colleges, particularly in that region for Princeton College where I finally received my training for ordination. That college, and the academies that have come to act as the preparatory schools for college, appear now as a planned network but they had considerable difficulty in getting started. Those of us who were directly involved can only make a firm acknowledgment of the hand of God in the struggle. These schools developed in the face of the conflict between the New Side–Old Side Presbyterians but now both those theological interpretations have come to accept, with different levels of enthusiasm, the educational base in place at Princeton. It is supported by the New Jersey Presbyteries and those in Philadelphia and New York."

I took a long breath. I had an audience but I did not want to appear to be lecturing to the uninformed. I was only telling my experience as a typical example of this merger of theology and education. "I think we will soon see a similar college proposed by presbyteries further south. My wife and I already conduct a classical academy in our home near our Buffalo Church because my congregation is so demanding of education for our children. It serves as a good financial supplement to my preaching but I am sure that we will develop it into an academy similar to the type I described in Pennsylvania. I believe that God has shown us the mechanism we should use to spread the Presbyterian Church in America."

There was a pause as everyone else digested the vision that I had proposed. Then Roger McNeill recognized that he needed to respond in the face of the resistance among the Scots to this type of vision. "I am inspired by your testimony, Pastor Caldwell, but I would be remiss if I did not respond with an honest interpretation of what I believe is the majority sentiment among the Cape Fear Scots. History tells us that the fresh wind of education, even offered within a religious seminary, can unleash conflict, radical ideas, even heresy. Our struggle in Scotland has taught us that we had to shed blood for our creeds and our covenants and, yes, they are our orthodoxy. Most of our people do not care a whit about the growth of our denomination, only about its 'purity.' Right now that drives them to insist on ministers trained in Scotland where they believe truth is preached. That attitude may not be appealing, but it predominates. Is that a fair expression of the situation? You others may disagree."

"Oh, I think you have expressed it very well," added Rebecca Campbell. "That is why I am so frustrated here. I feel so limited – in what I believe and in what I can say."

"I am afraid it is one of the encumbrances of predestination," I suggested. "Calvin used predestination to clarify Luther on the matter of salvation by faith alone. He could not go near the need for sinners to do good works to gain salvation - too Papist. Using Augustine, he expanded the omniscient nature of God, saying that God not only knew what choices each person would make, God already knew what those choices would be. Human free-will existed but God knew what we would choose because He had already chosen us. Therefore, God knew that certain people would live a Christian life and be saved. It was then wrong to say, however, that God decided who would sin and be eternally damned. All humans were depraved and unable to do anything to help themselves. Christ died, not to save everyone, but only to save that chosen, predestined elect. The elect were thus saved only by God's grace (or favor), not by their own choice. An act of faith was needed but God already understood, through irresistible grace, the way the elect would perform.

"Among the Scots, I fear we can glimpse the misguided response that can tragically emanate out of predestination. If we can satisfy ourselves that we are the elect, then we have reached perfection in the eyes of God and anything changed or modified risks our falling from grace. We have indeed dug our hole and now are pulling it in behind us."

Campbell then confessed, "I have to be careful but I try to show our people that such an attitude, manifest by them in their demand for a Scottish clergy, will in the end reduce our community to a small self-serving clique. That is not what God expects of us in this new land. I remain a Covenanter and I believe in predestination but I would add that I believe God is a loving God and wishes to save us all, not only the elect, and that individuals can choose to accept or reject salvation."

"I believe that makes you an Armenian, James," I said. "Some would call that heretical but I think more in our church find that a more acceptable position."

"Oh, enough of this talk of predestination and heretics," said Rebecca, knowing that the men would continue on into the night with such theological considerations and she and Suzanne would be ignored. "Please, Rev. Caldwell, continue."

"I was a contented bachelor at the time I married," I said as I picked up my story. "I would be quick to admit that I was transformed twice at a mature age, first by my call and preparation for ministry, and second by my marriage to Rachel Craighead. I had accepted my life up to that time as not unusual, rather conscripted by tradition, and satisfying. My calling had been the renaissance of my life, and my marriage had given it a new proportion. Previously I had been satisfied to be functional, as a carpenter, as a farmer. Now my life bloomed in response to an outer sun. I was restless without Rachel. She was my fruition and she had taught me to esteem the opinions of women. I knew that without her I could be consumed by the strictures of religion – the siren attractions of creeds and covenants that built castles of faith to keep the chosen in and the sinner out. I needed to hear women.

"My deepest apology, ladies," I pled, "for having led your

husbands into such esoteric theology. I am afraid it is the curse of preachers, too eager to expound, loath to harken. Can you enlighten us, Mrs. McNeill, from the female vantage point?"

"Preacher, you place on me a burden. I am afraid we women are seldom heard on such matters beyond the bedroom and I doubt I can, with certainty, give you their views as a category." Suzanne McNeill paused as if prepared to be silent if directed. Then she went on. "It does seem to me that our men become too blindly concerned about the details of the rules of men and too little aware of the reality of their own surroundings." She was an attractive woman, with very fair skin and a yellow-orange cast to her hair. The Scots might call her "fair made."

"We have been without a minister for ten years, since we came here. In all our planning in leaving Scotland, no minister was arranged to accompany us although we intended to be strict in our devotion to the Scottish Covenants. Once here, our dedication to the Scottish form left us with no ordained spiritual guidance. Now, we finally have Brother Campbell here, satisfying the strict conditions as a minister trained in Scottish schools, and all we want to do is dictate the theology he will preach. Should we not be listening to the message that God has sent to us through his preaching?"

When she paused again with an uncertain look, Campbell said eagerly, "please Suzanne, continue."

"Preacher Caldwell has spoken of imperative need within his congregation for education. We Presbyterians are often identified by our educational institutions as well as by the form of our worship. But again, around here, our children languished until Brother Campbell came, while we preserved Presbyterian orthodoxy. Now he is here, prepared also to teach our young, and little or no effort has been made to facilitate the organization of this school. I believe the frustrations of which I speak are commonly held among our women."

Faced with a profound allegation, which Rebecca Campbell confirmed, we all spent the evening searching for direction. When I was asked to end the conversation with prayer, before I returned with the McNeills to spend the night at their home, I delivered their concerns, now professed openly, to God asking for His guidance.

Some time later James told me how, on Sunday morning next, as they prepared for the service to be held at the Bluff Church, he and Rebecca discussed how interesting it might have been for me to have remained another day or so that I might have been able to attend. She had wondered, and he did too, if their Session would even have allowed me to attend without going through some form of testing. They are so protective of the word that they might hear, that both doubted if they would have given me much of a chance to poison them in some way with a new word. Rebecca imagined that my presence would not still Hector McNeill from challenging me on my proof-text of the scripture. She had concluded, "when our 'little ministers' start rising to question the determinism with which James casts out the devil, David might dash out and feel blessed to return to his contesting congregations."

That week, I was preaching at Buffalo church and much of my message dealt with the influences that our surroundings have on challenging our faith. I used the Scots as an example of placing our faith as a barrier to changing circumstances for fear of compromise. Instead, I suggested that they should accept the inevitability of ever–changing circumstances, and allow themselves the opportunity to be the faithful through whom God worked out His purpose in the current age. I ended this service for the first time with the ditty:

"If the Lord is willing
And I have the chance,
I'll preach next week
At Alamance."

CHAPTER FOUR **1774** Academy – Farmstead

I recall explaining to David Rankin, "when Samuel was six, Rachel and I had planned to give some form to his education, so I told him, to his great delight, that he could now attend the Academy that we had started several years earlier in our home. In those first years only members of the church who lived near to my farm had sent their children because I had to teach in my house and there was little room. It was so like one huge family. There was no other school within miles of Buffalo except the Quaker school at New Garden. So I began my academy in my home and it has grown."

More accurately, I had to admit, my academy had been an opportune necessity. I had bought my farm from John Blair although it was part of the Nottingham Company land. It had taken most of the money I had from my share of my father's Lancaster farm. My yearly salary as pastor was not sufficient alone to support us.

Rankin had replied, "it had always been our hope, Preacher, that if we could prevail upon you to come to Carolina as our minister, we could also convince you that you needed to be a teacher as well. We were probably not as open as we might have been on that point for fear that too much need might discourage your assent. You know, and we remember, how important to the flowering of our Presbyterian congregations around Chester were the academies and even those we less formally called 'log colleges.' They became respected throughout the colonies for the quality of their education. If the day will ever come when we can covet the wish to send our children to Princeton, we will have to give them a better education here in our neighborhood. Do you mind the dual role as preacher and teacher that you have taken on?"

"Absolutely not," I said. "I had been late in coming to education as the means of realizing the fullness of my own human calling. How could I then not see it as the revelation that all children should have available? I need the support of the congregation, however, and the participation of neighbors in order to have a facility to do the job. My home is not suited to serve a second function as a school. With our young family, Rachel needs all our space for crawling children. We need a separate building where I can have the surroundings to teach, and in case you have been thinking of it, the Session House at the church is not the proper place to be conducting a school."

"I am tolerable sure," said Robert, "that we can raise up a schoolhouse for you, Preacher, but for now, can you not make use of the church building?"

I said, "I do not believe that the church should be used in such a way. Besides, if it was once used, there would be no urgency in getting a school house."

"You are right there," he admitted.

Within the year the people of Buffalo and Alamance, along with other interested parents in the neighborhood, had constructed a frame school with fireplace and storage loft. In the first year the new building became overcrowded and by the time our eldest was in his teen years, a second building, also of frame construction, was complete with upstairs quarters for some of the students who lived at the school. Downstairs there were two classrooms and my office. We started just with benches but soon had built long desks across each row. Students used slates and I had an uneven slate square attached to the wall on which I could write. The academic model then matched the Pennsylvania academy, and the Latin and Greek classical curriculum was preparing students for college and seminary schools. But I get ahead of the story.

It was the first school of its kind on the frontier of Carolina, and although New Bern had an academy, many of my students came from the eastern part of the state. My only models for teaching had come through my own experience at Pequa and Princeton. I assumed my own techniques so they fit easily with my personality, and I was easily more at home in the school house than the pulpit. I discouraged frivolity but I was not very strict. I did not want children to learn out of fear but out of inspiration. Although I did have the rod well displayed, I was slow to bring it to use believing that the children should respect me but not fear me. I had to place more structure into the management of academy discipline as the student enrollment grew. Before the war I had about twenty students in all grades and with Rachel's constant assistance, I remember those days, as I said, as idyllic – well perhaps at least very joyful.

I was urged, likely more than others in Carolina, to begin such a school because I was serving a more cohesive group of newcomers, who had all left a region of outstanding educational opportunities, and wanted to have the same for their children in their new location. I had all the qualifications that they wanted. It was not a coincidence that my school should take on a special reputation for educating youth from a wide region of the central Piedmont.

These same qualifications that set me among the ranks of leadership and reputation, served to influence the organizational development of the Presbyterian church in the South. At first, I and the others in North Carolina were members of Hanover Presbytery in Virginia. That Presbytery, on more than one occasion, met within North Carolina in anticipation of the next step of expansion and the opportunity came in 1770

I greeted Hezekiah Balch and Joseph Alexander with uncharacteristic excess as they arrived at Buffalo that day. "We are now able to have a certified Princeton reunion. McAden is already here so 'where four are gathered, there also is a reunion,' if I might loosely paraphrase Matthew."

Hezekiah Balch and Joseph Alexander served Bethel and Sugaw Creek respectively. Hugh McAden was at Upper Hico in Caswell County. We were all graduates of Princeton. Henry Patillo was at Hawfields and James Cresswell was at Bullock's Creek in York County, South Carolina. Those men had all traveled to Buffalo that spring for the purpose of calling for a new Presbytery.

I told Hezekiah, "I had wanted to have James Campbell among our number when we organized but I suppose the Cape Fear Scots feared association with a colonial Presbytery as further isolating them from the church in Scotland."

"We are a stubborn lot, are we not?" Balch responded. "I suspect Campbell will be with us in spirit even though he considered it politic not to officially join us. We should keep him informed of all our actions and plans. He is a man of strong convictions."

" I know," I said. "I was at Campbellton just months ago and was fully exposed to the determination of that set of Presbyterians to maintain their links to Scotland and the Crown."

We met in the Buffalo Church, which could only be described as a rustic frontier log building quickly assembled and temporary. Buffalo was on a plateau above the North Fork of Buffalo Creek in the confines of the Nottingham Company purchase. There was a gradual rise in the land to the northeast. It was pleasant farmland not unlike our former home in southeast Pennsylvania. The air was good, usually well away from the fevers that were so frequent in the east of the state. This whole area drained into the Cape Fear River basin but the main immediate water sources were Buffalo and Reedy Fork Creeks. There were overtures presented to each meeting of Presbytery, from settlements of Scots-Irish spreading out from the route of the Great Wagon Road through North and South Carolina, requesting ministers to serve them. Log churches were many times built in anticipation of a minister and congregations were ready-made for formal organization. These pioneers had been able to bring so little of their material goods with them but they were possessed of their families and their traditions and they needed their church to root their structure in community. Mind you, the frontier was fragile for most people. They needed their God in familiar form. There were leaders and adventurers among them but for most, there was fear and uncertainty. A minister of their traditional denomination could restore their confidence. They needed their God but they also needed His representative in the form of a shepherd.

"We are meeting as Hanover Presbytery today," I began in explanation as we convened in the church. "It is the nature of the ever-expanding migration that there are no delegates from Virginia, but we have the authority for the action that we contemplate. Reverend Patillo," I said, "you have a report from your committee appointed to prepare the petition for the establishment of a new presbytery."

With that, Henry Patillo read the document that requested the establishment of Orange Presbytery. Presbyterians were known for our ecclesiastical organization which was based on a series of ascending courts. Congregations operated with a Session of Elders, elected from the membership, to whom was given the authority of governance. Each minister was a member of and delegate to the Presbytery which was intended to encompass a geographic area that could meet conveniently. The Presbytery had authority over acts of the congregations. Next in ascending order was the Synod, that covered a broader region. At that time the Synod of New York and Philadelphia would include our new presbytery. Later it fell under the Synod of the Carolinas. The Synod had authority over the individual Presbyteries. After 1788, the General Assembly of all Presbyteries would have ultimate church-wide authority in the United States. These courts all functioned in appellate order.

"You know that my people are of strong mind against Parliament," I said to Balch, Hugh McAden, and Joseph Alexander, "but we are infested in our neighborhood with an equally intense community of Tories. We may even have a few lukewarm Tories at Buffalo or Alamance but I think of them more as pragmatists, afraid of the insecurity that will certainly come with any effort at independence."

"I think you would agree that in the Mecklenburg area," contended Joseph Alexander as he turned toward Balch, "we are likewise divided but the Presbyterian congregations are very sympathetic with the Whig thinking in New England. There is talk of declaring for independence but I am afraid that is a radical thought, not yet an inevitable course of action."

Balch added, "I fear we are too aggressive and I preach order before chaos." He continued, speaking to me, "the declaration that you and Patillo and McAden sent to Tryon before the Regulator battle a few years back, did much to place Presbyterians officially on the side of the King. Now, I fear that Governor Martin and his Tories see us as uniformly opposed to England."

"You understand," I responded, "that declaration was an effort at pacification of the Regulator movement that was about to get out of hand. I do not see," I asserted, "Presbyterians as revolutionaries, or even as the discontented. We are the object of considerable opprobrium in the eyes of the English Church but we have been steadfast in our dedication to law and order. Tryon recognized that in granting us the authority to perform marriages."

"Yes, but we in Mecklenburg have failed to gain a charter for our college, in spite of the approval of the governor. Even under the guise of naming it Queens College, London feared to allow greater educational opportunities," said Alexander. "For Presbyterians that is anathema and our people are uniformly aroused." Speaking directly to me he said, "Caldwell, you have your academy. How would your congregations react if Parliament denied them a charter to organize a college?"

"I grant you, they would be firmly aroused," I admitted, "but we do not have, at present, that local defining issue with the King. We are still people of the Covenant and most of our members visualize that authority binds us with the temporal and the spiritual government. As for myself, I believe it to be only a matter of time before these exacerbating acts of the British Parliament and the Board of Trade will single out every congregation in a particularly unpopular action that will bring them into opposition. It is but a matter of time. Then, the obvious ineptitude of rule by an island nation, no matter how grand, over a colonial mass unlimited in territory and an ocean away, will seem absurd."

"We all seem to be speaking in terms of inevitability but we have a special charge as ministers of the word and the sacrament. We cannot mislead," said Alexander with an ominous tone.

"We will find our prophetic voice only as God leads us," I ventured. "Our prayers must be for peace and for human fulfillment. God will give us the insight to know when the one has overcome the other. Our effort must be to repress the devil within that would make militancy attractive or convince us of false pride. It will be a devious time of demagoguery and deception. God will demand that we guard against both and disown it wherever we see it. The good will not all be on one side but eventually we will have to choose one side or be banished from both."

"It is an unpleasant quandary but we act under a calling to service, no matter the circumstances," added McAden

"Having reviewed the quandary," said Alexander, as if to refocus the debate, "we must assume that approval of the petition to set up Orange Presbytery will create the only denominational church organization of its kind within the state outside the Anglican Church. That singles us out as the Colonial ecclesiastical entity, that is an alternative to the establishment position of the English church. We will be suspected and we will be watched. I do not say that fearfully but I believe we should all recognize our increased vulnerability. Any Colonial action that leans further toward independence, pushes us forward as among the disaffected. We are part of the current that is seen as opposing Parliament and the King."

The actions of that spring Presbytery meeting were approved by the Synod of New York and Philadelphia and Orange Presbytery was organized at Hawfields in September 1770, where I was elected as the first presiding Clerk. McAden preached the opening sermon and I placed the supplication before the Synod of the Presbyterian Church to send ministers to serve the congregations being organized in this new field.

"In the new and growing bounds of Orange Presbytery," I wrote, "there are churches eager for the service of ministers to preach the word and to mold them into community. Presbyterians can do that but as long as there is a vacuum, people will take advantage of the innocence as ignorance. They will stand and proclaim themselves called and they will distort the truth of God. We have got to provide leadership."

What we saw, meeting as Orange Presbytery, was the danger of a people poorly served by impoverished leadership and couched in the terminology of "the church." But similar dangers likewise existed in the political leadership that was available to the colonies. As pressure moved unevenly in the colonial mainland toward confrontation, the search for indigenous leadership mounted. If the conclusion of the building unrest was to be independence, from whence would the leadership emerge to demand such freedom? For the British government, their concern was where were the elements of organization capable of having significant executive potential in these colonies? One of the likely suspects, they came to accept, was the organization of the Presbyterian Church. So as pressure within the church forced the distribution of an educated clergy more broadly throughout the colonies, that also was developing part of the structure that would be active in the rebellion.

A year after our organization of Orange Presbytery, recognizing the strength of the Presbyterian community, the North Carolina Assembly organized Guilford County and designated it ecclesiastically as Unity Parish of the Church of England. 'Unity' turned out to be a paradox for a weak, ironic attempt to bolster the state church, since there were no congregations of the Church of England in Guilford anyway. The legislation required that twelve vestrymen and two wardens be empowered to levy taxes to build churches and employ ministers to preach for the Church of England. The county court simply elected twelve Presbyterians to the positions thereby making the vestry moot and two years later, the assembly dissolved Unity Parish.

My farm adjoined Thomas McQuiston on the east and further east was Buffalo Church. Sawit Branch of North Buffalo Creek ran through my farm, as did Centre Road, and to the west was New Garden Quaker Meeting. Immediately to the south was Dillon's Mill. Centre Road was the main north–south road through the center of the county. To the north it ran to the Court House and beyond that to the Iron Works on Troublesome Creek. To the south it went to Centre Quaker Meeting, from which it got its name. Near Centre Meeting that road intersected with the Kings Road to Hillsborough and with the Cross Creek Road from Salem down to Campbellton on the Cape Fear.

In the first decade, I established my farm, built my home, barn and outbuildings and the original academy. I didn't know then that I was establishing the physical surroundings that would sustain me for the rest of my life – my work as minister of two Presbyterian churches, my farm, and the school. My ministry was, in those combined functions, securely underwritten.

I remember one day that I told one of the boys, "fetch Mrs. Caldwell a fresh bucket of water from the spring, won't you lad?" I was speaking to one of my students who sat daydreaming under a monstrous oak. "While you are at it," I said, "splash some of that cold water on your face or you will be asleep in the shade."

"Yes sir," the boy said. "Right away, sir. Can I help Miss Rachel with anything at the house today?"

The boys knew that helping Rachel usually brought a special reward from the kitchen. That day, I think it was Tom Pinson. I said, "Tom, this part of the day you should be attentive to your studies. There are plenty of chores to be done and other diversions but you have to learn that work on your lessons takes priority. Mrs. Caldwell and I do not have you here to help with house or farm work. We have slaves for those jobs."

We did have some slaves assigned as field hands and house servants. There was some moral pressure at the time on those who owned slaves. For me, I invested in slaves to perform tasks that needed to be done and they in turn relieved me to concentrate on my teaching and my ministry and relieved Rachel for her family and kitchen chores. On a regular basis, Rachel gave Christian instruction to our slaves and I regularly gave sermons just for them at the farm. These services were usually attended by slaves from nearby Presbyterian farms. The Quakers, around New Garden, forbade the ownership of slaves and they held for the end of slavery. That was a subtle influence on our Presbyterians and particularly on me. I can tell you that the slaves were not ignorant of the situation.

Then there came the day I had to tell Rachel, "when we assembled to go to the fields this morning, Sam was gone." It was not so much information, as an indication that our frequently discussed moral dilemma had matured into a full blown incident. "I have advised Tom McQuiston and he advised me to immediately notify the Patroller, or he feared other slaves would follow our Sam's example."

"I hate the very idea of one human tracking another like an animal," I remember she told me, "but then it seems to me that we are more than considerate of our people and I can't see why they should want to run away."

I explained, as if to myself, "I need slaves to operate my farm and I convince myself that they are better off working here than anywhere else about. At the same time, I turn my back on the immorality of enslavement, by me and by those in my congregation. The Quakers call attention to the immorality. My people point to the economic reality of labor. Quakers and Presbyterians refer to the same Bible to underwrite their conclusions. My view," and I said I would speak so from the pulpit at Alamance that week, "is that freedom for slaves at this time would cast them out of secure homes, and the use of their labor would be of no use to them or us. There may come a way in the future that they will be able to sell their labor, but until then, the system serves black and white. I will have the Patroller recapture Sam."

Within the hour, McQuiston, David Rankin, and Adam Scott were at our door to make certain that I would quickly notify the Patroller to act. "Pastor, I suspect that somehow, Sam was encouraged to run by some of those Quakers up the road. They act meek and mild but they do interfere in our business just as they did in Pennsylvania."

"We like our independence," Rankin noted, admitting thus to that Scots-Irish prejudice of seeing all others as interference. "If those Quakers like working as a group to do their chores, let 'em do it, but I don't ask my neighbor to do my work. If I got more to do than I got hands to do it, I buy me a slave. Simple as that. I feed him and clothe him and I don't abuse him and that ought to be a fair bargain."

"If you don't have that Patroller out after your man, Preacher, I have a serious concern that some of my people will try to follow him," admitted Scott. "I've only got four men for my fields and if they were to run, I'd lose my crop."

"Point taken," I thought. "If you lose your crop, it will be the preacher's fault, right?"

Sam was away for only two days. On the second night, he was found breaking into a storage building on a farm near Dan River. The owner shot him.

"What point have we proven? What issue have we resolved?" I asked as Rachel wept on hearing the news from McQuiston. "The loss of my investment in another human seemed some kind of judgment rather than a financial reversal. I will have a poorly tended crop to remind me of this human tragedy but will we remember it next year or the next? Hardening of the heart is a progressive disease to be reversed only with prayer for forgiveness."

Rachel cried softly, "Oh, David."

I said to McQuiston, perhaps with more of a tone of judgment than he deserved, "you have your deterrent against runaway slaves for the time being. I don't think it will be remembered long."

The next day, I recall that two little black children played by the porch of the cabin occupied by Cleo, one of our cooks. Students played in the south field between lessons, laughing and calling out to each other. Billy Suttenfield whispered to Joe Sherrill, "my daddy tol' me that one of Pastor Caldwell's slaves ran away the other day and got shot."

Billy knew that planting such information with one of the

younger boys, would get results. When classes resumed, Joe Sherrill's hand went up and he blurted out, "Pastor Caldwell, who got shot?"

There was silence for a long moment. I knew what Joe had heard and I was considering how best to give the facts and an important lesson at the same time. "Boys, you may not know that my man, Sam, whom you all have seen about the place, ran away three nights ago. Yesterday he was shot on a farm up on the Dan River when he tried to rob food from a man's barn." The boys were stunned. I paused again. "Sam was a slave but he was also a human being. A human being means that he was just like you or me, one of God's children. A slave means that he did not have all the rights that you and I have according to the law." Again I paused. "Jesus tells us to love one another. Does that mean to love all human beings or just those who are like us? If we love everybody does that include slaves? If it means slaves, then how can we keep those we love bound in slavery? These are hard questions but I want you to think about them tonight, and tomorrow we will talk about our answers."

Joe was still excited that he had provoked this serious talk. "Preacher, can I ask my daddy tonight?"

I told him, "you can always ask your daddy, but I want to hear what you think tomorrow, not a repeat of what your daddy thinks."

On Wednesday, the boys were nervous about their thoughts and I imagined they had been restless much of the night. Some had mentioned the questions to their parents or talked with siblings or with other students before class began. Still, they were not used to standing before a class of their friends and expressing an opinion on such serious matters, as if their thought counted.

Soon after I had opened the morning class with a prayer, I looked long and slowly around the room at each student. I could easily tell, from the apprehension on their faces, that they had wrestled with the matter of slavery and they were confounded. They were experiencing the uneasiness of ignorance although at these young ages, they could not have identified the basis of their anxiousness.

"I asked you to spend some time last night thinking about a problem – what we might call a dilemma. The word dilemma is a combination of Greek and Latin – di, meaning two and lemma, meaning a proposition or an assumption. Thus, we have a word for a situation, when we are presented with an issue, about which, there are two or more alternative arguments or conclusions. The law in the colonies has allowed slaves to be imported from Africa. These slaves are black people, free in their homeland, who are captured, put in chains and brought across the Atlantic. Once here, these people are sold at public slave auctions and that is how white people come to own black people. Slaves are put to work at specific jobs, mostly on farms to do work necessary in order to have profitable farm crops. The owner is required to feed, clothe, house, and provide medicine for all his slaves. You know I have slaves and I believe that most of your parents have slaves."

Eight year old Eli Watson offered, "My daddy has six slaves. They have their own house. It is smaller than ours and they work in

78

the field and do work in our house."

"Alright, Eli, that is the way it is on most farms," I answered. "But many people are troubled that it is possible for one person to own another. I can demonstrate to you many places in the Bible where people owned slaves. Do you remember the story of the Israelites in Egypt, when Moses said to the Pharaoh, 'Let my people go'? Many people today are beginning to say, 'Let my people go.' Now my slave Sam wanted to go. He did not want to remain my slave and he ran away at night. I had a dilemma. What should I do?"

"Let him go," blurted out Robert.

"Can't let him go," countered Eli.

"If I let him go, who would do his work on my farm and who would pay me back for all the money I paid for my slave? I am not a rich man."

There was a pause as the boys saw that the quick answers were not going to be satisfactory but other answers would be complicated. I let them consider for several minutes. "I decided, after talking with my neighbors and spending some time in prayer, that I must report Sam to the Patroller, who is an officer of the court, and he would track down Sam and bring him back. I would not punish Sam but I would put him back to work in my fields. But before the Patroller found Sam, he tried to steal some food from another farmer's barn because he was hungry. The farmer shot him because he was stealing." I spoke more softly. "Now Sam is dead and I have no one to do his work on my farm and no one to repay me for the money I paid to own Sam.

If I had let Sam go, I would have been in the same situation but Sam would be alive. I am saddened and I feel guilt, because Sam is dead. According to man's law, I did nothing wrong, but we all answer to a higher law – God's law. God does not expect us, you or me or your parents, to solve every dilemma on our own. You will be faced with many dilemmas in your life including the dilemma of slavery. Work for a solution. Ask God to show you the answer and guide your actions. But in every dilemma, seek to make the situation better. You can do that. With the help of God, you alone can do that. In every situation, make it better. If it is a human situation, protect the least protected that it might be better."

I could not bring myself to replace Sam that year. It was difficult and I had to sacrifice more of my own time to the fields, but that was somehow atonement. In the spring I bought Casius from the slave dealer up in Caswell county. Everyone still had their dilemma.

CHAPTER FIVE **1775** Approach of Battle

My interests, and admittedly some responsibility, extended to my brother, Alexander. Alexander had left Lancaster when I did. We were the two eldest sons. Of course, I had trained for the work that called me as a minister and had 550 acres of Nottingham land. Alexander was a farmer and he had been an important help to me in the opening of the land and building the first house and school. By 1771, I sold to Alexander 275 acres of our land and he had married Margaret, and by January of the next year, they had their first son. Then it was my time to assist him in establishing his farm.

The replication of much that was familiar in Lancaster provided a solid foundation to the course of settlement and development along the Buffalo and Alamance creeks. To my mind, people found security in their neighbors, about whom they already had family knowledge. Even among the Quakers and Germans on the fringes, I always thought there was some comfort in having known our neighbors in Pennsylvania, although to some extent the petty hostilities that were familiar to Pennsylvania were brought to a new setting.

Alexander held me in great respect and I was re-enforced in my work by his uncomplicated and buoyant spirit. He was slightly taller than I and had a healthy, rugged body. His personality attracted admirers. He too had attended Pequa Academy but was not much of a scholar. When I had determined on the ministry as a calling and needed money to attend Princeton, Alexander convinced our other brothers to advance the money by purchasing my share of our parents' farm. I believe my later success was a vicarious confirmation for Alexander.

Having Alexander and his family nearby gave me an extension of my family by blood that was a comfort as more hostile times approached. Rachel was my wife, my confidant, and Alexander was my companion with whom I could deliberate on my thoughts without needing qualifications. We shared the common starting place of our lives that only siblings can appreciate instinctively. On the frontier a man can selfishly leach into himself and soon find he has no interest beyond his own needs. My prayers of thankfulness were always for God's gift to me of Rachel and Alexander. They were the instruments for defining the purpose of God in my life.

Alexander and I tended to wrestle earnestly with public issues and having concluded the authenticity of one side or the other, became vocal adherents to a cause. No newspapers were available to any of us then on a regular basis, but we devoured eagerly those that did appear by post from the North. After the defeat of the Regulators, the Nottingham Colony gradually, but with resolution, took the side of the New England radicals. Some of the motivation came from the structure of the Regulator community. After all I had, in a rather official manner, assured Governor Tryon that Presbyterians were not behind the Regulator activities. I really believed that my efforts to qualify the actions of the Regulators had an effect on retarding Presbyterian interest in that cause. Presbyterians like Forbis, the Gillespies, and Rankin had attached themselves to the Regulators, but their enthusiasm was curtailed. I believe they were more active in the early stages of the movement because they were leaders, and the Regulators were the only organized group that was challenging the actions of government, and the only group outside the government that desperately could use leadership. Their support wilted as the cause was directed more locally, and disappeared in the face of the defeat at the battle of Alamance. They continued to be suspicious of government and now that distrust gravitated to distant government. They had no natural interest in the concerns of the radicals, especially those driven by the rivalry of wealthy merchants of the East. Government, however, never served them well and their specific complaints were used by others to draw them in to common cause against all aspects of government, indeed to the inbred suspicion of law itself.

When Josiah Martin took over from Tryon a few months after the battle, he made a concerted attempt to listen to and assuage the concerns of the people of Stinking Quarter, Sandy Creek, and the Germans at Salem, and demonstrate his good will. He made no similar effort among the Presbyterians. Governor Martin thought that he had basic support among the Presbyterians on the Cape Fear that would surely influence those in the Piedmont.

Alexander Martin said, "What I read from Lancaster and Chester certainly indicates that sentiment grows for some kind of break with England. The point is made that although the economic impact of the increased taxation of colonial goods by Parliament may be more on the commercial interests of the East, sooner or later higher taxes will lead to more laws that restrict our trade everywhere. We are left here, across an ocean, without any input into a debate that determines our fate. We Scots know well enough what danger there is when our laws come from far away London."

"Ho, Ho, Ho. 'We Scots' indeed," I chided him. "Since when did a Jersey man like you consider himself a 'wee Scot?' You were born a Colonial. What transpired with our Scottish ancestry serves us falsely in this land, I'll tell you. I have seen it on the Cape Fear. They are more Scots than Bonnie Charlie and it will likely dry up the energy of the Presbyterian church in their midst. At the same time, they have bound themselves so solidly to the Hanoverians that they cannot make an independent decision even today. We should, in truth, preserve some of our good old German and English and Irish and Scots ways but we are Colonial boys now and we must find the means to be our self-sufficient selves."

"Do I hear a rebellious priest then?" Alexander said to me in mock amazement.

"Rebellion is a word I fear," I answered, "but independence is a condition I consider inevitable. My problem is, I can't see how to get to the one without going through the other."

At that moment Elders Thomas McQuiston and Hugh Wiley arrived at the door of the manse and I greeted them. "Come break up a political discourse, please," begged Alexander.

"God knows our fate but He still encourages civil discourse." observed McQuiston with a wry expression that contested Presbyterian doctrine.

"There you go, Tom," I said, "crucifying us on the cross of the elect."

We all sat down with serious faces understanding that as leaders of our church, we must be able to speak the truth in the face of insecure times.

"I want you to know, preacher," began Hugh Wiley, "that last week a Baptist brother, whom I will not name, challenged me as a 'blue stocking' saying, with a serious face, that since I believed in predestination, I shouldn't worry at the prospect of rebellion. He said since I was no doubt already chosen of God, it shouldn't make any difference to me which side I was on in this earthly struggle. I would still get to glory. I laughed, of course, but it concerns me that my beliefs can be used by such a fellow to mock me."

"Poor Wiley," I said with a touch of the ironic. "You should have answered that since he was once saved always saved, you should expect he was equally certain of heaven and you would expect to see him as well at that glorious moment." Hugh, a little restrained, joined in the laughter. "I will bring out my predestination sermon soon but right now we were discussing our colonial options in this growing crisis."

"I am resigned," said McQuiston with a firmness that invited debate. "Parliament seems bent on our subjugation, but if we can be subjugated, we can also be free. The sooner our debate turns to who will lead us and when shall we start, the better we will be prepared."

For a moment, I was afraid that the opinion of the clerk, the chief lay officer of the congregation, startled the others by his belligerent tone. "The sooner the better? Tom you are indeed resigned," said Alexander Martin. "When I hear it said so bluntly by another whom I know to be a man of personal faith, I must say that I recoil a bit. I presume, for each of us, we need to hear it said. We need to encounter the literal. Fear builds rapidly in the face of uncertainty. I believe it comes to you, David, to be the guiding light for these people. I am satisfied that God will use you."

The discussion continued into the night. It was no longer a decision-making debate but many little debates on adverbs: how, when or why. The next day I spent the morning in the Session House outlining my Sunday text. I sought to give my people something that they could place in the context of their known circumstances, that would lead them to conclusions they could continue to support and that would support them. It would not be didactic but confirming. After all, around the county Whig sympathizers were attaching deer tails to their hats to show their opposition to the government. My people yearned for direction.

I began my sermon with taxation as the measure of harmony

between government and the governed. "When we pay a tax to the support of a government whose constitution we approve and in whose measures we have a voice, it is paid cheerfully," I began. "When it is paid to a foreign government, and especially if it is paid from compulsion and not from choice, it is always considered as degrading." I demonstrated that when such conditions were tolerated, people were, "in a degraded state of subjugation." Persons, however, "are so constituted that vigorous and well-directed exertion is necessary to the attainment of anything that is valuable." I concluded, "We are surrounded by enemies and dangers of various kinds, and to avoid being overcome, both vigilance and efforts are necessary; if we refuse, however, to watch and to take the necessary precautions, or to defend ourselves when attacked, captivity or ruin will be the certain consequence."

I continued, using a paraphrase of the Calvin ethic. "The creator long ago implanted into man's nature a capacity for civic responsibility. God taught men to consider themselves His stewards, and gave them talents and opportunities, and expected them to make the most of these endowments." Then I applied that argument to the issues being raised by the Whigs. "It is not enough to practice thrift and self-denial in the patriot cause. The people must gather and exert their psychic energy; they must focus, concentrate, and obey their own self-consciousness and thereby move with swiftness and grace instead of habitual heaviness, clumsiness, and indecision."

Then I gave a name to this antithesis to psychic energy – the sluggard – my enemy. "The sluggard, as a worthless being, destitute of merit, and doing no good to himself or anybody else, is really as much an object of reprobation as the miser, the spendthrift, or the highway robber; deficient to his duty to his God, his king, and the country."

I could not bring myself to speak treason against the King, but Parliament, never the friend of the Scots-Irish, was a natural target. I reviewed the experience of the Stamp Act, but I concluded that even Parliamentary repeal of that action was suspect. Parliament in fact seemed so "maliciously zealous to obtain domination over us that they officiously stepped in and stripped his majesty of his prerogative," with the result that "we are reduced to the dreadful alternative either of immediate and unconditional submissiveness or of resistance by force of arms."

Then came my challenge to action. "If we stand up manfully and united in defense of our rights, then in the strength of the Lord, who is mightier than all, we shall prevail. We expect that none of you will be wanting in the discharge of your duty, or prove unworthy in a cause which is so important in itself, and which every patriot and every Christian should value more than wealth, and hold as dear as his life."

I admit that this was less the stuff of a sermon and more a political rallying call. Delivered in both congregations with slight modification, it confirmed that I was on the side of the Whigs in a nearly equally divided colony. Rachel heard the words and was filled with fear but she knew well the struggle that I had worked through in prayer. She was certain that I had divine guidance and she was content.

At this point, leaven was taking the place of inertia within the Colonial interests. Cautionary concerns were being pushed aside. The tenor of conflict was as contagious among the New Side at Alamance as with the Old Side at Buffalo. Although I led my flock as war approached, frequently I was in the position of holding back their aggression. There were no British troops on the soil of this province. The Tory in the neighborhood was physically the closest thing to an enemy and if emotions were allowed to overtake reason, I feared that Civil War could result. It was necessary to maintain the debate in order to vitiate the emotional pressure of distinguishing an enemy, a delicate task for a minister.

Much more, the Craigheads and Alexanders in Mecklenburg were embroiled in deliberation that would precipitate a revolution. After Alexander Craighead's death in 1766, his pastorate at Rocky River was taken up by another of my Princeton friends, Hezekiah James Balch. The denial of a charter for Queens College and the closure of that school in 1773 by the Crown, had hardened the hearts of the Mecklenburg Presbyterians. Royal authority was insensitive to the devotion on this colonial frontier to education and that merely confirmed the indifference that could be expected from distant government. The Presbyterians, meeting in General Assembly in 1774, instructed local congregations to press for the dissolution of ties with Great Britain. On May 20, 1775, a convention of Mecklenburg delegates met at Charlotte to consider a formal defiance of the King. More than twenty of the delegates to the convention were Presbyterians, connected with the seven churches of the denomination in the county. Abraham Alexander, who had been whipped at the time of the Sugaw Creek War, chaired the convention. The resolves of this convention were dispatched by the end of the month to Congress then meeting at Philadelphia.

Captain James Jack, one of the Presbyterian delegates, was selected to ride to Philadelphia and present the Mecklenburg resolutions. He started the last day of the month and his first stop was Salisbury where a General Court was in session. The Whigs responded to a reading of the resolves with enthusiasm. Jack stopped next at Salem and a few miles further came to Buffalo to share the document with me.

Jack's ride was considered a risk as he passed through the deeply divided colony headed north. His stop at Buffalo was only for a brief rest and to advise me of the actions and sentiment in Mecklenburg. "I can tell you that most of the text is the work of your Princeton friends, Balch and Waightstill Avery and especially Ephraim Brevard," Jack confided. "It is a call to action directed by our Committee of Safety and we intend for it to encourage our delegates in Congress to action."

"I have no doubt that it will have such an effect," I responded. "Are more such declarations to come from other Committees?"

"We have no such correspondence but I suspect that the sentiments are widespread."

"Widespread sentiments do not have the political impact of a declaration voted in convention," I noted, "but we near the precipice and it is time we assert our conviction with the greatest clarity. It will be a hardship on people who struggle daily at survival, to anticipate the probable impact of war upon their circumstances. I am torn by my sympathy for those who are always trapped into being the munitions of war and my certainty that we cannot longer tolerate union with this dominion pressing down on us. I am called to speak kindly concern from the pulpit, while I smolder in rage against tyrannical behavior. May God speed you on this mission, James, and use your labor to a worthy result."

Jack's departure was as dramatic as had been his arrival. I thought to myself that he had been like the whirlwind dropping uncalled into our lives with unknown consequences. Then I became conscious of the eyes of students and adults around the barnyard who were absorbing the sight in uncertain fear. There would be days, when I could help them to understand but at this moment, I felt called to plead with God for direction and energy.

By September of 1775, the Provincial Assembly provided for a single company of Minutemen to be raised in Guilford County. The next April, the Fourth Provincial Assembly appointed field officers for the militia in the county. Most of the officers in both cases were Presbyterians. Tories understood that I, as minister for many of these men, was the strongest influence on their decision to arm. They accused me of acting like a popish priest by absolving those who had been Regulators of the oath that they had taken after the Battle of Alamance, to support the King. It had not been absolution that I had found for those who had accepted Tryon's oath of obedience to King George. I gave them the means to see that the oath had been coercive, because the alternative to signing was hanging. Now, they had to ask themselves, if the British government continued to grossly and repeatedly violate our rights, are we to be bound by the second oath? Obligation and duty are reciprocal conditions. The home government had notoriously, and with increasing frequency, violated their oath to us and they showed every indication that they would continue to do so. Therefore, at some point that becomes the justification for our release from our obligation to obedience. These are no less the terms of a covenant that is broken when one signatory breaks the conditions of the agreement. Reports of my association with the Whigs singled me out as a leader of this building insurrection.

Down on the Cape Fear, James Campbell was having an experience that contrasted with mine. He had struggled under the pious and devout Scots Presbyterians, trained as they were in their old Scottish fashion, repeating their catechisms, and lining, word for word, the text of the minister at all services. They were called by some, "the little ministers of Barbecue." Some relief had come eventually to this pressure on Campbell, when Rev. John McLeod arrived with a new colony of Scots about 1770. After a few years, McLeod declared "he would rather preach to the most polished and fashionable congregation of Edinburgh than to the little critical carles of Barbecue," and he sailed back to Scotland. Campbell's sympathy was with the rebels and he found strong opposition from the Scots. In this case, their roots as Covenanters were interpreted as committing them to the cause of King George, with whom some had taken an oath of allegiance after the defeat at Culloden. The Scots saw this as a civil and religious covenant by which they were bound. Minister and congregation were at such hostile odds that ultimately a Gael named Munn threatened, "Preacher I will shoot you dead if you ever again pray for the success of those rebels." Campbell accepted the threat as literal and left with his family for Guilford and the friendlier confines that surrounded me.

It was these Scots on the Cape Fear, along with the still hostile Regulators in Guilford, around whom the Governor intended to fashion the defense of the Royal Prerogative in North Carolina. Governor Josiah Martin was depending on the shifting support of the Highlanders for the British government that had assisted in settling them in this new land. It was an alliance united only in its dissatisfaction with the Whig leadership of the colony and the fact that some in both groups, having been defeated by the Crown, had pledged their oath to support the King in the future. Late in the year the British sent two officers to organize the Highlanders and in December the British commander in the American colonies, General Sir Henry Clinton, dispatched 2000 troops from Boston.

On January 10, 1776, Governor Martin called on the

Regulators and Highlanders to raise the royal standard and march to join the British at Brunswicktown. By now, James Campbell had become active as a leader of the rebellion and he was co-operating with the Cumberland County Association in opposition to the British.

At the time of the battle at Alamance, key men in my congregations like Ralph Gorrell, William Mebane, John Forbis, and William and Hugh Wiley were active and energetic in the Regulator cause. None responded to the call of Governor Martin to the King's colors.

Our Patriot troops made up of Minutemen and local militias and commanded by Colonel James Moore, met the Highlanders at Widow Moore's Creek Bridge, 12 miles above Wilmington, on February 27th. The forces in the battle were small and untested under command. General McDonald, at the last minute, was declared too ill to march and Colonel McLeod accepted command. Finding the Highlander units ready for battle, he ordered the advance.

McLeod wheeled his mount and advanced toward the bridge. Drums rolled and the clanking of equipment and the stamping of feet in that swampy setting sounded strange. In full regalia, the Scots stepped upon the exposed logs that now spanned the waters. The flooring of the bridge had been ripped up by the Patriots prior to the battle. Patriot marksmen opened fire and in the first fusillade, McLeod was shot dead from his horse. The Highlanders, in their soft shoes, slipped on the damp, mossy logs even as they attempted to rush the bridge. Patriot sharp shooters from a slight rise on the other side had unsteady targets of their choosing and the Highlanders slipped, fell, screamed, and died in a pathetic attempt at crossing. The action, exposed to full view of both armies, sent panic through the Tory ranks

The Governor was present to see his Carolina strategy collapse. The Highlanders had not received the Tory support they had anticipated from the rest of the colony, but Whig support also had been slow and many units arrived after the fighting. British confidence was stunned and the Highlanders disheartened.

I had followed eagerly the news anticipating the battle and I received first hand descriptions of the battle from members of the Guilford militia. James Martin, a member at Buffalo, and younger brother of Alexander Martin, commanded some forces of the Continental line. I also heard from my former Regulator members, who knew people who had sympathized with the other side.

"It was a battle in a swamp," was James Martin's summary. "The Guilford men would have made a poor report on themselves, I fear. Half of them came into camp unarmed. We had to impress others along the way, who wanted no part of fighting. Captain Alexander Hunter seemed to lose all reason when faced with their indifference to logic. At one point along the march he deserted his men, then became so tyrannical and lawless toward them that he had to be restrained. He was accused of tying two of his men to a tree and levying a charge of £10 for drunkenness without ordering a Courts Martial. By the time we arrived, the battle was essentially over, only a few small signs of stubborn resistance remained. My brother, Alexander, and his Continentals, were better trained and equipped than were the militia – at least they looked better. They came later still and were only used to supervise the prisoners."

I asked if our Guilford men seemed to be ready for war. "They looked like such a motley lot when you marched them out. Can they act as a dependable fighting force when real war comes?"

"They are good for shooting squirrels and Indians but if they faced British regulars, they would be soundly whipped," admitted James Martin. "I have no confidence. If our woodland boys are fighting woodland Tory boys, I am sure we will hold our own. Our families can take some comfort from that. But a militia force is no match for regulars in spite of their bravery. My discussions with other officers while we were there at Moore's Creek satisfied me that we had effectively defeated the Highlanders as a fighting force in support of the British. We were fortunate, because that fight could only be considered a brawl."

"But the Highlanders were better trained and equipped," I pointed out, though that seemed to imply that the victory was more than just chance and insignificant. "I know these Scots to be hard and stubborn and they will not easily accept defeat."

"Defeat may not be the best measure of the result," Martin told me. "The Scots will not be a cowering defeated people. The battle did, however, settle what ever desire there was to support the cause of the distant King. At least for some time to come, they will lick their wounds. Now the Regulators, I believe, have been completely eliminated as a Tory fighting force. They remain as Tory bands in pockets throughout the district but they still have no leadership. And our boys – all they talked about on the way home was their spring planting. There was no question that they were farmers, not fighters."

In the middle of a school term, I can tell you, it was difficult to retain the attention of young boys on their school work, when their minds swirled with images of guns and fighting men and charging horses. News of the Moore's Creek battle consumed their imagination. In the few weeks after the battle they received less organized information than I did about the fighting but they picked up, and communicated repeatedly, every scrap of news they heard. Some news was from a parent who had been there. Other news came from passing travelers and peddlers. They eavesdropped on every adult conversation. Two or more talking adults were shadowed by small boys, attempting to be inconspicuous, but near enough to catch every word.

There were about twenty students now at the academy. We had no official name. That was unimportant when everyone knew it was Rev. Caldwell's Academy. Word just passed around that I was accepting students, and parents negotiated terms for their children depending on how many days, how many children, and if they were to be boarded with us. About half were boarders, and they took their meals with us. Our children adored these older boys whom they could constantly follow. The boys were dependable companions who, by playing with the children, gave Rachel much needed freedom to accomplish all the other duties of running an extended household. Parents contracted with me to teach their boys but they got for free the influential teaching of Rachel. She served as surrogate mother, and also as moral and spiritual advisor. I was the pedagogue, but Rachel was the guide to conscience and virtuosness. As for the school's influence, in the early years I would have to describe the school model as "sitting at the feet of the master." Parents sought the influence of what they considered learning and God-like living. It was a classical school model. Latin and Greek offered structure to learning. Skills in vocabulary and rules of declension and structure, were transferable to all learning and to the organization of life. There were almost no books for the students, only the Academy and Princeton texts that made up my personal library, from which I lectured. Older students shepherded the learning of the younger ones, transforming instruction into interpretation, into knowledge. There was a certain Biblical rhythm that penetrated the process – a sharing of the talents.

A pseudo-courtyard created by the main house, barn, school house, and outbuildings was the center of all activity outside the school room. Under three spreading oaks, a grove of cedars, and some pines, boys played games, ran races, and shared their lessons. They each had assigned chores that were periodically rotated so that skills were learned and more difficult work was shared. Boys loved to work with the animals but I did not allow them to do field work. They were allowed to ride the horses but they also had to curry them afterwards and clean stalls. Their clothes were loose- fitting homespun, cotton or wool, or linen. Dyed in natural colors, they were never bright and rarely clean. The aim was to keep them clothed, not clean, and I can tell you, a room full of smelly boys just in from play, could distract for a moment.

In April of '77, Presbyterians in Mecklenburg County made an even more ambitious effort to establish their academy by act of the Assembly. They still smarted under King George's rejection of Queens College and as a consequence, were provoked to name their new school Liberty Hall. To gain broader exposure to the academy, they asked me and other Presbyterians outside the county, to be trustees. I thought it well to encourage more education in the state wherever it might be proposed, so I agreed. They prevailed on Rev. Alexander McWhorter to assume the presidency. When Cornwallis moved the revolution into the South in 1780, the school was closed and never resumed.

On a Wednesday morning three weeks after Moore's Creek, news that Colonel Martin and his Continentals had returned from Cape Fear and camped near Buffalo, excited the students. In mid-morning, the Colonel and three of his aides rode up the Centre Road and into the yard before the school. The excitement could not be contained and the boys burst through the door to see these handsomely uniformed soldiers, the first soldiers that most had ever seen up close. I followed them out of the school house and strode up to my friend. "Alexander, or please pardon me, Colonel Martin. I am so pleased to see your safe and victorious return."

"David, I fear that 'victorious' is an undeserved exaggeration, for our company arrived several hours after the battle, and the closest we got to the Tories was to transport them as prisoners to Campbellton."

Alexander Martin was a King's Attorney at Salisbury when Captain Jack had passed with the Mecklenburg Resolves a few months earlier, and now he was the appointed Lieutenant Colonel of the 2nd North Carolina Regiment of the Continental Army. Although he was fifteen years younger then I, he too was a Princeton graduate, class of 1756, and had still been a tutor there when I had entered as an older student.

I urged him to come in because I knew that Rachel would be anxious to see him. She had asked me about him just this day. Martin handed the reins of his horse to one of his men and followed me into the house.

"Oh, Alexander, how pleased I am to see you well and returned," called Rachel as the Colonel dipped his head beneath the door jam. She threw her arms around him in pure joy.

"This is the homecoming I knew I could depend on from this house. How are you, Rachel, and the children?" he questioned.

"All healthy and energetic, thank God. We have had our first concerns about the fighting but it seems we have come through it."

"Rachel, would you find us some tea and then perhaps Alexander will stay to join our meal," I ventured. "The boys are so excited to see soldiers that I know their thoughts of study are gone for this day."

"I apologize for such an interruption to your routine, but I promised that I would return here with a report after our foray into Cape Fear."

"You did and we plan to enjoy this opportunity to the fullest."

Alexander and I went into my study to talk more seriously, away from the preparation for the meal. It was not a large room but it was where I often prepared my sermons and usually my lessons. My library of books was small, only about fifty, and they were strewn about on the writing table and a smaller table by the window. I offered Alex the upholstered chair before the table, and I took up my usual seat behind it. After a further exchange of compliments and mundane questions, I wondered, "Are you at liberty to tell me about your recent activities? I will not share any news," I hesitated, "that you might feel compromising, I guess."

"I have no concerns about your loyal interests, David, and I will be glad to speak about my adventures as to a good friend," Alexander replied with ease. "The Snow Campaign into South Carolina in the winter was our first trial as a military unit and I believe that, fresh as we were, we acquitted ourselves with honor. The Scovillites were Tories and they slipped out of the fort at Ninety-six in the middle of a blizzard, attempting to escape. We caught them and in a brief battle took more than 400 prisoners. I think our action sorely discouraged sympathy for the British cause in the up-country. Since our return, I have been vigorously involved in filling the ranks of the 2rd Regiment to full muster. At times it has been a comedy to encourage these ignorant farm lads to enlist in an army that might take them far from home. I don't know whether they abhor leaving their farms, their girl friends, or their livestock, but the duration discourages most. They are supposed to arrive armed and mounted, and that presents further misunderstanding. Some come without guns, just hunting knives, some with nothing. Others have mounts that can barely bring them the distance into camp so they have to wait for new mounts to be brought in by traders. They can't write or read and few can take directions. If you command them too harshly, they become disheartened and will sometimes just go home. Individually, they are brave and they are capable hunters and marksmen, but I have to make my best effort with my sergeants, hoping they can mold these rubes into anything fit for an army. Some make you laugh at sight and others make you smile when they open their mouths. They know nothing outside the realm of their squatter homesteads and anything new is confounding, for a time at least. How we will stand against British regulars is an unknown."

"I declare," I pointed out, "that is an analysis that would discourage Alexander the Great."

"And I am no Alexander the Great, I tell you. As I said though, the early enlistees acquitted themselves well at Stono, and this foray against the Highlanders would have been more valuable to our training if they had seen actual battle, but they learned to march, oh, and march," he laughed. "In motion, they are a sea of bobbing heads that would make a sailor retch. And their shoes soon fall apart but they don't mind being bare foot. It seems more natural to them. If they have to relieve themselves, they just walk away from the ranks when they see a tree and eventually they come running back. But most can place a bullet through a tuppence at a hundred yards. My job is to convert all that into the standards of an infantry manual."

"And you a simple lawyer. Why, dear Alexander," I wondered, "did you seek command under such circumstances?"

"David, you are my confessor and I know that with you I can be frank with my foibles. I saw this conflict as inevitable and I truly believed that when it was done, there would be a new nation like nothing ever seen in the confines of Europe.

"We are of the birthing generation. With God's help, we will be able to create all things new. I am schooled and politically positioned to be an active part in that evolution, and I flatter myself that I have some degree of talent along that line. Surviving a successful career as a soldier in winning our independence will be a respected qualification when the time comes. As I speak, it does seem like boasting, but I believe that I am being objective in my analysis and I am at ease saying this to you as my friend and as a respected influence on character."

"You have, to me, one of the most ordered, proportioned minds I have ever seen," I said. "You reason with equanimity, with a controlled temper. There is a harmony in your thought process that balances the impact of ideas and this I see as essential in a politician, and not amiss in a preacher. Yes, I wish sometimes you could have been a minister as was your late brother. But, alas, if you must go into politics, I am honored that you will represent me and I am confidant in your action, although we might not always agree on the details."

"Oh, I assure you, our debates on details are the source of many of my cultivated opinions. I sometimes feel poorly prepared when I have not had the chance to argue the finer points with your analysis, and I don't mean just your theological input, although there I look on you as my master."

The first Provincial Assembly back in 1774 elected North Carolina delegates to the Continental Congress. Guilford County, which had been formed two years earlier, sent no delegates to New Bern but when the second assembly convened there in April 1775, Alexander Martin had made his move to the new county and was sent as a delegate. He had acquired land where the Centre Road intersected with the New Garden/High Rock Road north of me and later, he would acquire more by confiscation.

In June 1775, Josiah Martin, the last royal Governor, fled his palace at New Bern for the security of Fort Johnston near Wilmington. By August, when the Third Provincial Assembly met at Hillsborough, seven delegates represented Guilford including Alexander Martin, and the Assembly represented the Provincial government of North Carolina.

When the Fifth Provincial Assembly met in Halifax in November, 1776, I was elected one of the four delegates of Guilford.

I was absolute in my opposition to the eligibility of any minister for election to any civil governing body. In this case, however, I became convinced that this assembly would not have at issue any business except the creation of a constitution and to that cause, I considered I could make an important contribution. So I agreed to allow my name to be put forward. The resolution of independence had been introduced in the Continental Congress on June 7th and passed on July 2nd, with the Declaration proclaimed on the 4th. The Fifth and final Provincial Assembly, therefore, had the task of writing a constitution for the new state under the newly proclaimed independence. As Martin stepped out of the political arena, I stepped momentarily in, but not as a politician. The question of form would be decided and I considered myself as well versed on the covenant form. Religious freedom would be an important debate and I had strong opinions on the sacredness of the Christian faith that I believed could be ignored in the debate over terms, if there were no clergy present at the assembly to see that it wasn't.

As Alexander and I continued our discourse, I said, "now, having lauded your skills as a politician, you are abandoning politics for a military career and I am elected virtually as your replacement in the Assembly. A war seems to place people in unfamiliar or, at least, untried roles." I told him, "I am accepting this election as I see God calling me to be an influence in the formation of a just and God-centered government. I may not be adept on questions of court reform, or structures of a parliament, but I believe we Scots, in our covenants, have created the Biblical form for a satisfactory ruling order."

Martin reacted. "You do then intend to introduce, or should I at least say, 'work for,' a type of covenant relationship for civil authority?"

"I do," I said. "It is my responsibility."

"I have no serious objection about such a form being placed on the table for consideration. It is my own feeling that covenants do well in binding churches, denominations, even small countries, but in more expansive situations, covenants cannot be made broad enough to accommodate a variety of thought in vast territories. Our nation will be vast and increasingly diverse. I think our governing must stretch to embody as great a diversity of the views, prejudices, preferences, and political experiences of its people as is possible."

"And do covenants not represent the will of the people?" I demanded.

"Absolutely, but they do not tolerate well diversity of opinion. They can easily become a tyranny of the majority that can wipe away any opposition view. A covenant can improve on a royal prerogative as a governing order, but it seems to me that it stops short of the free expression of ideas that should exist in a representative government."

"I applaud your altruistic intent," I told him, "but I fear that such unbridled authority cannot be vested in our human ignorance. We must have covenants that define our basic principles or people will simply gravitate to irrational doctrines and heresies. We are a Christian people and we have the Bible to give us the truth. We must build that truth into our form of government or we will operate outside the will of God. That would be a sin for us."

"Many of us are Christians, David, but our government must protect religious belief of all kinds."

"All kinds?" I erupted. "Do you mean to imply that our government must protect Jews and heretics, non–believers and Mohammedans? You go too far."

"Our government, simply because we have an overwhelming majority of Christians in our land, will reflect the tenets of the Christian faith, one of which is to love one another. I don't think Christ meant to deny anyone the full realization of equal protection under the law."

"Then they must not be able to hold office," I countered.

"Why should they not? If they are to be elected by a majority, then they should face no exclusionary bias."

I confess I was bewildered. I said, "Alexander, you go far too far. I thought to sit in your place at Halifax and to echo your ideas as my own but we are not together on this. In this case we have opened a debate that we will be a long time in reconciling."

"That is why I value public debate so highly. It is often laborious but if good will can be maintained, placing a wide net of ideas into deliberation can bring about a most equitable resolution."

Rachel walked in on cue just in time to hear Alexander's last remark. "Well, I always heard that the test of good friends was that they could shamelessly praise and directly curse each other and their friendship would be reinforced either way," she said with infinite wisdom.

Alexander stayed through the meal, which was shared with the students and the young soldiers who had accompanied him. There was no serious talk. The boys wanted to hear stories of blood and fights and the soldiers really had none to share. The boys were sure that we had discouraged such stories as the soldiers must have experienced. When Alexander said that the next campaign for the militia and some of the Continentals might be against the Indians, whom the British had armed to attack the frontier, the boys were awash with visions of scalps and flying spears and arrows. Alexander said it was important, at this early stage, to neutralize the Indian tribes or they would loom as a potential threat over the mountains every time there was a campaign in the coastal colonies. We understood, but the boys imagined Indians in their bedrooms that night.

Talk of war had suddenly introduced the unknown realm of mystery yet to be mastered with adolescence. Floors creaked and any crack in the chinking in log walls magnified the whine of wind on a cloudy night. On moonlit nights it was the shadows cast by trees or furniture that could outline a perfect Tory, even though the boys had never knowingly seen a Tory. They had all grown up with explanations of the sounds and shadows of their remote homes and this knowledge acted as a wall of security satisfying their untested imaginations. Rachel particularly attempted to be a calming presence with the younger boys. With some who were older, it was a more delicate nuance that balanced between external bravery and the concealed terror within, and she had to learn to minister without exposing either to the ridicule of their peers.

I was not able to attend the April meeting of Presbytery but I proposed through Waightstill Avery that they should write a letter to the next Assembly asking them to consider relief from all the conditions that bound the Church of England to the government. We should oppose any state religion in any new constitution. Avery wrote such a letter and the Presbytery sent it to the Assembly. At that time, I didn't know that I would be a member when that Assembly sat but I was glad I had anticipated the point.

After the crops were harvested, I bid farewell to my family and congregations and rode off to the Assembly with Isham Browder, Charles Bruce, Ralph Gorrell, and Joseph Hines. We took the high road across Granville County along the south side of the Roanoke River basin to Halifax. Gorrell was a member of Alamance Presbyterian and Charles Bruce was a Scot living at a cross road north of our farm, near the Haw River. Gorrell and Bruce were concerned with the legislative form and with the local courts that would function to bring order to the legal system. By the time we all reached Halifax, I knew that I was not going to be supported in my views of a covenant government. I did have the support of my delegation, however, concerning the protection of the Protestant majority against the influence of heathens and heretics.

I considered myself influential as a Presbyterian because even the enemy singled us out as part of the leadership of the revolution. As a Princeton graduate, I was one of the better educated of the delegates. I deliberately placed copies of the Scottish National Covenant of 1580, the Solemn League and Covenant of 1643, and the Westminster Confession of Faith, among the seminal documents to be considered when the committee was writing a constitution.

Then when I gained the floor, I recommended the efficacy of the covenant as a form for a government based on scripture. As a cleric, I had been chosen several times to offer a prayer at openings and special sittings of committees but it was clear that my theological background fixed me with a bias against secular civil authority. But even delegates, who dreaded to see me rise to a point, could not ignore my interpretation of religion as fundamental to the character of those that they sought by this document to govern.

I remember I began rather formally. "I stand before you as preacher and revolutionary but it was not always so. I am a product of, and I represent, people who suffered much under the usurped authority of kings. I believe that God has given us in the Christian Bible, the clear and blessed format by which he intends people to be governed. I know among the Scots that it was only when they returned to the covenant, for both religious and civil authority, that they achieved a satisfactory time of peace. You see, a covenant demands that each party, government, and those to be governed place their aims on a table, and after debate and examination, agree to amalgamate those positions into a single understanding. Both are vested, both are committed, one to the other and before God. Such a covenant recognizes that, when in the passage of time, one party o'er steps the rights of the other, and when called to account, refuses to recant, the other party is released from that covenant and must declare independence from it. I declared myself released from the covenant made by King and Parliament with the mainland colonies of America when King and Parliament no longer represented my interests in covenant and refused to allow me to be represented in debate over issues in which my interests were involved." I had been heard with respect but I could see my reasoning fell on some untrained ears. I feared I had not measured my audience very well.

In the evening the parlor in my tavern, where I shared a room with three others, was more crowded than usual with delegates. In addition to those who had taken rooms there, others had come over after an evening meal for the debate that followed every session. I found myself the center of one of the swirling discussion groups around the room, after my comments about covenants. With me in discussion were my Princeton friend, Waightstill Avery and his mentor, Hezekiah Alexander from Mecklenburg; Alexander Mebane from Hawfields; Matthew Locke, an Irish Presbyterian from Salisbury; and Thomas Burke, an Irishman, new to Carolina.

"Although I am a product of the Scottish Covenant through my family," began Hezekiah Alexander, "I cannot see, how a simple covenant, no matter how expertly crafted, can serve as a form for a government whose prospects of scope are so great."

"My experience with the covenants, Pastor Caldwell," offered Thomas Burke in a noticeable Irish brogue, "is that they were necessary to keep the obstreperous Scots from fighting among themselves, but of little value in equitable government. I would put to you that you speak more of a philosophy of John Locke than as a covenanter. I could almost hear Locke extolling 'all government exists for the good of the governed,' in your words today. Particularly, your personal justification for a rejection by a colonial government of a mother country was more out of Locke."

"You have me exposed, Mister Burke," I admitted. "I have considered Locke to offer very insightful philosophy as to civil government. I am a particular exponent of Francis Hutcheson's philosophy, as it seems a perfect product of the Scottish covenanting tradition. These, and other enlightened thinkers coming out of Scotland, are most influential in my reading, but as a minister, I am led to begin with the Bible as my rock. There I see a covenant as the fundamental structure that God uses in the Old and New Testament to establish understandings upon which to build community. I can accept the more secular thinking of these men, and of Voltaire, Montesquieu or Diderot, as to their influence on revolutionary thinking, but I solicit a divine presence in the governing of our new state. As a Christian, I must seek to envision God's will in our actions." I immediately saw that I had discouraged debate, a reluctance to appear to suggest any alternative to the will of God. I sought to lighten the air. "Matthew Locke, I had never thought before of the connection but Matthew, surely you can say a word for your British kinsman, John Locke."

"Oh, I am unable to claim any knowledge of a kinship with the brilliant John Locke," said Matthew. "If there is, I must have descended in the younger brother line, with the name, but not the fame."

Leaving a moment for a general laugh to alter the somber edge that I had given to the discussion, Waightstill Avery directed at me, "you sat at the feet of Finley, Davies and Witherspoon at Princeton. I know that you are not captive to the Old Side. You must appreciate the opportunity to create government based on the will and the interest of the people represented. We have no such form yet, but what we are elected to create cannot be restricted to a theocracy."

"Absolutely not, " I responded with admittedly a certain edge of surprise that Avery would suspect me of such an advocacy. "I do not advocate the swing of the pendulum toward a theocracy but I feel as a minister that I must guard against a vigorous swing to the other direction, toward say a secular denial of a government under God. I am not politician but preacher. Ultimately I am more than willing to leave those experienced in law and government to formulate the design of government. I see my role as representing the Godhead that must be present in a government. That does not make me omnipotent, only an instrument of God's will."

I was not alone in pressing for a statement defining individual rights in relationship to the power of government. Others would defer on the use of my term "covenant" but in the end the North Carolina Constitution had as a preamble, "A Declaration of Rights made by the Representatives of the Freemen of the State of North Carolina." Where the Scottish covenants focused on the limitation of the power of royal and parliamentary authority and in defining the usurpers, the North Carolina declaration concentrated on enumerating the individual rights of freemen that would be protected. In this form, government would be designed to function in protection of the rights of the governed. The covenant form was used to institute the enlightened psychology of human aspirations. In such measure, Article XIX of the declaration said, "That all men have a natural and unalienable right to worship Almighty God according to the dictates of their consciences." This was the definition of freedom of worship that was a fundamental vision held by most of the delegates, including me.

I did not have to lobby for a constituency. I defined the roll from which I would advocate so that when I rose, delegates heard me as a chastening instrument poised against extremes of debate.

Only once did I structure a specific article of the form of the government that was set out after the declaration, and in that case I did define an issue in law. Article XXXI of the finished constitution prohibited clergymen from election to the legislature or the Council of State. The next article was written by me, and I must admit to you that for more than half a century, it was to define religious bias in the state:

> "That no person who shall deny the Being of God, or the Truth of the Protestant Religion, or the divine authority of the Old or New Testament, or shall hold religious Principles incompatible with the Freedom and Safety of the State, shall be capable of holding any Office, or Place of Trust or Profit, in the civil Department within this State."

One other article forbade the establishment of any state religion or preferential funding of any church or minister. My influence had denied to me and other clergy the right to legislative office, and had ruled out a state religion. It was my heavy hand that denied the full rights of citizenship to Catholics, Jews, and any other non-Christian religious faith. The article echoed the Scottish definition of errors, heresies and schisms but did not go so far as to single out Deism, Moravianism, Quakerism, Anabaptism, and others as had its earlier covenant models.

"You have effectively denied me election to public office, sir," said Thomas Burke to me when Article XXXII was approved. "Do you consider that religious freedom? I am a Catholic."

"If you do not deny the truth of the Protestant religion, you may still serve, and any other office is open to you," I responded, a little embarrassed by the point Burke had made personal.

"So I won't taint lesser offices and, if I deny my own religion, I can even be Governor or legislator. Sir, that is not freedom."

On one other issue, I had a strong influence in keeping with the traditions of the Presbyterian Church. That was education. Hezekiah Alexander and Waightstill Avery took the lead in this case motivated by that refusal of the King to authorize Queens College. At the time reopened as Liberty Hall, Avery had that school in mind when he proposed the inclusion of an article supporting the funding of higher education. The only other institution existing in the state that might qualify for support under this article was my academy. But neither he nor I sought passage of a higher education bill to obtain state support of our institutions. Ultimately this was the seed-bed article that led to the chartering of the University of North Carolina. It had the effect of committing the state, as soon as possible, to the establishment of a university.

I returned home satisfied that I had been a positive guide on the course of this state toward a government influenced by strong Christian principals. When I was most objective with myself, I even knew that I had instilled Presbyterian principles that I believed preserved the covenant values of our tradition. Convinced that I had acted as an instrument of God, my inner soul wavered. Had I forced my will or His?

In 1771, Governor Tryon had sought to isolate the Regulator concentration of Orange and Rowan counties when the county of Guilford was established. In 1779, after war had begun, the southern third of Guilford was cut away to form Randolph County, as if such a county line might contain the spread of the infection. There had been Regulators among the Presbyterians at Buffalo and Alamance, but as a party, Regulators were expressing their anger with the extortionate fees and exploitation of the poor farmer by the officers of the court. Now the Presbyterians and their neighbors were faced with an emerging revolution as the governing authority of the crown in the colonies was severed, and as domestic civil authority established dominion. The churches of Orange Presbytery were already firmly within the Whig community, although a few isolated members might still be ambivalent. Whether I mounted the pulpit at Alamance or Buffalo on any given Sunday, I was preaching to the converted. My duty was to fortify the intensity of their resolution. I believed earnestly that God had sanctified their right and their obligation to free themselves from tyranny. But these were not belligerent people and this kind of war required that their neighbor might take on the function of enemy, where earlier there had been little enmity. Even within the family, that kind of confrontation might arise, arming father against son or brothers against each other. So the church had to be a refuge where one could be certain that, having to choose, the choice was founded on the will of God.

When I rose before my flock at Alamance, I was surrounded by faces combining fear and uncertainty with righteous indignation. It was a time to give them a confidence in their future, a confirmation, that the risks they or their parents had made in committing to a colonial life could be confirmed in a new type of government, and that the liberation of independence was worth the time of testing through which they would have to pass. "You have your misgivings and concerns," I said, facing their earnest, trusting faces. "You have your God, ready to hear your concerns through prayer, who gives you a promise of redemption from any of the world's ills. Uncertainty is debilitating for those who try to find remedy in themselves. It is as if a whole load has been suddenly deposited on your back and the fear is natural that you will drop your responsibility or be crushed by it. God does not treat us so. Your neighbors will not treat you so. We are a people of the book and we can see over and over in the text of our Bible, the action of a redeeming God. We have a covenant, in the redemptive blood of the Christ, that is poured out for us and for our salvation." I continued to diminish their anxiety not by minimizing the reality but by reinforcing their own power to prevail. I did it gradually so they could absorb it fully into their understanding, like feeding a child not so rapidly that the child spews it back.

The people of Alamance wanted to hear soothing words.

Then they demanded to hear a call to purpose. When they were calm, they were people who reasoned with a confidence in their faith. The Bible was their foundation that liberated them to be dynamic disciples who wanted to be instruments of the will of God.

To the congregation at Alamance, the sermon was usually an exposition on a Biblical passage. They expected me to develop the immediacy of the text applying it to a response drawn from the individual. Early in the war, as an example, I would dwell chiefly on the Old Testament, defining God's first covenant with Abraham and His covenant with David, before I left to attend the Provincial Assembly. I relied much on judgment when I encouraged men to march against the Tories at Moores Creek or when Tory raids perpetrated bloody incidents of fratricide. When the new army needed leadership and when the militia needed to train to a level of skill that could respond to Tory deprivation, I used hero stories of David and Joshua. My style was plain but robust. I did not gesture wildly but used my arms and hands to drive a point. I always entered the pulpit in a black robe, unadorned, with a white collar which cast the serious nature of my words. Never was I casual in this role, never entertaining. From my two congregations, in addition to Alexander Martin, of the Second North Carolina Continental Regiment, came his brother, James Martin, Colonel of the Guilford Minutemen; First Major John Paisley; later Captain Arthur Forbis and James Gillespie; and Charles Bruce, who was in charge of recruitment in the county. At any time there was to be any military activity in the Piedmont area of Southern Virginia, North Carolina, or Upper South Carolina, I was preaching courage to warriors and fortitude to families. At the end of my sermon at Alamance I would remind them that I was responding to my duties in the face of the demands of war, using my alternate doggerel:

"If the Lord is willing
And the water is low,
I'll preach next week
At Buffalo."

The transition every other Sunday to Buffalo required mostly a change in my presentation. The congregation was a little larger and it considered itself the parent church, organized six years earlier than Alamance, in 1756. It also never forgot it was the church where the organization of Orange Presbytery had been proposed. It was thought of as Old Side Presbyterian which carried the connotation of conservative, in the sense of more orthodox. Old Side Presbyterians had not responded to the awakening influence of George Whitefield. They had stronger ties to the Scottish Covenanters, through which they held closer to the links with the Scottish church and a ministry trained in Scotland. They lined their hymns, which were Psalms. The Scot term "dour" laid comfortably upon them and they had no apology for being obstinate or unyielding. They insisted on proof-texting my sermons with their Bibles. So when I came to Buffalo, my sermon was a scholarly, Biblical exegesis that required an educated congregation for understanding. Of course that also discouraged people without education from attending, and in a frontier setting, that limited the appeal of such a Presbyterian Church.

Having gone through the rigorous exercise of examination of the authority of my scriptural analysis on one Sunday at Buffalo, I could, on the next at Alamance, expostulate my message on the same text in such a way as to awaken my hearers to the opportunity of being Christ's instruments in a troubled world – same text – presentation, presentation, presentation. I had an abiding understanding of the depth and nature of the struggle between the Old and New Siders and I saw it as my duty to preach the word so that the congregations would not focus on the content of my words as division. To me, God was working both sides of the debate. In my two–congregation pastorate, it was education that was always the unifying agent. My school was not at either church so it was never a source of competitive ownership. I was a Presbyterian pastor and I operated a classical school. That satisfied all shades of Presbyterians and did not discourage Christians of other persuasions.

I had established my life as minister and teacher on my farm on the banks of Buffalo Creek in Guilford County. It might have been possible to replicate in this location much of the settlement experiences I had known in Lancaster and Chester Counties in my youth. I would have had familiar benchmarks of accomplishment. I could have tied back into the earlier settlement successes in the Valley of Virginia and in Pennsylvania. But Revolution intervened, and that era of settlement was forever significantly altered. In the course of that revolution of colonies against mother country, there was a channel of events: into civil war, into inter-faith quarrels, into individual liberty, into new themes of government. My capacity as minister and teacher dictated that I be drawn into each fluctuating tumble of this upheaval. I don't imply that I was victimized by the Revolution, or that I disliked being drawn thus into it. Actually I was inspired that I was in position to be an instrument in the midst of unbridled turmoil. What man goes into the ministry without an ego driving him to accomplish? To find oneself offered the opportunity to influence the evolution of a nation was energizing, I must admit.

Watching rain upon a window pane in the dim light of evening, I noticed drops channel into tiny streams of water running down the glass. Most lines of water ran in a wobbly course down to the frame. At one place there was a small bubble in the glass and the several courses of water that reached that bubble had to go right or left around it. The bubble was there before and would be there after the rain imposed itself upon the pane. I imagined myself like that bubble. I wondered, would my presence have any consequence?

A few of my parishioners during the revolution chose to enter service with the national army, the Continentals, and over the years they were sent wherever in the country the battles were fought with the British military. Alexander Martin was such a man. Others lived elsewhere at the beginning of the war and they entered their local militia units and some, moving as the fighting shifted from place to place, ended up in our neighborhood and a few joined one of our congregations. Militias were called out as regional threats arose.

The first battle, at Moore's Creek Bridge, was colonials against mostly Highlanders. A British victory at Moore's Creek would have emboldened the Tories throughout North Carolina. Instead, the defeat of Governor Josiah Martin's plan for an early successful southern strategy led to the first spell of barbaric infighting between Whigs and Tories and to cold-blooded atrocities of the war.

At moments, I imagined that I was the only force in my community that stood between patriotism and bloodthirsty rebellion. In the early incidents, both sides were little more than bands of bullies. Military order was maintained with difficulty when to each action there was a more savage reaction.

The Whig militia, assembled at places like Charles Bruce's Muster Ground, Spring Garden, and Guilford Court House, and trained according to old infantry manuals and the common judgment of men who had the appearance of leadership. They struck out first against Tory Colonel William Fields and his brothers in southern Guilford. Most of these men were former Regulators whom the Governor had expected to rally to the King's Standard at the Cape Fear. They had failed to appear and were said now to be skulking around in the woods and swamps, living off the land. Most of these men were captured and sent to Halifax, while their impoverished families pled for their lives and their return, claiming they were only trying to support their families. Men returned to Buffalo with tales of seeing Whig farmers hanging from a tree and returning the following day to see twice as many Tories hanging from the same tree. We heard stories about women and their screaming children, left alone by hot-headed husbands, to defend their log homes from neighbors bent on burning them out. It is not necessary to preach hatred to arouse anger, but it is difficult to preach compassion when anger has already taken root.

By fall of that year, these same militia men were called to march against a more distant enemy over the mountains. The Cherokee were said to have been persuaded by British agents to begin deprivations along the colonial frontiers against settlers who had already entered treaty lands and taken land as squatters. The Indians knew that they could be defeated by an American army of sufficient size. They were also aware that the white settlers were able, on a piecemeal basis, to drive them from their land as easily as an army could do by force. The British convinced them, at the same time supplying them weapons, that while their forces waged war to the east, this might be the only hope the Indians had of pushing back the settlers. Their consequent ravages had proceeded as far to the east as the Catawba River, when the Council gave orders to General Griffith Rutherford to proceed against them. As one of the more heavily populated frontier counties, Guilford sent about 400 militiamen. They crossed at Swananoah Gap, to the Pigeon River, the French Broad and to the Tennessee where they found the Indian towns. So well supplied were they, that their commissary alone included 3000 beef cattle and about as many pack horses loaded with sacks of flour.

When they camped at one town, they found the next morning that the animals had destroyed all the Indian crops down to the stump. At other towns the militia destroyed all the houses and burned the corn. The estimate that I heard most frequently was that they destroyed sixteen towns. They killed only a few Indians because the natives never could put a force together large enough to engage them in battle. On their return, having defeated Highland Scots, Tories, and Indians in the first year, my people felt secure in their homes and more than a little invincible. Still, a man like Mathias Swing, who lived down near what was known as the dividing line between Whig and Tory farms in the south of Guilford, went armed at home and when he went to church. When he went to his fields, he took two guns and left one at each end of the field as he plowed.

We were safe enough in our area that the boys continued to come to school. I remember it as a difficult task to retain their attention on studies as their heads were filled with stories of men fighting. I assumed it as a personal project that I should not allow them to become savages merely because they were surrounded by savagery. Wars do interrupt the order of a society but they end, and then it is important to have intelligent men who can restore order in the face of chaos. Rather than buffet against the inevitable, I allowed the boys' natural interest in fighting to work through their lessons. In Latin studies, we devoured the history of the Gaelic Wars, and for Greek studies, Sparta and Troy. In Bible study, we found ample brutality in the Old Testament, but I was able to modulate that with the compassion of Jesus. Still, those who came each day went home to new tales of tragedy, real and imagined.

The second year of the war turned out to be more orderly in North Carolina. Most of the fighting was being done by the Continental army against the British troops and their mercenary units in the northern colonies. It wasn't until October that Rachel and I had another, longer visit from Alexander Martin and we heard, directly from him, his own exploits and those of Washington's army. He rode over several days after arriving at his home at the Court House and a day after visiting his mother on the Dan River. We were dismayed when he dismounted and we had the opportunity to see closely how physically aged he had become in but a year. He was not in uniform and his clothes were loose on his frame. Dark shadows circled his eyes and there was a hollowness to his cheeks that made him appear undernourished.

"Before you belabor me with concerns about my health," he began, "let me assure you I am at the bottom of a pit, physically and emotionally, and I am reaching out to begin my re-ascent to the level of humanity." Just the statement seemed to have exhausted him. He slumped in the chair that was offered and appeared to gather himself.

"You are home, friend, and that at least answers our prayers," I said to give him a moment.

"Yes, I have wept over the news from the North, wondering each time where you were and how close you were to the danger," added Rachel.

"I was at all times bolstered by the knowledge that you and my family were concerned," said our visitor. "Had I not had that, there were moments when despair was like a beckoning meadow into which I longed to disappear. Now, the army is a part of my past, whatever be the consequences of that reality. I have resigned." The late afternoon sun provided a back-lighting through the window behind his chair that made his face even more darkly shadowed than it might naturally have been. There was a pause as fact froze for a moment, waiting for an explanation to be placed under it, before it crashed to the floor. Rachel and I were poised to listen.

"A year and a half ago, when I was last here," he began, "I told you of likely military moves against the Indians which, as you know, did take place. I spent most of last year in recruiting and training Carolina men for the 2nd Regiment. In March, our commander, General James Moore, was arranging plans for us to march north to join General Washington at Morristown. The Continental Congress had abandoned Philadelphia as too near the British. To our great sadness, and as if to foretell disaster of some kind, General Moore returned briefly to his Cape Fear home and there died suddenly. I was devastated personally by this loss. Francis Nash was quickly appointed his replacement, and just as quickly, I became a very good friend of that gentleman. He was to me as a brother. We continued General Moore's original plan and left Salisbury for New Jersey.

"The Continentals had successes at Trenton and Princeton and spent the summer in campaign in New Jersey where we joined them.

There was already much infighting among our officers, many of whom had never been part of an army. We were faced with desertions, and insubordination was common. On the way north, I had informed the President of the Continental Congress, John Hancock, that my men were badly armed and much of the equipment I should send back to North Carolina because it was scarce worth having. Lt. Colonel Ingram, of the 8th North Carolina Regiment resigned, and finding myself the senior regimental officer, convened the field officers to choose a successor. I found army politics immediately and shamefully corrupt, filled with petty cabals and false loyalties. Added to that was the interference of civilian politicians in the operations of the army. For me, one of the earliest and most vocal such characters was the Irish delegate from Hillsborough, Thomas Burke. He seemed to consider that his recent arrival in this country somehow gave him a better grasp of British intentions than others far his superior. I swear, he was a pompous jack-in-the-box, appearing everywhere, an authority on every detail."

I said that I knew Burke as a member of the Provincial Assembly. "I thought him very intelligent if a bit over-sure of himself. He did seem to assert himself as an authority on every thing. He strongly opposed my Article on clergy elected to public office. You know he is Catholic, and I successfully managed to keep Catholics from eligibility to run for high public office."

"He became more than a burr in my saddle," replied Alexander. "It became clear that Howe and his British intended a move on Philadelphia and the army moved south to block him. It was Washington's intention to attempt to bolster the moral of the citizens of Philadelphia, with the numbers he was now able to put in the field, in spite of the fact that many units looked more like marching rabble that a national army. In the best order we could assume, we marched through the city, the largest by far that my farmers had ever seen. They were so awestruck that, had a sudden halt been called, they would have compressed into a single pile before the officers could have gotten them stopped. Howe landed at the head of Elk River and Washington formed to block him at Brandywine Creek. This was our first action against a British army. North Carolina regiments were part of William Maxwell's corps under the division commanded by Nathanael Greene. The initial British attack was carried by Hessians who were repulsed by Maxwell with heavy loss. Appearing to be reinforcing the thrust of the Hessians, the British, in a successful outflanking maneuver, crossed the upper fords of the Brandywine. Sullivan, Stephens, and Sterling were rushed in to repulse the crossing but they had no high ground to hold. Only the arrival of Greene with the reserves, including our regiment, prevented a rout and allowed an organized withdrawal. In the midst of the battle, I was seated on my horse but a few feet from General Lafayette when he was wounded. Washington had failed to block the British but in turn, Howe was slow to press his advantage or we might have been routed.

"I could not fathom the battle of words that followed the military defeat. The counterclaims in the face of defeat I anticipated as a possibility, but the character charges I thought never to see among men fighting for the same army. Poor Sullivan almost lost his command as a result of the direct attack of our old friend Burke."

This was not a very reassuring picture of our army, and Rachel and I could make no informed comment.

"After retreating from Philadelphia following the defeat at Brandywine, General Howe camped his army at Germantown, content on leaving the occupation of the larger city to Cornwallis. Washington had reconnoitered thoroughly around Germantown the positions that Howe now assumed, and felt that we were in a very favorable position and prospect to initiate battle.

"In the very early hours of October 3rd, our units were supposed to have moved into their positions but some were late and we were losing our element of surprise. By 5:30 the sun was beginning to rise on a dense fog which Washington hoped would further conceal our movements. Sullivan moved forward as planned in a bayonet advance through the fog and we listened for the full volley of firing that would signal that the British had joined battle. For nearly a half hour we waited, hearing scattered shots from their pickets. Finally convinced by the sound of shot and shell that we were engaged, our army moved forward."

I noticed that Alexander had gradually tensed as if feeling the building climax of his own experience. He rose suddenly, circled to the back of the room as if to leave; then he came forward again, and as if he had forgotten himself, returned to his seat and resumed.

"We were held in reserve with the New Jersey brigades near a Lutheran church but were pushing forward, keeping pressure on the retreating British." Again he paused and shifted nervously. "A single shell, perhaps a parting shot, passed over Sullivan's Pennsylvanians and over Washington and his staff and fell among us. The wayward ball bounced off a sign post, through the neck of General Francis Nash's horse tearing into the General's thigh, and struck Major James Witherspoon in the head killing him instantly." I heard a soft compulsive gasp from Rachel. "As our commander's horse fell, Nash was caught beneath the animal. We stood shattered by this bloody slaughter." He turned directly toward me to say, "David, Witherspoon was the son of our revered Dr. John Witherspoon, under whom we were both students at Princeton."

"Oh, God, I remember him," I blurted out, "I remember him as a boy."

"General Nash attempted to bring order, claiming his wound was not serious and ordering that we continue to push in behind the advance. The battle was now centered on Cleveden, a massive stone house heavily fortified by the British. Some of the shots from the Americans on both sides went over the house and fell among their own men. The smoke was mixing with the morning fog and as the one dissipated, the other moved in. General Anthony Wayne, in command of Pennsylvanians, having progressed beyond the house, heard the concentrated firing and wheeled about. Brigades lost track of each other in the smoke. General Stephen's troops from Greene's division fired and were answered with a withering fusillade. We were firing on each other. Out of a whirlpool of smoke and the popping sounds of hammer on cap, lead balls flew with indiscriminate aim into responding flesh. The army, which Washington had thought on the verge of a significant victory, lost all perception in the fire and smoke. My men were firing into friendly troops, trying to beat them back as they had turned to retreat. I was commanding in a swirling sea of terrified humans, beating them back with my sword and calling for order. The American retreat to Pennypacker's Mill was anything but orderly.

"At the end of the day, I declare that I felt the most unspeakable fatigue I have ever experienced. My uniform was covered in blood and the smoke of battle hung upon it. I continued to experience the sensation of bodies bouncing against my legs, with my horse, terrified by the sounds, muscling his way round in circles against the beating force. I was left by then with the vision of the headless Witherspoon and my mortally wounded commander braced against his horse. I wept bitterly – unable to control my emotion.

"In the wake of defeat, irresponsible as well as sometimes appropriate charges of cowardice and ineptitude rang out. General Stephens was cashiered for drunkenness. Several officers of the 4th North Carolina charged me with cowardice, concocting the story that in the heat of battle, I was seen pulling a terrified soldier out of the trunk of a tree and hiding inside myself. I was so outraged that when I was advised of the charge, I immediately demanded a court-martial be convened. I was cleared of all charges but I was sorely tested by the provocation of the charge."

"It is a malicious charge on its face, Alex. I can imagine how perplexing it was to you after such a battle."

He did not comment but resumed, "The question of replacing the fallen General Nash may have appeared to others as an opportunity before it came to me as a responsibility. As senior colonel of the North Carolina Brigade, the only way for any other regimental commander to gain the vacant position of brigadier was to bring me down. The motivation behind the cowardice charge was now clear to me. I hope you can understand why I absolutely refused to undergo the further assault on my personal integrity that others had shown themselves ready to commit. I resigned my commission. I can assure you that as my man, Ben, and I rode home in the late cold days of November, I agonized over circumstances that had demanded that I leave my command when it was in such precarious circumstances. Only with the distance of that ride did I recognize how physically I had been broken, as you see me now." There was a flutter of leaves against the window. His head bowed with these last words and tears ran freely down our cheeks.

On June 24th there was such an extraordinary event of nature superimposed on our melancholy lives that primal emotions fed on our uncertain age and more than one person interpreted cosmic signs of end times. The eclipse of the sun happened near mid-day with a fairly clear sky and without forewarning the sun began to be obscured. The decrease in light cast a gradual pall. I was in the classroom and I had a strange uneasiness but it was our young Samuel who first cried out, "Papa, something strange is happening outside. It's getting dark." The boys rushed for the door, some barging out and others holding back until they could shadow me. Nature seemed to have a sudden, sickly face. Rachel was out already with the smaller children, at least one of whom was crying. The tumult of questions suddenly hushed as the eyes of the beholders took in an awful scene. Total darkness awakened the stars and rushing coveys of birds sought shelter in their nests. "It is an eclipse of the sun," I told them. "For human beings it appears as an anomaly of nature but it is caused by the orbit of the moon in its course. It should not be feared. It should be a glorious wonder. Children, I will teach you all about it this week but for now, observe it. Do not stare at the sun but watch it at an angle and watch how the other parts of nature respond."

Rachel and I had moved toward each other and our children had closed in upon us. As the sun had left us, so it came again and man and beast appeared stunned by things they could not control and events for which they had no reference. Wonder of this kind, in a world at war with itself, is debilitating. Even if we understand the orbits of the solar system, we internalize fears converting them to marvel, the supernatural, fable, superstition. The stunning effect percolates through our intellect and eventually it will come out seasoned by all our bias.

That night I told Rachel, "I will be a busy man after this. I am a teacher so I will have to lead my students into a scientific understanding of these events and at the same time calm their childish fears. Many of them will bring into their homes the only factual explanation of what simple people have seen as miraculous or portentous. I am the source of understanding and I am well aware that my knowledge is as through a glass darkly."

"The children will take time to gain understanding because they will hear all of what you call miracle and portends," said Rachel. "May I tell you, David, that one of my first recognizable reactions today was to connect the eclipse to the war. Was it a sign? And then I thought how many others must also be thinking in the patterns as was I. I thought how natural."

"Natural, Rachel, yes, but also dangerous. Ignorance is like a filter that can block truth or shade our vision. It is destabilizing. We live in a world of great uncertainty. Everything I do is an attempt to overcome ignorance – I preach, I teach, and now I am even becoming something of a physician and a politician. It is as a minister that I have concern. I know in my heart that at this moment there are laymen and ministers who are rummaging through the book of Revelation. They will claim that it is for insight but it will be for signs, those opaque images from which they can excite the minds of the uninformed to believe monstrous and spurious fantasies. They do not rise to the level of heresy because they are without theological form. They elevate the dependence of poor people to the words of the preacher, not to the message of the Bible. I know such vanity will come to pass and I already must contain my rage.

On Sunday I will speak about the reality of what has happened. The gospels of Matthew, Mark, and Luke all speak of the destruction of Jerusalem as a defining moment of cataclysm, persecution, desolating sacrilege, and

> "Nation shall rise against nation, and kingdom against kingdom;
> and there shall be great earthquakes, and in divers places famines
> and pestilence; and there shall be terrors and great signs from heaven."

We face such a defining experience as our nation struggles in war against kingdoms and neighbor. The heavens seem to recoil at the prospect and we are called on to do and see terrible things. But we must not forget that like the Israelites our task is ever watchfulness.

> "That ye may prevail to escape all these things that shall come to pass, and
> stand before the Son of Man."

In what will come to pass, we must not lose sight of our task, blinded by these terrors. When this war is past, we will be the remnant who must lead our people back to stand before the Son of Man.

Then it may be possible for me to guide my flock back to the Biblical roots that may have been tested today but that are unshaken. This has been a memorable event in there lives. It is awesome as a demonstration of the majesty of God's creation. The creator God has ordained from the beginning the course of our salvation. To His purpose I must direct my ordination as a shepherd."

"I thought just an hour ago about poor Alexander Martin,"

said Rachel. When he left us in such dejection, I was concerned. In such a state he must be sensitive for guiding signs to help lead him to recovery of his self confidence. He must wonder at such an event as this in terms of his own condition."

"That had not occurred to me, dear. Even strong people who in normal circumstances have complete control over their emotions can be over awed by a cataclysm. The army has given him such a blow and now even nature seems to contrive to destabilize his reason. Thank God he is with his family. We must seek him out."

Alexander appeared in my Buffalo congregation on the next Sunday. He showed no ill effects. "I have to tell you, David, that when the lights went out, even though I knew the cause, I wondered what I was being told. Then the lights came back on and I knew. Even in the depths of the deepest pits of life, be certain that light will return and my life is in good hands."

"May I quote you, Alex?"

CHAPTER EIGHT **1780** Conflict Moves South

In the next two years of the war, my people continued to be called out on expeditions against Indians and designated bands of Tories. There was no central command for the Tories, but individual forces would coalesce around a leader, and these bands were capable of causing significant damage and terror before the state would order out militia forces to intercept them. Gideon Wright commanded a very illusive Tory force in Surry County. The Moravians, attempting to remain non-belligerents, were always concerned that Wright's men would raid in Wachovia. I was in Salem in '79 when there was a report that Wright was about. The Moravians became suddenly very guarded in their dealings with me, knowing my sympathies. Certain supplies of meat and clothing became unavailable, hidden I supposed, until the report was proved false and my money was again sought. There was little way of determining a stranger's sympathy unless he said something and even then, he was possibly creating a diversion. People were paid to provide information. Neighbors were known to purposely accuse those they had lived around for years, and by that false action, have them hung by the other side in order to try to steal their land.

Daniel Gillespie was considered a scourge to the Tories. Early in the conflict he was raised to the rank of Colonel by the Rebels but he was considered too impetuous for large command. He often operated against the Tories around Deep River and in one poorly planned encounter, most of his men were captured. He had too few men left to mount a rescue raid, but in spying on the Tory camp, he overheard them tell John Hall, one of his captured men, that they were going to hang him. He refused to wait for reinforcements but sneaked up to the edge of the camp where Hall could see him and gain reassurance that he would not be left behind. The Tory commander demanded of Hall if he knew Gillespie. Hall said he did not. "Do you see him?" they asked. Hall looked away and said "no." This was repeated several times then Gillespie sprang up, jumped on his horse and rode off. Most of the Tories followed directly after him leaving the camp so little defended that the few remaining Rebels rode in and retook their fellow soldiers without loss of anybody.

Colonel David Fanning had his own regiment of Tory Loyalists, who operated most effectively then out of the Carraway Mountains, referred to as the "high hills of Randolph," a perfect place of concealment. They plundered and pillaged into Guilford and Orange, Montgomery and Moore. "Going Tory hunting" was the repeated description the Whigs had for their campaigns against this Tory strength. I remember a story told to me by Thomas Lovelady, a less than noble warrior, about an encounter with Fanning. Thomas was commanding a company returning from South Carolina when they stopped at the home of an "old Dutch Tory" on Stinking Creek in Randolph, named Apple. They asked for some water but they were refused. Justified by their hunger and thirst, they helped themselves and after eating, all lay down to sleep except Lovelady and the Dutchman's daughter. He tried to persuade the young lady to go to bed, assuring her they would not be interrupted but she refused and he, knowing this to be a Tory house, determined not to sleep. He tried to keep his eye on the girl so she would not arouse local Tories but he fell asleep in the chair. Awakened later by some sound, he realized she was not in the house and he tried to waken his companions but was unsuccessful. About daybreak, the house was surrounded by Fanning and Tory Major Bill Nichols. Fanning shot one of the men and was about to shoot Lovelady, when Nichols interfered and said he had been raised with Thomas and knew him well. The remaining eleven were spared and forced to take an oath, administered by Fanning, not to fight again against His Majesty, and thus they were released on a parole of honor. They set out on their way home and on the way met a company of Whigs. Six of the Whigs joined them, when they told their tale, and together they returned to the house of the Old Dutchman and his daughter. Fanning and his party had left and the Whigs proceeded to take the young lady into Stinking Creek and there gave her a sound dunking. They left her in a situation, "not in the best suited to carrying speedy expresses."

One day a company of the militia marched by our farm coming from William Brazelton's house to the south. When we asked, they said they were taking two infamous Tories to the courthouse to a courts martial and they would surely be found guilty. The insinuation was clear. They were to be executed. Only later did we find that the Tory, Hugh McPherson, had been executed. His second in command, a man named Campbell, had been "spicketed," a brutal punishment where his foot was pushed into a sharp spike in a log and he was twisted until the pin was run through his foot. Thus maimed, he was released.

Such stories made the rounds of public houses and even our Presbyterian academy, as great entertainment. By such casual concern for other people and human dignity, everyone became accustomed to lenient moral attitudes. I often believed that I spoke from my pulpits without the slightest influence on anyone else. War not only kills and maims the combatants, it strains the moral fibre of people, some beyond their limit of honor and decency. For others it may be a release of the rascal within, that in peacetime, law and the community are able to keep contained.

By 1780, our friend Alexander Martin had succeeded in recovering his health. He had entered politics and, just a year after his resignation from the army, he was elected a member of the North Carolina Senate from Guilford. By the time he was elected to his third Assembly, he was selected by his peers as President of the Senate when the sitting President, Abner Nash, was chosen Governor. There was no Lieutenant Governor under this constitution, so he was the second highest elected officer in the state and the most obvious political spokesman for the frontier people.

We heard that the British, under Generals Clinton and Cornwallis, had taken Charleston and that among the Americans captured were almost all of the North Carolina Continental soldiers and about 600 militia. General concern spread when it was recognized that the British intended to concentrate militarily on the South and that the state had few troops to place in their way. Reinforcements arrived from Maryland and Delaware in the form of 1400 troops under General DeKalb. Horatio Gates, who had made his fame with his great victory at Saratoga, was sent by Washington to take command. Former Governor Richard Caswell took command of all North Carolina state troops and militia. Imitating what the national government had attempted during a crisis situation, the legislature established a Board of War to help the Governor, and Martin was one of the three members of that all-powerful committee.

In August, Gates met Cornwallis in battle at Camden and suffered the worst American defeat of the war in the South. The Americans were routed, and old Gates ran so fast back through Charlotte and to Hillsborough, people said he must have been in a steeple chase. Even Caswell, unable to rally his Carolina men, fled the field. If it hadn't been for our nephew, William R. Davie, who was late in arriving with his command and succeeded in reorganizing the retreat of the Carolinians, the whole army would still be running. It became clear throughout the state that times were desperate.

There were members of my congregations fighting at Charleston and Camden and at other places like Monck's Corner,

143

Ramseur's Mill, and Hanging Rock. By winter, we were sorely tried. The American commissary had drained the state of all extra provisions. The army had lost almost all its baggage at Camden and everything had to be replaced. Those who had not been called on yet to reenlist, knew that they might not be available for spring planting. All my services were well attended and my people expected me to have words of re-assurance. They suddenly got very religious. This time it was less enthusiasm for theology and more willingness to depend on any force that might save them.

Conversely, the Tories, who had been pretty much driven into the woods and mountains, reappeared with new prospects and the civil war got new vigor. Colonel Fanning rebuilt his command and was able, by stealth and deception, to create the prospect of a successful linkage with the British troops in South Carolina. General Gates was replaced by General Nathanael Greene, whom Washington had dispatched with orders to reform the American strategy to block Cornwallis.

That winter, when Alexander Martin returned from a meeting of the Council of State and was staying briefly at his home on the Dan that he called Danbury, I visited him with the intention of gaining a first hand understanding of what we were now facing in the war. With so many people depending on me to give them leadership and inspiration in their time of need, I needed something myself, for I could not keep building their confidence based on no reservoir of my own.

I found Alexander Martin completely recovered from his military experience and now a man robust with confidence. No doubt the care of his mother and family had brought him back from his depression and given him back the determination that was his signature quality. He seemed as resolute as I imagined any commander of an army or of a sailing ship should be. Civil command operated within the control of laws and the courts, and even in times of desperate war, that structure limited the indiscriminate exercise of vendettas and cabals as the means of gaining promotion. I had always known that Alexander had the character and stamina to go against political competition. It was the filthy, coarse tactics of half-witted uniformed fools that he could not abide. He cursed only his own inability to disdain such people in the military but he knew how to get the better of those same types in a civilian political atmosphere.

He stood before the fireplace with the glow surrounding him. I sat in the Windsor chair by a drop- leaf table on which he had spread books and official looking documents.

"We have no functioning government," he announced with resolution. "I am one of a committee of three charged with facilitating the state interaction with the army. Legislators fear to meet with no force to guarantee their safety. Cornwallis and Tarleton blazed their way through South Carolina and we are their next objective. Fanning strikes behind our back and we are left to swat at him like he was a big blue horse-fly."

"It is a classical testing, to be sure," I added.. "There are preachers and Tories alike telling uneducated people that we are experiencing God's curse for our challenge to the anointed King. My elders want me to proclaim that God will fulfill his covenant with his chosen people and will smite those who would deny our freedom from tyranny. I will proclaim only what I know, that God has his purpose to work out and that He will redeem his people. I cannot define his plan or describe His method but I can proclaim that having created us as free people, we must defend our free nature, even at the expense of our own lives."

"David, you must be untiring in proclaiming that message," Alexander said. "I can outline for you our plans to repel the British, but it will succeed only if our leaders can inspire timid people to do extraordinary things. For the first time, I believe, we have in the South at the head of our forces, a man capable of brilliant strategy. I know General Greene. Some declare him slow but I know him to be deliberate, attentive to details of terrain and commissary and numbers, the things that make for successful campaigns in war. I know something first hand of Cornwallis also and I judge him to be bold and determined, the perfect general to pressure a frightened, dispirited foe. Cornwallis will not relax his pressure in victory or defeat in individual battle, but I am convinced Greene will not give battle until the terms are his. The Board of War is exerting every resource of supply but the state larder is almost empty. We are pressing our neighbors who understand that if Cornwallis succeeds in our place, he will soon besiege theirs. General Washington is sending all the force that the northern army can spare."

I asked innocuously, "where do you suppose Greene will stand against the British? Will it be in North Carolina?"

Martin looked at me earnestly. "Cornwallis approaches Mecklenburg, but I do not believe a stand will be taken below the Yadkin River. The British are aimed at Virginia but Greene intends to take them on before they reach the border. Since Cornwallis is now on a south to north course, battle should ultimately come very near here."

I was expecting to hear that the fight would be near to Buffalo Creek, but the direct news, that it was a likely location, shocked my system. I must have been conditioned already, however, because my mind was not dazed but energized, almost inspired. I astonished myself. "What can be done in our section to prepare?"

"First, do not act upon what I have told you. In fact, this information should be confined to only the most trusted of our American friends. Knowing about what I have said should be used for the purpose of general alertness for the time when Greene will direct action to be taken and not before. Think about who might serve well as guides for portions of the army, where river crossings can be made easily or supplies might be stored with best safety, how civilians might be protected in the time of greatest danger. People will be concerned about being displaced from their property, so be ready with instruction for their own protection. Don't hoard food but also, don't let the Tories have it. As to the Tories, obtain as much information as possible about their maneuvers and their strength and concentration. David, do now what you can do best; preach inspiration and pray without ceasing."

For some time, at least since the fall of Charleston to the British, friends and family had sought sanctuary on our farm. Rev. James Edmunds escaped Charleston and was the first we took in. Then two of Rachel's sisters, Mary Dunlap and Elizabeth Crawford arrived with their husbands and young families. Fortunately, they quickly rented a house and small farm nearby. Our brothers-in-law, although recent arrivals, tried to be active participants in the patriot cause and were much away with the army using their wagons and teams.

I held nothing back from Rachel. She showed concern for the safety of the children but otherwise was prepared to preserve everything as normal. I was diverted from teaching frequently now and she learned to step in and carry on the lessons if I had to be away. The students wondered about my frequent absences but they were perfectly happy to hear from Rachel who had been educated literally at the knee of her father, one of the great Presbyterian teachers. At first we discouraged the "forts" the students insisted on building and the military games they played after class. It appeared counter-productive to discourage them when everyone else that they knew was consumed in their own way by the nearby war. But the more nearby the war came, the more observably subdued the general atmosphere.

Encouraging news came in February that General Dan Morgan, our own frontier general, had won a stunning victory over the British at a place called Cowpens. Greene was now in a position to truly embark on his plan to bring Cornwallis into a defining confrontation.

Morgan had the 700 prisoners and all the equipment taken at Cowpens and Greene sent him north with them, toward Virginia. They crossed the Catawba, with Greene giving covering support, then they left General Davidson to hold Cornwallis from crossing as long as possible. Davidson was killed. Cornwallis got across. Then, in the same sequence, both armies crossed the Yadkin River. I got the news of Davidson's death and the successful British crossing of the Catawba, the same day that news came of the death of my close associate, Hugh McAden at Red House. We had sent his son, John, home from our school just a few days earlier, when we heard of his father's serious illness. I was deeply saddened. I had now lost McAden and Henry Patillo, who had left Hawfields a year earlier for Granville County. I would have depended on these two men to be stalwart supports in any looming crisis, able to inspire their congregations to patriotic leadership.

I happened to be in my study one day when, hearing a commotion outside, my sister-in-law, Mary Dunlap, our house guest during this uncertain time, burst in to say the house was surrounded by Tories. Before I could reach the front door, they were inside and had made me their prisoner. Their intent was to turn me in to the nearest British force and share the bounty which Cornwallis was reputed to have placed on my head. The house was searched and they piled before my feet the items they intended to plunder. Rachel was with me and Mary came in with a serious look and whispered in a voice too loud to be ignored, "is it not about time for Gillespie and his men to be here?" The Tories froze as they knew the name of Daniel Gillespie to be my congregant and Captain of the Guilford militia. The Tory in command, demanded to have her repeat what she had said but she allowed as how "it was a private communication and none of his business." Now whispering quietly but urgently among themselves, the Tories were soon frenzied to leave before the rebels were "thick as hell." They abandoned prisoner and plunder and were gone in an instant.

Another Tory company appeared a few days later without identification and demanded my English mare, my favorite animal. Presuming they were sent by General Greene as an impressing party to round up horses, I requested to see their authority. The man in command, drew a sword and announced it as his authority. I let him ride off with my mare and he left a wretched, lean animal in exchange. The next day, I came upon the same group and asked if I could pay them for return of my horse. Instead, they took away the replacement they had left and handed me an animal with such sores on his back that they could not be covered by a saddle. I was outdone, as you can imagine, but learned later that my mare was in McQuiston's stable. So I spoke to my man, Sammy, who is very black, and convinced him to go to the stable on a moonless night, sneak in and get the horse. He did, and at my direction took it to a hiding place only Sammy knew about. I strongly suspected that these rogues would come after the horse. I persuaded my brother-in-law, along with Sam McCorkle, Robert Hall, and Daniel Thacker, all my senior students, to come over with their guns. When the Tories came up, my friends stayed out of sight. The rogues quickly became abusive claiming that I was lying when I said I had not seen my horse since they had ridden off with it. One man cursed me and said I was a liar. McCorkle stepped out and took offense saying that the man had better calm down and refrain from such abuse. When the others also stepped out, the Tories were chapfallen. They became very quiet and moved off without their prey. Several days later, Sammy brought my horse home. Regretfully, they seem to have had the last word anyway. Some Tories, maybe even the same bunch, came back and retook the mare and I never had it in my possession again.

I was once more at Salem when Patriot units began to arrive. With good cause, these German Pietists saw with dread any approaching armies. Patriot soldiers particularly had used the Moravian towns badly in the course of the war; stealing horses, supplies, getting drunk and destructive, and giving no respect to the Moravians for their refusal to take sides. Although I had no regard myself for the Moravian beliefs, I considered it my duty as a clergyman to do what I could to arbitrate their grievances with Patriot soldiers in a number of distasteful circumstances. I left the day that the first Patriot headed north but I did have the occasion to meet General

Greene. When I advised him of my friendship with Alexander Martin and my position as minister at Buffalo and Alamance, he took me aside and we discussed the instructions that Martin had given me earlier.

"Very good," said Greene. "You can be a critical asset to whatever happens. I have been several times over the terrain between your creeks and I believe that location would be the most advantageous for the type of defense we will have to mount against Cornwallis. Of course, I cannot guarantee that I will be successful in drawing him to it but I would value your help if it should happen. Right now, I must protect my army. We are yet to be prepared for the battle that I envision. By use of the upper and lower fords of the Dan River, I intend to move temporarily into Virginia to await resupply. Already we have boats all along the river commandeered to ferry our men across. Once across, we will let the high water, and corresponding lack of transport, stall Cornwallis on the south side. When we are ready we will cross back and move into Guilford."

I assured him of my support and that of the Presbyterians in the area. He countered that although he had been renounced as a Quaker, he hoped those in the area might at least be sympathetic to his army.

Days later, having lost this ponderous race across Dan River, Cornwallis dropped down to Hillsborough where the state government had been meeting. There he raised the King's standard and summoned all loyal citizen to join him. Each army thus awaited reinforcements.

By February 28th, Cornwallis had exhausted the supplies of food in the vicinity of Hillsborough and broke camp moving toward the Haw River. Five days before, Greene, having succeeded in reinforcing his army to 2000 men, crossed the Dan and headed south. Greene reached the Haw River and camped at High Rock Ford. Between Troublesome Creek and Thomas McQuiston's farm on Buffalo, they were able to replenish food and supplies in large measure because the Scots-Irish Presbyterians, the old Nottingham Company, rallied their resources. At the Iron Works on Troublesome Creek, Greene tactically prepared fortifications as a secondary battle site. If he had to retreat from a reverse around Guilford Court House, this would be a defendable position to halt a British advance.

For nearly fifteen days, the woods were alive with moving troops. Small skirmishes were fought between foraging parties. Rachel kept our children inside whenever possible. We had six boys and a girl. The youngest was John Washington, just a babe. Most of the students were sent home for greater safety. Those that were here lost their enthusiasm for war games. The American camp on Thomas McQuiston's farm sprawled next door over onto our place and especially onto brother Alexander's. Camp noises at night and the smoke and flames lighting up the night sky were eerie portends of disaster. While the Americans were here we felt some security but more skirmishing, and particularly pressure from the south, caused Greene to retrace to the Iron Works.

General Harry Lee and his Light Horse were a constant shadow and harassment to Cornwallis' main army. They were like a squad of flying Scythians, each hour executing some little partisan exploit. On one occasion, Lee and about sixty of his men came to Charles Bruce's at the crossroad north of the court house to get breakfast and have their horses fed. They were received heartily by Bruce and had sat down to the meal when Isaac Wright, a neighbor, rode up on a flea-bitten pony and said he had seen Tarleton's Dragoons just down the road. Lee told his men they could not eat until they had checked out this report. When Wright then went to leave, the General became suspicious of his information. Lee commanded half his force to head toward the reported location of Tarleton's men and he ordered Wright to accompany them. Wright said he would go but he would not be able to keep up on such a small pony whereupon Lee had him exchange horses with his own trumpeter, James Gillies, since he expected no fighting from the boy. Gillies, unobserved, decided to go along anyway on the pony to keep an eye on his horse. They had traveled beyond the point where Wright said he had seen Tarleton and they were about to take Wright back to Lee for giving false information. Wright convinced them they should go just a little further and they went about a half mile when they did spy Tarleton but too late to turn and escape. The poor trumpeter, using spurs and his hat, saw the pony was going to be overtaken and began to cry "quarter." The response came back, "damn you. We will quarter you," whereupon they rode him down and cut him to pieces. Wright and the others reached the doomed boy too late but cut down seven of the dragoons. One of the patriots named Johnson, in single combat, saw a dragoon force his sword beneath Johnson's saddle and flip him so he lost balance. Precariously laid back and defenseless, he felt the splatter of blood and brains and thought he had been struck but, righting himself, he found instead that a friend had seen his predicament and struck the dragoon just above the ear nearly severing his head.

I had to leave my house to avoid capture and to make my family less vulnerable to retribution if I had been found there. On Sunday, the 11th, I risked capture to preach at Buffalo knowing that Cornwallis camped across Alamance Creek from my other congregants. There was an emotional tension that is rare at a Presbyterian service. Women could not control their weeping and children were terrified. Men attempted brave countenances that exceeded their individual capacity. There were so many American soldiers that the aisles were filled and others just lingered outside to be in proximity to a religious service. I attempted no theological treatise, which was their usual preference with these people, but tried to speak to their fears. No one sought judgment or sanctification. They wanted the comfort of forgiveness and to experience the palpable presence of God. They viewed themselves as suffering servants and it didn't hurt to be reminded that they were people of the Covenant. The service was also briefer than usual, again as a precaution against intrusion.

General Williams fought a battle at Wetzell's Mill to the east as Cornwallis crossed the Alamance and camped at sites on the Buffalo finally at McQuiston's. Fortunately, I anticipated that he might move directly into the area that Greene had vacated and where I was in hiding. Before I had left, Rachel and I gathered the children and prayed with them. We tried to explain, in terms that some could understand, that I had to leave them and that people might come who might frighten them. I would be near by and God was going to be with them and with their mother. They should be brave but it was all right to be afraid. "Stay near mother and do not wander off with anyone. Do not speak to a stranger even if they offer to give you something. If you hear loud noises, go to your mother." We knelt and I prayed and then Rachel prayed. Before I left, I gave them each a small portion of candy wrapped in paper. Leaving my family was the personal trial that I anticipated would nearly unhinge me. I was correct. I think it ventured very near the limit of my faith and I was staggered emotionally. We took all the horses and left just enough livestock as might be needed immediately. Nothing was to be left for the British. I used that night, and on several other occasions, the large stone drain that we had made from the basement kitchen under the west half of the house, as my route of escape. We were certain that the Tories already kept watch on our house and this drain opened beyond the house toward the creek. It was tall enough for me to crawl through easily. Any spies would be watching the two entrances to the above ground sections of the house, because our entrance to the basement was inside the east room.

I went first to Troublesome Creek, near the Iron Works. The Haw River, at that point, was little more than a creek but it was high in the winter. There I learned that a young boy who had been a prisoner of the British had escaped and returned to the army before he broke out with smallpox which spread rapidly in the American army. I had added fear for my family.

I went to McBride's farm on Reedy Fork and sought refuge but McBride was a man of limited courage who feared for his family. He said that he could not allow me to stay the night but he would camp with me nearby. I was piqued at first but came to understand his concerns. We found some low ground and spent the night and the next day went down about two miles to McQuiston's Bridge. It was the 14th and near the bridge we met some unruly militia troops without command, fleeing in anticipation of the fighting. These could not be our men, I convinced myself. I was sure that with men I had known as Christian believers in command, like James Martin and John Paisley and Captain Forbis, our men would be steadfast.

My brother, Alexander, had been an active Whig leader. In 1776 he had been placed on the Committee of Safety for Guilford. He was a partisan but he also struggled with the necessity to pursue neighbors with whom one differed. He signed a petition to the North

Carolina Council of Safety meeting at Halifax, to free Jeremiah Fields who had fought for the King at Moore's Creek and was imprisoned in Maryland. Alexander read me the petition and I was amused by the claim of these Whig leaders that Jeremiah was "far less criminal in that case than most of those infatuated persons that formed that diabolical scheme of subjugating the Province." Such a rationale betrayed the early ambivalence of neighbor against neighbor as enemies.

Alexander had to remain with the army all during the period of Cornwallis' invasion of the state, and while I tried to oversee my family from a distance, I had to also watch over his. There were seven children in Alexander's family and his wife, Margaret, was much like Rachel in her determination to protect her brood. One day, around sunset, I spied two men wandering toward my brother's house. I was told that they were foraging for the British army, which was passing near at the time, but I decided to observe them. They reached the house ahead of me and ordered Margaret to prepare dinner for them as they assembled items they intended to steal. It was the same pattern that had been used before when such a group had invaded my house. As I approached the cabin, I was met by one of Margaret's servants with her mistress' request to know what she should do. I told her to say Margaret should fix them the best possible meal and watch where they stacked their guns. After they were seated, as far as possible from the guns, and enjoying their meal, she should send word to a particular haystack where I would be hiding. All went according to plan. I slipped into the side door, took their rifles and declared them my prisoners. Later I turned them over to an American officer.

Men like this were not the most objectionable of the offal cast about in the wake of any army. The camp followers were ever a presences difficult to be ignored. Officers took no concern for them, about their welfare or their function. Some were prostitutes and acquired families. Others were simply wives and children who feared to remain in their homes without the protection of their husbands. They cooked and washed and sewed and satisfied. The worst were known to reflect gonorrhea on the march. At this place they would spread smallpox, but anywhere they spread any virulent pestilence without discrimination. They were left in the van along with the disregarded straggler. I confess that I could not bring myself to think of many of them with sympathy. I could satisfy myself that I was too busy to care. Later they might provide me a powerful sermon illustration. I would have to meditate long hours before I could decide, of what.

I was notified that General Cornwallis had indeed placed a £200 bounty upon my head and I hoped that news would not reach Rachel. It is a strange feeling to know that you have so angered another person, that they would provide money to see you captured or killed. I did not feel that I was such a danger. I had spoken truth where I had seen error. Was I not called to such a task by the vows I had taken as a minister of the Gospel? Who would be my judge and in what court might I be tried? I did not know then that the danger through which I was passing was not as great as that through which

Rachel was to go.

Two days before the battle, Cornwallis and a large company of troops rode into our yard. It was one of those beautiful March days with a chill that makes life appears tense with expectation. On such days, your hasty steps seem somewhat more vital and you never linger. The General came forward but did not identify himself. Rachel was confused and although suspicious, she told them where they might find me, believing she was speaking to Greene or to one of his commanders. The General wheeled abruptly about and Rachel knew instinctively that she had informed the wrong people. She agonized that night with no way of warning me of the danger. By some intuition, I had decided that the camp I had planned nearer my house was not safe and that was the day I had gone to McBride's.

Cornwallis' army spread over Gorrell's, McQuiston's and my farm for several days, during which they took all the supplies that were left, then burned fields, even fence posts. The McQuistons were placed in a lean-to in the yard and watched as their furniture and personal belongings were burned. Tories had singled out the McQuistons, but Cornwallis did not need Tories to direct him to the home of the Presbyterian minister he had already tried to capture. Repeating the indignities at the McQuiston farm, British soldiers claimed everything at our farm except one old goose which they left sardonically to prove they were not uncivilized. They took iron rods and probed in every location looking for contraband or a concealed preacher. With special significance, they turned Rachel's large brick oven in the yard into a burning pyre of household furniture, clothes, the contents of my desk, all my papers and my sermons. Then by the armload, they carried out my library and tossed in the books and finally the family Bible with the family record. Unable to silence me, they seemed to believe that they would succeed by burning my words and the sources of my inspiration. At one point, Rachel cried out as she saw the soldiers about to throw into the fire a tablecloth worked and given her by her mother. As she literally wrestled for the cloth, she asked, she pleaded, if there was not someone there who had a wife or mother and if they would stand to see her treated thus. A British doctor stepped forward, touched by the sentiment, took the cloth and returned it to Rachel. "Yes, I have such a wife," he said, "and you shall not be treated with such indignity."

For two days, as Cornwallis occupied the farm, Rachel and the children stayed huddled in the corn- crib with nothing to eat but some dried apples and peaches. Samuel and Alexander were old enough to assist Rachel in entertaining the younger children in their cramped quarters. It was difficult because everyone was dealing with their own response to fright. For the little children, fear became real when they cried. They could not give what they feared a name, but their little bodies reacted to being uncertain. The older children were more specific in what they feared: loud noises, unpleasant looks, horses and soldiers moving hurriedly in groups to unknown destinations. Rachel could pick out the specific soldiers that she should avoid by such signals as the indifference with which they satisfied a command directed against some of their property.

During the day when battle was finally closed, I was used several times as a courier between field commanders and militia units that were arriving late. I was dressed in black as I ordinarily would be, and I realized that anyone would obviously take me for a minister. By now though, the concerns to punish Presbyterian ministers as seditionists had faded, replaced by the personal concerns of the combatants. It was William Lasley who first advised me of the brisk battle that occurred in the early morning at New Garden. Cornwallis had headquartered at Deep River Friends Meeting House some twelve miles from Guilford Court House.

In the wee hours of the 15th, Cornwallis started his limited baggage south to Bell's Mill on the Deep River. Greene had sent Colonel "Light Horse Harry" Lee to stalk Cornwallis' movements. Lee's cavalry pricked at various picket positions. Then one of his companies, hearing the sound of the moving baggage, reported that Cornwallis was on the move, and that was transmitted to Greene. The British did not really start from Deep River until 5:30. Lee, still shadowing, made contact with Colonel Tarlton's Dragoons along New Garden Road northeast of the meeting house. It was not more than a lane, but worn down so that it was banked on either side and topped with split-rail fences, a dubious place for cavalry. Lee chose the location knowing that Tarlton had smaller mounts of poorer quality. Tarlton made several assaults but in each case he could attack only a few of Lee's men in the narrow path. Then Lee countercharged with such force that his men unhorsed the British, cut them down and swept forward taking prisoners of the unhorsed. Tarlton retreated and Lee suffered no losses. Tarlton was moving back toward the Quaker Meeting House by a wooded detour, and Lee struck out on the road planning to cut them off from the main army moving up from Deep River. Lee arrived at New Garden just as some of Cornwallis' guard units arrived in the vanguard of his main army. There was a second battle around the meeting house that lasted about thirty minutes, with roughly 1000 men engaged, and produced heavy casualties on both sides. The sun was now up. The Quakers, living in proximity to the meeting house and declared non-belligerents, were eye-witnesses to these battles in their farm yards and were left to care for the wounded of both sides and to bury the dead, which they did, usually where they were slain. A third battle occurred later in the morning at the Cross Roads on New Garden Road between the Meeting House and the first encounter in the lane. I heard later that William Hunt's sixteen year old son had gone out to observe the soldiers and hid himself behind a split-log fence. When a troop of British light horse came into view, he took his smoothbore gun, aimed it at the Captain that he supposed in command, and fired. The Captain fell dead and the company, supposing they were facing Greene's army behind the fence, turned round and fled. Lee with his support infantry, that had joined him at the meeting house, were in good position and took on what John Barringer told me were probably four-fifths of Cornwallis' army.

The one hour encounter was broken off when Lee, facing a superior force, retreated.

This morning, fighting could be heard easily at some distance, even at the Court House, and to General Greene it was satisfying that his adversary was being constantly harassed in his progress. The direction of the sounds of battle also gave him a clear indication of the position of Cornwallis through the morning. Rachel and the children could also hear the noise of battle throughout the morning as it moved from just west of our farm, around to the north. From time to time they also saw small units of soldiers passing toward the fighting and retreating away from it. They never knew whether they were going to find the fighting right in their midst.

A number of the women of Buffalo Church, met that morning at Robert Rankin's and they spent the day in prayer. At Alamance, others of the women did the same. Many old and young in both congregations were down with smallpox, adding to the anxiety of those who waited.

Many of the Buffalo men and boys assembled near John Allison's house with their women, children and old men, and waited. They were to the left flank of Greene's first line. When the firing started, the young men sprang for their rifles. The women tried to hold them back in a scene of much drama. The young men fell in with Colonel John Campbell's mountaineers, so immediate was the conflict.

The non–combatant, Quakers and Presbyterians, women and

children, heard and viewed the battles with disparate eyes and ears. Throughout the Revolution, the greatest fear of the Quakers had been that they would somehow be drawn into fighting. Some of their number had taken arms for the patriot side and had been disowned. I've heard it said that as many as 600 took sides. Some few may have known that Greene, a Rhode Island Quaker himself, had been disowned for taking arms. The battles around their meeting house left them responsible for the burial of many dead on both sides and the care of the wounded for days thereafter. Almost all the Presbyterian homes heard the battle, knowing they had at least one family member involved directly in the fighting. They were emotionally committed to the outcome. They had hatred for their Tory neighbors and the fighting only intensified their desire for revenge and retribution. The Quakers cursed both Whig and Tory with equal vigor seeing little difference between the moral intentions of either. As Scots–Irish, the earlier generations of Presbyterians had come to a dislike of the Quakers in Pennsylvania. Having earlier invited them in as immigrants, the Quakers soon rued their benevolence and came to see the Scots–Irish as a scourge. The Scots–Irish saw the Quakers as closing them out with higher priced land and strict political control of Pennsylvania. In Guilford, these two denominations lived in uneasy proximity without hostility but also without harmony.

CHAPTER TEN **1781** Battle of Guilford Court House

It was Lasley who also gave me the first description of the start of the battle at the Court House. It was about noon and he recalled how Colonel Lee, after all his morning activity, rode up to the first line and in a voice of complete confidence said, "my brave boys, your lands, your lives and your country depend on your conduct this day! I have given TARLETON hell this morning and I will give him more of it before night." At that very point a British cannon was heard to roar. "You hear damnation roaring over all these words and after all, they are no more than we." Then Lee took up his position anchoring the left flank of the army while Colonel William Washington's cavalry did the same on the right.

Colonel James Martin still lacked sufficient ammunition and equipment for his militia command as the battle approached. In those last days he raised about 200 more men than he could arm, and on hearing that Cornwallis was on his way to Guilford, some of the newcomers deserted. Martin had joined Greene at the Iron Works in command of the regional militia. Together, the Americans had proceeded to the Court House. Greene now knew that Cornwallis was marching up the New Garden Road toward him. He drew up his men in three lines with 100 to 500 yards separating each. Greene had learned to be suspicious of the unreliability of any militia facing British

166

and Hessian regulars. He placed the locals in the first line, backed by two regiments of North Carolina foot, about 1000 men, under Eaton and Butler. He hoped that this line might fire about two volleys but did not expect more. The second line could give little cover to the first and was distant enough that it did not serve well as a fall back line. Because they had such limited military training and experience in battle, there was no way of knowing how competent these farmers would be when facing an organized enemy. Some were very good shots and they were as brave individually as any American force, but the application of bravery responds to the circumstances, particularly with inexperience. The third line was near the cross roads at the Court House. Here Greene had his regulars: 1400 Continentals from Maryland, Virginia, and Delaware. This was the power of his army upon which he would anchor this plan.

Captain Arthur Forbis was in command of scarcely a complete company in the first line. Many of his people from Alamance Church were included. He commanded his men to sit down until the British came close enough for effective fire. As they got closer, Martin asked Forbis if it was possible to take down the British Captain who was driving his men forward with drawn sword. He said confidently that he could, and Martin told him to do so at 50 yards. Forbis was good as his word.

Greene, alerted so early by reports from Lee of the movements of Tarlton's cavalry, ordered a quick breakfast for his men so that they would meet the British on full stomachs. Advancing early, Cornwallis had not been able to provide the same advantage for his men.

Greene sent all his baggage and provisions, to be guided by Thomas McQuiston, to the Iron Works site. Cornwallis sent his sick and provisions to Bell's Mill on Deep River. Marching northeast along the New Garden Road in the damp cold of a dark, late winter morning, the British could hear the firing at New Garden. It was certain then that Greene was committed at last to a battle.

On the field, Greene too walked the line of the wood fence behind which the militia now crouched. Urging calm and steady shots he asked for two volleys, just two volleys, and then they were released to retire. He was aware they would be facing for the first time the image of bayonets in a charge by veteran European soldiers. The sound of fife and drum was heard even before they saw the flags. Greene spoke as soothingly as he could to the farm boys about to face combat. Then they stood alone and up the grade of the path that was called New Garden Road, came the mounting sound of several thousand tromping feet, then tops of flags billowing, then a shimmering light on rows of shiny sword–tipped rifles, and finally blocks of red and green and blue companies of the enemy.

It was about two o'clock when the British came in range of some of the best marksmen on the first line. Scattered shots rang out and men in tattered, brightly colored uniforms began to drop. To the fife and drum was now added the strange sound of the Scots bagpipes whining over the open field. With the British about a hundred yards from the fence, the Americans fired their first volley with respectable success. A few steps further, the British fired their first volley and militia men dropped along the line. Still they held. The British were now at a run and having closed half the distance, suddenly pulled up. They recognized that the Americans were not going to break as they had much earlier at the battle at Camden. They were facing a point blank barrage from the fence line. For just a moment men on both sides seemed suspended in anticipation. Their Lt. Colonel Webster rose to the front and high in the stirrups rallied his men in an inspiring voice and they moved as a man. I later learned Webster was the son of a Presbyterian clergyman from Edinburgh who was on occasion the moderator of the General Assembly. The second volley was then delivered with fair precision by the Americans' militia. The Fusiliers charged forward into what was judged dreadful havoc on both sides. One half of the Highlanders on the east side of the road were said to have dropped on the spot.

Having delivered the asked for two volleys, the militia turned in retreat. Many just broke and ran, dropping weapons and any equipment that might slow them. Others fell back under their officers to the second line. Several American officers, seeing what appeared a rout, tried to block their flight threatening to shot them down if they continued. No one listened. Commanders in the second line warned their men that this mass of rugged frontiersmen was descending on them and not to get caught up in the image of a general rout. The Americans on the flanks, anchored by the cavalry of Colonels Lee and Washington, did not break, and since he was drawing into the center,

Cornwallis had to turn and face them as a threat to his flanks.

In the weeks after the battle, there were many debates, some bitter fights, about this retreat. It was claimed by some that the North Carolina militia companies ran in panic. By others, it was asserted that it was not the volunteers who had run but the North Carolina Foot under Butler and Eaton. It was said that the volunteers did not run because they defended their families. It was the Foot who had enlisted, who risked punitive action if they were caught, that had kept running. Captain Forbis claimed that it had been the Virginians in the second line who had actually shot him, so chaotic were the circumstances.

About this time, before the second line had been reached by the British, I was directed along with about a dozen other civilian volunteers from the region, to move up to the Iron Works Road. There we were to try to intercept as many of the locals who had fled as we could and try to persuade them to return to the field. Retreat in battle is a seductive option, particularly after a man can convince himself that he has completed his assignment and he sees his neighbors in retreat. Sending us, people they knew in the community, even a minister, to put their action into question, did cause them a second thought. There were some who felt shame and turned immediately to go back with new resolution. Others told them, if it were such a good idea, to do it themselves – a reasonable suggestion.

In the process of my assignment, I ranged nearer to Speedwell Iron Works, and the men I was encountering there had purposely retired to the place they knew Greene had prepared as a fall-back position. There were groups of men standing in anticipation. Some were assigned to the army's baggage and ammunition train. Others had found friends who, like them, had been in the battle, and they were effusive in their conversation comparing experiences and rebuilding their self image. Small groups of men, like those I had encountered in the more rapid retreat, lingered in the trees on the edges with little to say. There was no one there to assemble them into a unit force again so they watched, some considering still the option to continue to run. The road to Speedwell approached from the south down a long descending hill of open farmland to a bowl where the mill stood along with the miller's house, and branches of Troublesome Creek converged. Then on the other side the land rose more sharply and I could see recently constructed trenches and redoubts. Even without any military experience, I could see the defensive advantages of such a position. I would not recognize for many months, the similarity of the Speedwell site to the terrain of Greene's third line defense at Guilford Court House. I was eager to return to the Court House where I knew the battle must be fully engaged but I had no directions to do so. I thought it best to stay at Speedwell, at least until later in the afternoon, in case a retreat became more precipitous and I would be needed again. I went to the miller's house and there found some food and a welcome respite.

The American second line at Guilford was designed around Generals Edward Stevens and Robert Lawson and the 1300 man

Virginia Brigade. At Camden, Stevens had seen his Virginia Brigade vanish from the field and he was determined that they would make a dependable show of themselves this time. It was his turn to pace the line, encouraging his boys and showing them the most advantageous factors of their position. The British were advancing now into the wooded area that had been behind the first line. In here the cavalry had to dismount in order to proceed. Unit order was broken. This time it was the Virginia farm boys, many of them veterans who were fine shots and had the more stable protection behind trees and they were giving Webster and O'Hara scalding fire. A hail of lead, knitting in crossing patterns, clipped twigs and thudded into heads and bodies. The woods were so thick that bayonets were useless. General O'Hara fell from his horse, shot through the thigh and the chest. So close was the fighting that St. George Tucker told me later that he was attempting to rally his Virginia Company, when he was bayoneted in the leg by one of his own men and never knew if by malice or accident. In spite of his best efforts, and those of other Virginia officers, the brigade was in full retreat.

The third line was on a ridge in an open field, a kind of amphitheater. The Welsh Fusiliers, the Jagers, the 33rd and the guards company, and on the east side of the New Garden Road, the Highlanders began to emerge from the smoke and haze of the trees. The natural undergrowth had broken up their usual close unit order but as they cleared the trees they re-formed. Cornwallis' men, some of whom had been through more than one of the five confrontations of the day with various American units, hungry and tired, faced now Greene's seasoned Continentals above them. Cornwallis was nowhere to be seen and General Webster, unwilling to delay until his commander appeared, moved the columns forward. Down a small hill they moved over open land crossing a small stream, then up a final hill they marched toward the rested, fed, and ready Americans. Within one hundred feet, the Continentals opened fire in a withering volley that ripped into the British, cutting down scores of men in heaps. They fell back from the slaughter in complete disorder. General Webster was painfully wounded in the knee cap but insisted on remaining in command. At the very least, Webster's advance had been imprudent, taken against a very secure position, heavily outnumbered, commanding tired and hungry men, leaving his flanks wide open, and without reserves. Colonel James Stuart and his 2nd Guards Battalion broke out of the woods, and with a company of Grenadiers, advanced up the same hill in a bayonet charge that breached the ridge and sent the 2nd Maryland into panic. Firing a volley as they topped the ridge, Stuart's Guards overran the Marylanders and some artillery units. A counter charge by Colonel Gunby and the 1st Maryland fired point blank into Stuart's men. Both sides were blazing away at each other, sometimes so close that it seemed the fire from their barrels met in mid air. The Marylanders this time mounted a bayonet charge into Stuart and some of the fiercest hand-to-hand fighting occurred, with the Americans beginning to slaughter one of the best of the Guards units. Cornwallis now appeared, and seeing the critical position his troops were in, ordered his artillery to fire grape shot directly into the melee. The artillery was of course indiscriminate in its decimation, but it succeeded in breaking up the pitched battle and the British rallied to the rear. General Webster made one more, even less successful, attack and fell back. The British were bloodied and fatigued. It may be that at that moment, Greene might have brought up reserves and carried the day. Instead, having accomplished his purpose of the day by mauling Cornwallis' invading force, he began retreat at about 4:00 in the afternoon.

Cornwallis was left on the field, the ordinary measure of victory, but at a terrible price. His prized Guards battalion had 50 percent casualties. The Grenadiers had lost all its officers. He started the day with 3,300 men and at the set of the sun could field fewer than 1,450. Not a single field unit remained field ready. Five of his senior officers died including Webster whom he called "his scabbard."

Cornwallis retired to New Garden and camped near the Meeting House, where the wounded of both armies were being treated. His best military experience told him to pursue, but the reality was that Greene had accomplished a strategic success and his was an army unfit for further combat.

Greene retreated to Reedy Fork Creek and waited for stragglers. He had lost 20 percent of the best of his army, but no senior officers had been seriously wounded. Of course, most of the militia was gone, many because their enlistment was up. It was not until the late hours of the night that Greene reached Speedwell Iron Works on the Haw. He camped in positions, including trenches, that were already prepared to repulse Cornwallis in the event of the expected second battle.

Rain that night fell on friend and foe alike. The dead lay unburied and the wounded cried and moaned all night. Families searched for survivors among the bodies. Surgeons of both armies worked the fields trying to assist those they could. What served for hospitals were set up at New Garden Meeting House, at the Court House, and at the McNairy House near the morning battle at the cross roads.

Captain Arthur Forbis was wounded near the first line and was left on the field. Since it was on the edge of the battlefield, he was overlooked at the end of the day. Tories swarmed across the field as the Americans retreated, and one who knew Forbis found him and gave him a hat full of water. Another came upon him later and mercilessly cursing him as a rebel ran his bayonet through him. For thirty hours Forbis lay thus with multiple wounds upon the ground until a neighbor woman, searching for her brother, came upon him and with great difficulty got him on to her horse. Leading the horse toward Forbis' home, they met his family in the coach out seeking his body. The family took him home. One of the surgeons helped me with him. Had he not been left without care for so long, we might have saved his life. It was a tragic scene as he began to fade. His mind wandered about the details of the fighting. He would cry out commands as if he were still on the field. Two days after the battle, he died in his bed. For our community, Forbis was our hero. The Tory who had found him wounded and had run him through was named Shoemaker. After the battle he was one of the first to be sought for retribution and he was hung. Three days after the battle some of the Americans were yet to be buried.

After Greene had reached Speedwell, he asked me to return to the battlefield and to assist with the care of the wounded. Before the war, as is the case with most ministers, I had learned to be informed about common medical conditions just because a minister is looked on as generally knowledgeable about life sources. I had a particular penchant for medicine and sought books on the subject to increase my knowledge. When we had children, I had another practical reason to be knowledgeable. Beginning on the battlefield that evening, I was immersed in the intense battle fought by surgeons off the field against death. Battle was an assault against the intensity of my faith as a Christian and also turned out to be a confirmation of my latent fascination with medicine. I worked that night with several American surgeons and their assistants. At one instance, I found myself working closely with General Cornwallis' chief surgeon, Dr. Jackson, a demonstration that we were assisting wounded men, not friend or foe. I recall Jackson was sawing off a soldier's leg. The man had been screaming in unbearable pain and suddenly fell silent in a faint. Jackson had me holding the mangled leg as he worked and said to me, "I see by your dress that you appear to be a minister but you have some skill in medicine. Were you in the fighting, too?"

"No, I am the minister of the Buffalo Presbyterian Church just over there." I pointed in the direction of the church. "I have been assisting as a civilian courier for General Greene for several days and I have not seen my wife and children for now three days. I am afraid you British have placed a price on my head so I have been careful but now I can put some rudimentary skills I have acquired at medicine to use for these pitiful victims."

"Are you Caldwell, perhaps," he said to my surprise.

"Yes, David Caldwell," I replied.

"Such irony. I am Dr. Robert Jackson of Fraser's Highlanders and just yesterday I met your fine wife at your home in rather strained circumstances." Then he recalled for me the destruction of my papers and the struggle for the table cloth and his part in its retrieval. I was grateful for his service to Rachel but I was only further concerned for what she and the children might be suffering.

At one point that evening I went with Dr. Jackson over to the McNairy House, which was filled with wounded. We continued to operate, amputating so frequently that we tossed limbs through the door into a wagon parked just outside for the purpose of bone collection.

With only quick and infrequent naps to relieve my exhaustion, I labored under various surgeons through the night and the next two days, binding wounds, amputating limbs, dispensing medicine, and praying with the dying and dead. Many times I considered the surroundings as the depths of Sheol. Death in battle, I came to

177

understand, was more to be wished than death as a result of battle –
death that lingers, turns gangrenous, putrid, toxemic, fissured,
hallucinatory. From that experience, I knew that for the rest of my life
I would never shrink from a struggle with death and I was confirmed
in my belief that "nothing, in life or in death, can separate me from the
love of God in Christ Jesus our Lord."

I finally got back to my family on the 17th. The exaltation of
reunion, played out in the physical atmosphere of devastation, was
absolute. We had all survived. Much of what we had accumulated,
much of what we had labored to make up into our farmstead, was
gone. Our memorial past, my old sermons, my library, the family
record in our Bible, had been consumed. We wept for our loss and
were consoled by our survival. I understood that it had been Rachel
who had preserved our children. It was she who had the direct
encounter with the armed and appointed soldiers of domination. Her
actions had confirmed the balance between the wanton destruction of
personal, precious property and the preservation of beloved life. She
had intended to accomplish this task so that I could be free to function
in a more public capacity available to me as a minister of the Gospel.
It was a capacity bestowed on me by God and by my community but
it was available to me only because of Rachel. It was in the symbolism
of that hand–made table cloth that Rachel had envisioned her calling –
she saw her identity. She claimed it against the forces that would deny
her and she had passionately claimed it. "Love endureth all things."

On that Sunday, the 18th, I stood in the pulpit at Alamance.

Cornwallis was preparing to finally leave New Garden. Greene, knowing now that Cornwallis was unable to pursue him, left Speedwell Iron Works just a few miles north, beginning now his pursuit of the crippled pursuer.

The church could not contain another soul. Rented pews overflowed with invited strangers and wounded soldiers. Outside, crowds strained to hear at every window. I looked out on that multitude aware that they, as I, had each been backed to the limits of despair and had survived. It would be years for some to process the experience, the slow grinder of their reason, assisted when I could by my words of intercession. I stated my text, Romans 8:33–35.

> Who shall lay anything to the charge of God's elect?
> It is God that justifieth; who is he that condemneth?
> It is Christ Jesus that died, yea rather,
> that was raised from the dead,
> who is at the right hand of God,
> who also maketh intercession for us.
> Who shall separate us from the love of Christ?

The Quakers were not able to use their meeting house for two Sundays, while it served as a field hospital. During that time, and at other Friends Meetings in the near by, they found much comfort in recognizing the March events as visions of the chastening hand of God. The fact that several British soldiers they had cared for brought smallpox into their families did indeed seem to give some credence to that interpretation. I was not ashamed, for my own part, to speak to the elect who had survived and to see for them, as time revealed the reality of the battle that had been fought in their midst, God's purpose fulfilled. The people who faced me had survived. I had to give them some fortification to carry on. I would not be so shallow as to claim God to be on the side of the Americans, and it was important that we not try to ensnare God in our ambition. I wanted them to have confidence in God's plan, the security that God makes intercession for us, and that we are loved. Victory is not in our triumph of intent but in God's design for humanity. In God's house, we would not have a victors rally, no glorious banging of drums or dedication of captured battle flags. On this scarred and bleeding Sunday, I had to help them make out the vision of God in their midst, not triumphant like the generals they had seen committing the fate of common soldiers to the blast of rifle and gun; even here, especially now, God was present and intercessory. The experiences of this week would brand my messages for the rest of my pastorate. On that first Sunday, I had only to bring them ashore out of the quagmire; we needed to feel the firmness of foundation upon which to stand.

Before leaving Guilford, Cornwallis issued a proclamation declaring to all citizens his success in defeating the Whig forces and calling all North Carolinians to return to their allegiance to the King. He declared a victory that he had not won in order to make possible a result he could not expect. It was a political shell game. Nathanael Greene played something of the same game with the Quakers as he came through Guilford Court House. He directed to them a letter in which he presumed their support as a birthright Quaker, and praised their humanity in the face of the flotsam of war. He made no mention of their neutrality which had not only denied their support to the British but also to him. He pointed out that the British were deceiving when they claimed that this was a religious dispute and he insisted that only Americans could bring religious liberty. This, he declared, was a political struggle for power and if the British won, the colonials would soon see that their freedom would be denied. The only British purpose was to create division as they had in "the horrid disorders among the Whigs and Tories." Finally he begged them to continue to care for the wounded that he had been forced to leave behind.

The Quaker response to Greene assured him that they would do all in their power to aid the suffering among them, who still represented over a hundred wounded in their meeting house alone. In spite of the fact that the British had almost foraged the resources of the New Garden Quakers to the bone before they had departed and left even more of their soldiers in their care; they would not make a distinction as to party or cause. They were not beyond noting that both armies had been responsible for the burial of their dead and the care of their wounded, according to accepted rules of war, and that they both had placed an imposition upon the Quakers that took advantage of their Christian commitment.

I did not fault the Quakers for the tone of their response. It seemed to me that in this conflict there was a deep paradox of the nature of the Christian calling in the face of political reality. If one were to attribute to the parties of the immediate conflict an identifying quality, we might say that the Tory's quality was loyalty, the Whig's was patriotism, and the Quaker's was humanitarianism. The Scots-Irish Presbyterians could be grouped with the Whigs but individually, their attribute might be considered as that of independence. None of these characteristics is offensive; in fact under normal circumstances, each would routinely be coveted by the other groups. More important, each quality would be essential to the nation each side hoped to construct. At this moment, however, the insinuation of each group was that their dedication to their defining attribution implied that the others were lacking in that quality. If you were not for that attribute, you had to be against it. Ironically, in war it is not enough to accentuate your best nature, you must with the same vigor deny that nature to your adversary. We Presbyterians did care for our own, that is, those of our immediate families who died or were wounded, but we almost ridiculed by our attitude the humanitarianism of the Quakers that held high the Christian calling to all the needy in distress. The Quakers refused to fight for the religious freedom they sought, and similarly seemed to imply ridicule to the Presbyterians who were willing to die in order to be free. Tories were loyal to a tradition that had repeatedly betrayed them, and Whigs were patriotic even when they were hanging their neighbors. And it was not over.

CHAPTER ELEVEN **1781** The Aftermath of Battle

At my first glimpse of the farm, as I rode down the hill on the 17th, it appeared unchanged. The buildings were all in place, some of the fencing was down, and then I noticed that the school door lay on the ground and the windows were out. Just as I began to grasp the extent of the damage I saw the first two boys chasing around the side of the barn. I heard the cry distinctly, "PAPA, PAPA, Papa's here! Mama, come now!" I rode through the gate and by the time I could hastily dismount, it was into the swarm of wife and children. I believe that was the happiest moment of my life. I was pulled and pummeled and tears of joy splashed across my face.

"Rachel, my dear one," was as much as I could say as I reached for my wife.

"Oh, David, do we have you back at last?" she wept.

The children pressed around me grabbing at me and pounding on me. Sam was fourteen, Alex was twelve, Andrew was ten. There was Patsy, my one girl who was seven, the twins, David and Thomas who were four, and John, just seven months, a tiny package who squealed his excitement. Could a man ever have so much joy in one moment? I let the emotion flow over us unabated and kissed each one tenderly.

When we had finally satiated our joy, come to a balance of our emotion, I said, "Now, we must thank God who has made this moment for us. Do you remember that when I left, we asked God to spare us and bring us back together after a time of trial? We must thank Him for this gift." We all knelt and I poured out an expression of our joy before the author of that joy and we tried to remember all those who had lost lives and loved ones and those whose death had no mourners.

Taking stock of our material losses was difficult but somehow it was done without grief. We were all experiencing the lesson on values in life. We believed that we had survived the definitive life experience of this family. It had been physical and immediate, not a second hand influence on our emotions or just a threat to our security. In March of 1781, with our neighbors, we had literally walked through the valley of the shadow of death and God had been with us. We had been protected by His rod and His staff. We were on the other side. What we did not fully appreciate then was that we were present at the creation of a new nation. God knew, but we were still gazing through that dark, immediate mirror.

There was little left in my library, my sacred space. Rachel decried the indignity of the assault on a man of God. I told her, "I understood, when I called my congregations to resist tyranny, that I gave those who would support that tyranny, the right to see me in terms of enemy. I could not expect to have it both ways. It was the price I offered to pay and now, having paid it, I certainly could not curse those who exacted the toll. My library, our school, God's churches, will all emerge stronger because they have been in the flame and they have been tempered."

"But your sermons, David, and all your writings and your Bible, they are gone."

"Dear, you give me the opportunity to pontificate shamelessly. The Bible is not gone. If my sermons spoke true, those words live in the ones to whom I spoke. The words written down on a paper scrap are not important. My thoughts survive. I survive, more tempered by the experience. Oh, give a preacher such a time of testing, and you have given him the sermon metaphors of a lifetime. Rejoice!" We shared a wistful laugh.

"Daddy, look, one of the soldiers gave me his whistle and Samuel got an old gun that doesn't work but it has the name of the King of England on the stock." Andrew was not slowed by his experience.

"No one took my dolls, and, Daddy, they tried to take Mama's table cloth and she took it back and said they could not have it," reported Patsy with great pride in her voice.

"I heard about the table cloth from a fine British doctor, named Jackson, whom I was assisting in an operation on the battlefield that night."

"You mean my British doctor?" blurted Rachel. "That fine gentleman who saved my mother's table cloth, and I suspect, may have saved an hysterical woman who I suppose had gone into shock. What a mysterious instrument of redemption he proved to be. After it was

185

all over, I thought to myself, 'a table cloth,' I drew the line over a table cloth?"

"Don't chastise yourself, Rachel, the country drew the line over some tea and stamps."

We were fortunate that all our buildings survived and soon doors and windows were replaced. Much of our furniture was broken or thrown into the fire along with our split rail fencing. Even our grape arbor had been torn down and burned. Of course there was no hay in the barn but then again, there were no animals either. Of more immediate concern, all our food was gone. It was planting season but we had to survive until harvest. Even the slave quarters had been raided. Ironically, our slaves had refused to consider themselves freed and did not go with the British where they were promised food. They stayed on the farm to help us rebuild, but in that process, became more mouths to feed.

In the afternoon, Rachel made a list, as we walked about, and later that night, by the light of several candles, we planned together the order in which we had to execute our recovery. We did not have solutions for everything. "How do you get milk for the baby without a cow or a goat? There is no plow to cultivate our own food needs and none to plant a crop to sell. No one has money." Still, when we considered the full list together, we were not discouraged.

I held Rachel that night and we were as passionate in our love as we had been as newly-weds. The difference was that we were no longer innocents, tentative and afraid of mistakes. We had been transformed, as had the world around us. What now could possibly happen that would shake our world ever again and cause us such testing? Our trials were over. The next morning I told Rachel in the spirit of a little boy, "I think we planted our first seed last night. Harvest will come."

Rachel laughed.

We prepared to leave early on the next day for church because we would be walking. We had no carriage or wagon. This was our regular Buffalo Sunday. Rachel had dressed us all in clean clothes and we sauntered up the path as if we were headed for a family picnic. As we passed the McQuiston farm, we were hailed by several of their boys who had been sent by their parents to ride us in their spare wagon. The McQuistons followed in another. Tom had gotten hold of two British commissary wagons near New Garden and brought them back to replace his farm wagons that had been confiscated. The six miles passed through the pastoral setting that had a few days earlier supported armies in battle. Approaching up the hill from North Buffalo Creek, we could see the church yard already awash with a strange collection of old horses, patched wagons and even rough field slides. We were received with hurrahs and applause as if we were a confirmation of survival. The children were lifted down by Presbyterians animated beyond their typically subdued nature – they were absolutely impassioned. At that moment, I recognized in their faces that they were secure in faith.

Our church bell was small but on this day the peal could be

heard all across the valley of Buffalo Creek in the crisp air of March. Was it because the bell was more alive than normal or was our hearing so much more vital? Leafless trees seemed alive with anticipation. Spring wheat was splashing green across the red clay on distant banks. That same redness appeared in the cemetery on the north side of the church where fresh graves held the neighbors who had died as soldiers that week and Mrs. Alice Burris, who had died an anticipated death in the bed at her home, on the day of battle. Wreaths of ivy and garlands of holly berries and magnolia leaves decorated these places where we had prepared the earth to contain their bodies and mark their being. That morning, I added to the order of service a memorial to those dead and remembered them individually as I had not been able to do earlier because of the circumstances. I saw my children weeping with others when I mentioned some of the names. Young people do not process death well in normal times but they knew these people were mostly dead as the result of something they had known as a game from which you bounced up only to be downed again. A children's game in the hands of adults was a grievous experience. Adults should not play war. They always forget the rules.

I had hoped that my sermon might begin to stabilize life at Buffalo. Faith had gone through, and would continue for some time to go through, some testing. But it was that same faith, full blossomed, that would be the substance on which we could each recover. I could not give them answers to questions that I too was yet processing. I could lead them through that labyrinth of shadows and sharp angles and high barriers, with a loving God and a compassionate Jesus that would make us all whole. Of this I was certain.

After the service, I was greeting members individually when Samuel came running up trailed by his brothers and urged me to "come look in the wagon." As I rounded the corner, the congregation surrounded our wagon in a wide circle as if to spotlight their response to my efforts to shepherd them. Leaving just enough room to seat the family, the wagon overflowed with barrels and packages and jars of processed food, two hams, rice, sugar, wheat and barley. A cow was tied to the tailgate. Three chairs, a table, and a small sugar chest and flour box were under all the food. Frank Rankin spoke for the others, "We didn't any of us have much, Preacher, but we each had a little and we wanted to share that with you and Rachel. Frank Wiley, he come over from Alamance last night and he brought some from your people over there. Don't you worry about what you shall eat or what you shall put on. You care for us by sheltering us in the love of the Lord. We will care for you in the only way we know how and we will all be fed. Thanks be to God."

"Thanks be to God indeed," I answered. We were all materially bereft at that moment, but there was a harmony in our relationship with God and with each other that was palpable. Fear and tribulation had been vanquished to a dark corner.

The McQuiston boys went home with their Daddy who had intended all along to see that we kept the wagon and team on which we had ridden to church that morning. We rode slowly home with cow in tow and Rachel sniffling in joy and appreciation. The unloading of the wagon brought order again to our farmstead. Our plan for recovery had all the means to get started. There would be times when we would laugh at items that we used to have but now did without. We were confident that the day would come when all that and more would be ours. We had demonstrated for us on Sunday the makeup of the necessities of life – God is love.

I called a meeting at each church of all the men and we took stock of what seeds we had available among us. When we divided it, we found that we had enough for each farm to plant almost their usual spring acreage. Then we took a census of our available manpower, and where anyone had a real need for some extra hands, we shared their burden. Then we put aside ten percent of all our seeds and an estimation of extra manpower and asked the Clerk to offer that to others in the neighborhood, not only of our communion, who had special needs.

Rachel organized a meeting of the women of both churches and they made an inventory of available food, meat, clothing, fabric, and shoes. Then they redistributed so shortfalls were overcome and enough was left over to add to the Clerks list of items to share with the neighbors. Then the women made a schedule for canning and shucking to match with the planting schedule of the men.

We grouped the lone pigs and cows that had not been taken off, into a few little herds and assigned them to particular farmers, and we made a schedule for community slaughters so that everyone would help with the preparation of meat in season. We took an inventory of our wagons and surviving farm equipment and everyone knew where they could borrow what they needed, when they needed it, with a little scheduling.

On Sunday, I blessed every crop and asked God's help in the harvest and each Sunday we had Thanksgiving prayers for our survival. It was not lost on these people on the Buffalo and Alamance that they now had not much more than they had when they arrived in this place in immigration. The difference was that this was their home, not a place they intended to make into their home. They belonged here and they had been preserved here in a great testing. There was powerful assurance in the certain knowledge that they were God's chosen.

It was Patsy who first complained of a "bad smell" when she came near the mill. At first we discounted her senses but then others noticed a distinct odor. A few days later, Andrew and several of the students were playing near the creek and came upon a decomposing body. It was clearly that of a man who had been in the battle but we could not tell if it was a militia soldier or a Tory. Andrew had found his shot bag and insisted on keeping the relic. We buried him there near where he fell and I held a brief service attended by my family and some of the boys. The children were all subdued by the experience. They had not been on the battlefield to see the many dead and wounded after the fighting. This body had been so gruesome an image. Ours was not the only story of the discovery of a soldier's body well after the fighting. In the fields nearer the court house there were fresh graves all around – single graves and clusters.

Through the summer, we were consumed with rebuilding and cultivation. There was no school. Children were a vital part of the recovery but by late August parents wanted their children to return to their interrupted lessons. The school house had been repaired and broken furniture replaced. In the evening I had worked on new lessons and replaced what I could of the teaching materials. We would have to share the few books we had put together and we had only a few slates and almost no writing paper. There would not be enough money to purchase the missing supplies and books for several years but learning was the hope of independence, not its victim. We made the announcement that our Classical Academy would resume for the Fall Term on September 15th.

Cornwallis had remained at Guilford Court House for two days after the battle. He claimed victory, but we knew that his army was no longer formidable enough to draw Tory colonials to his support. Everywhere I heard, "he is beat, Preacher." The general still declared that following his "victory" he would be heading into Virginia to continue to destroy Whig resistance, but when his army moved out of Guilford County it was east toward Wilmington.

From James Martin, Paisley, James Hunter, Gillespie, and

Forbis, I collected the impressions of General Greene's next moves. He had reassembled his army at the Iron Works in good order for a "defeated army." Although they had been sorely tested in battle, he could still muster substantial numbers of colonial militia, particularly now in Virginia. In the first twenty-four hours, Greene anticipated pursuit by Cornwallis and manned the Iron Works trenches he had built prior to the Guilford battle as that fallback alternative. By the third day, he knew that Cornwallis would not follow him and that reality told him that he had seriously incapacitated the British army. Pursued became pursuer and Greene broke camp to find the British to provoke the battle where he now considered that he had the advantage. Cornwallis was already on the move to New Garden where he abandoned his wounded in the care of the Quakers, and proceeded to Cross Creek. Greene was his shadow. The Highlander support in the Cape Fear, that the British had hoped would recoup their losses, were not available in men or in supplies. Finding the Cape Fear now a growing Whig hornets' nest, Cornwallis immediately moved on to Wilmington still anticipating resupply.

Nathanael Greene saw this as his chance to reclaim lost territory in South Carolina and broke off the pursuit. During the summer, as we concentrated on restructuring our farm economy, we followed the maneuvers from a satisfying distance. Our only tangible concerns were the bands of Tories in our midst who were now desperate. In spite of all the magnanimous efforts within my congregations to love one another, to share what we had with each other, very little of this newly confirmed community went beyond the bounds of our denomination. The Tory menace seemed to over- shadow circumstances and to preserve a high level of suspicion and distrust, even hatred. Without the presence of the British Army, the Tories became cornered animals, perhaps in a more dangerous stage than they had ever been before. "Tory hunting" was now left to the North Carolina Militia which moved in sorties against obstreperous bands of the disaffected who struck like terrorists with little objective except to create fear and distrust. Captains Burke and Bryan commanded Tory companies around the Yadkin. Without doubt the most effective Tory commander was Colonel David Fanning, leader of British troops in Chatham County, and his second in command, "One-eyed" Hector McNeill. Fanning I had never met but I knew his reputation as a raider and bushwhacker for General Cornwallis and "the object of the greatest opprobrium." When I first heard of McNeill, I feared he might be that noble Presbyterian elder in whose home I had been generously entertained at Campbellton in '72. I soon confirmed that gentleman had been called Hector "of the Bluff" and that indeed this British officer was not closely related.

By July, we had news of the temporary capture of Pittsboro to our southeast by Tories and increasing skirmishes throughout the Carolina sand hills. Fanning had been given a set of rich regimentals, with suitable epaulettes, sword, and pistol by Major Craig at Wilmington, and a commission as Lieutenant Colonel. Together with Colonels McNeill and Archibald McDonald, they sought to convince the Highlanders once again, as they had before Moore's Creek, that the British Army was well financed and hearty and that the Scots should respond to the colors again. After the British had won, they would be handsomely rewarded. In August, they temporarily seized Campbellton and on Wednesday, September 12th, Fanning and McNeill rode into Hillsborough in broad daylight with 1200 men. They captured the Governor, Thomas Burke, (that Catholic Irishman who feared my article in the North Carolina Constitution might keep him from the office), his Council of State, many members of the assembly, 70 Continentals, and the Governor's military guard. The government of North Carolina was virtually deposed, but in an irony to my delight, Alexander Martin was not among those taken prisoner. Martin, as one of the Senators from Guilford, was still Speaker of the Senate. As the second highest civil officer in the state, after the capture of Burke, Alexander became acting Governor of North Carolina. At Cane Creek, a day after the Hillsborough mass capture, 400 militiamen under General Butler ambushed Fanning and attempted to recover Governor Burke and the other state officers. Fanning's arm was broken and "One-eyed" Hector McNeill was killed, but the attempt to free the prisoners failed and they were taken under guard to Charleston.

Martin sent me a letter on the 15th, soon after receiving the depressing news that the attempt at rescue at Cane Creek had failed. He listed the detailed losses at Hillsborough. Then he added, "I find myself the sole government of the state. The Council Extraordinary was abolished last Assembly session. We have no army to call upon. Greene is in South Carolina asking for us to continue to supply his troops. There are not enough legislators to call an emergency session of the legislature, even if there were a safe place to have it meet. Without a state capital, all the state records, which follow the Governor and the Council of State in wagons, were taken by Fanning. Dare I use the term, destitute? Some state troops have already come to my protection here at my Dan River home, and Pleasant Henderson has volunteered to act as my private secretary. I have written to all the elected officers of the state whom I understand to be still free, and advised them that I am assuming the position of acting governor in the absence of Governor Burke. I have written to Burke to assure him that I will exert my every effort to gain his freedom, and that I will immediately return the office to him upon his release. Greene has been advised, as have the Governors of South Carolina and Virginia. For the time being, I do not plan to appoint a temporary Council of State, considering that will only make for later difficulties, if Burke is released quickly. I do seek your prayers and your council and I will ask several others to serve as my private council as issues arise."

"Has ever history given any man a 'shadow government,' such as the one that has been conferred upon me? I must be careful not to exaggerate my mandate or appear to be usurping authority; while at the same time I have to grasp every thread of legal government in order to prevent anarchy."

I sat dumbfounded at my desk, the letter dangling from my hand. I had been reading it to Rachel, who stood before me without comment. The moment was drained of resolve and I began to pray. As she knelt beside me, we sought guidance for ourselves and for Alexander and our state. Our earlier euphoria of our "victory" was at serious risk.

School had begun again that very day and we anticipated a fine harvest in our neighborhood. We had been shown dramatically, however, that war was yet our companion and uncertainty our constant condition.

Colonel Daniel Gillespie and Captain William Bethel called up militia men from our congregations and they joined troops from

Rowan, Mecklenburg and Bladen counties under the command of General Griffith Rutherford. In total, the Whigs put 1400 men in the field, and the Tories had in excess of 600 at a point in Robeson County called Raft Swamp on the Lumbee River. From a causeway that must have been reminiscent of that bridge at Moore's Creek that had seen the earlier disaster for the Highlanders, the Whig cavalry, well mounted on large horses, pushed the tiny Tory ponies into the swamp. They floundered with their noses barely above water. Riders were unhorsed and the standing order of "no quarter" saw many a Tory head cleaved to the shoulders. Stragglers were tracked down and cut down. The Patriot victory was decisive over the best remaining organized band of Tory troops and really ended what people now call, the Tory War. In a few more days, we had news that Cornwallis had surrendered at Yorktown.

We knew then that the only effective British Army in the South had been defeated. This was glorious news but no guarantee that England was prepared to surrender the North American colonies. We remained in a condition of near lawlessness. I am afraid that we operated our lives with a permanent air of uncertainty. The academy had fewer students because parents were unwilling to allow their children to be far from home, so there were no students to board. Students who could walk to school daily joined our children and five of my brother Alexander's seven.

My poor brother, Alexander, had returned from the army

suffering from camp fever and did not long survive. I sat vigil with him as he died, drained by a war that now took an immediate member of my family. His young brood was left destitute and I, who had tried to be their guardian during the dangerous period of the battle, took on a more permanent task after his death. I hardly had time to grieve for this lost brother, my confidant. He had come to my aid when I had wanted to go to college. He had shared with me the adventure of transporting to this place from the sweet land of Lancaster valley. I may have provided some service in proclaiming revolution, but it was he who left his young family and faced the bullets and swords of the men of Cornwallis. And he had paid the final price. It was a consolation that he had been able to spend his final days among his loved ones and we laid him to rest beside Buffalo church.

Alexander and I had often talked of our lot, how we spent our youth and the forces that shaped our adult choices. He once told me that he had considered it part of his adult calling to see that I had all the opportunity possible to preach and pray. I will never forget that statement because I consider it a perfect expression of complete sibling love. Physical separation from that brother was the ultimate price I had to pay in the time of testing, greater by far than the loss of my books and papers or the destruction at the farm. At the depth of my tribulation was the loss of Alexander.

As if to magnify his loss, we received a post from John Witherspoon at Princeton with details of the tragic death of my first cousin and Princeton colleague, James Caldwell. I had not seen James since he and Witherspoon had made a fund-raising tour of the South in 1769, and had visited us here at the farm. On his return to New Jersey, James had accepted a call to the Presbyterian Church at Elizabethtown, married Hannah Ogden and they had ten children. He became a trustee of Princeton and clerk of the Board of Trustees, in addition to his duties at Elizabethtown. With his family, he had to flee the British as they marched across New Jersey in 1776, and they hid in the mountains. He preached when he could but also took on the task of assistant commissary general. In 1780, while as refugees living in Union, the British sacked the town and Hannah, who was standing in a window, was shot and killed by a British soldier. In November the following year on a trip to Elizabethtown, James had an altercation with a drunken American soldier who shot and killed him. Witherspoon said they were considered civilian martyrs of the Revolution. He told the story of an incident near Springfield in 1780, as the Americans were in retreat before the British and ran out of paper with which to ram powder and balls into their muskets. James jumped on his horse and rode to the village church and returned with his arms filled with Isaac Watts' hymn books exclaiming "Now put Watts into them, boys!"

Heroes and martyrs, we had more than enough. I remembered James as a fine student about ten years my junior. We had known little of each other as children since my father had settled in Pennsylvania and his had gone to Cobbs Creek in Charlotte County, Virginia. We wondered how James Caldwell's orphaned children would be able to make their way.

While we sought to re-establish community along Buffalo and Alamance Creeks in Guilford County, Alexander Martin attempted to accomplish a re-establishment of the civil government of the state. He spent days in the saddle riding the circuit as a lawyer, applying the law and keeping the courts functioning. Between court sessions, he personally visited political leaders, senior officers of the state militia organizations, and key politicians who were not prisoners in Charleston. With everyone, he emphasized that he was acting in the place of Governor Burke and with the remaining members of the Council of State who were not incarcerated. He was receiving no directions from Burke, only pleas that Martin continue to attempt to obtain his release.

Fortuitously, in the previous August in his role as Senate Speaker, Martin had prevailed upon his friends the Moravians, to invite the North Carolina Assembly to have their November meeting at Salem. "It will be to your considered advantage to have members of the state government who are unfamiliar with the nature of the Moravian beliefs," he told these religious dissenters, "to see what valued citizens you really are." Seeing only marginal value to being thus better understood and certain that their routine way of life would be compromised, they nevertheless finally agreed. Governor Martin arrived on the 8th with his own military guard and waited through the month as legislators straggled in to Salem, never enough to even represent a quorum to call the session to order. Now the acting governor was expected to operate without a functioning legislature. He announced another special assembly to gather at Salem the end of January.

From Halifax, Martin issued a Proclamation of Pardon in which he took the first official step toward a restoration of normalcy. Then, he dispatched General Rutherford to drive the last remaining British force out of Wilmington. Back in Salem on the 25th of January to await a legislative quorum, everyone was astounded on the fifth day of waiting by the arrival of Governor Burke, who had escaped Charleston without parole. Civilian legislators were joyous with his return, especially Martin, but the military officers were incensed. General Greene, when informed of the escape, was also advised that Burke had assumed the office of Governor from Martin. He condemned the action, not the escape, because Burke said he feared for his life. The condemnation was that without having received a parole, he had assumed an office. Under the rules of war, this threatened the mutual acceptance by the belligerents of the system of parole. This precipitated a rising feeling of disdain in the state for Burke. Again the assembly failed to attain quorum at Salem and adjourned to the next scheduled meeting which they chose to hold at

Hillsborough. There Burke refused to be a candidate again for Governor and Martin was elected to the first of his terms as Governor of the state.

At Buffalo, we were overjoyed. Rachel and I danced and whooped so, that we frightened the younger children. The older children remembered well our friend Alexander Martin who now was Governor of the whole state.

In the light of the emerging victory of revolution, I saw with more clarity every day the guiding hand of God. Each bit of news, each event in fruition seemed to come to me with the insight. "Yes, that is it. That is it!" There seemed such harmony, but even more, direction and purpose. We were witnesses to the emergence of a new nation, brand new in world history, with the potential to be what all others had not been able to attain. People began to individually perceive elements of this national euphoria. They came to me with questions and I believe that had I ever sought prophetic status, they would have followed my every word with happy expectation. I continued to build a structure of faith on which they could build. We were the chosen people. We had been led through a process of refinement and we now were prepared to establish our destiny; my term was always that we were in a position to fulfill God's purpose for us. By profession, we were Christians and by denomination, Presbyterians. By revolution we were Americans. We could feel on the inside what those terms meant and we were eager to confirm ourselves.

But seeping in, on the corners of this certainty we were building was the concern about those who were not Christian, or Presbyterian, or American, in our midst. Where is their place in this new national identity? What about the Tories, some of whom are still our neighbors but who "lost"? What do we do about the British? We can discard a King, even a parliament, but what do we do with English law, or the network of economic links, or the protection they once provided from other empires that might even now covet us? If we describe this country as Christian, to what position do we relegate those who are not Christians? How do we share space with the Indians? The Church of England lost. Can they remain Americans? We have been in conflict with Catholics for generations. Can they now be welcome in America?

I read. I prayed for guidance. I had discussions with those whose opinions I valued, particularly Rachel's. Weekly, I stood in a pulpit and tried to guide others with common beliefs to find direction. and in that exercise, find self-illumination.

The new Governor, on his way home from Hillsborough, stopped by our house and Rachel and I sat with him for a long discussion of the circumstances we faced: we as citizens, me as a Presbyterian minister, he as Governor of a newly independent state.

"We are so proud of your election to such high office, Alexander," began Rachel. Martin shied deferentially. "You know that I am not being patronizing. I am proud because, of all the less than fulfilling events in which we seem to be suspended at the moment, the events which have placed you at the head of our new state government seem to be the only positive accomplishments."

"You know, Alexander," I interrupted, "that we have committed ourselves to the cause of revolution largely because we felt betrayed by an insensitive, almost repressive government, all the way across an ocean. But like others on the frontier, we have felt none too satisfied with the political power of the Whig cause as it came to us from our powerful eastern Carolina brothers. It is hard to see their interests as reflective of ours and we have been uneasy. I do not consider your election as a power shift but I do recognize it as acceptance of more equitable representation in the future of the state. It is reassuring."

The Governor was struggling to speak to us as trusted friends, determined that he could still step away from the office and find parity with those whose friendship he valued. He told me much later that on that meeting, he was concerned that his sudden elevation as a public official would mean that he would lose our intimate relationship, by his own insensitive action or by the reluctance of his friends, to speak unadulterated truth. He desperately needed people whom he could depend on, with whom he knew he could safely drop his anchor. "You two know that I value your good wishes and I know them to be sincere. I need you both now as I have never needed you before. We have bonds of understanding with which I could wish to be surrounded, but instead I find myself in an instant sea of sycophants. I like to believe that it is partly because of my innate ability that I have risen thus in state government but I am not so vain that I do not see that circumstances have peculiarly swept me up and pushed me ahead of any normal elevation to office. I have no intention of modestly demurring the opportunity. This happens to be my time. I do not question it. At the same moment, David, I will not accept that I am some kind of chosen one. My qualifications are sound. I am no fluke of circumstance and I have work to perform. But as I say, I desperately need good friends who will ground me to reality, especially because our era is so experimental, so full of opportunity for a magnificent future but so surrounded by pettifogs and prostitutes of the public purpose. Can I count on you both to help keep me grounded?"

"Alexander, need you ask?" Rachel wondered, somewhat chagrined. "You know that David and I are deep set in our faith and we will speak out of that core which does not always mean we will be tempered by exigencies of politics. Since you come from the same denominational background, you will be able to interpret with ease the nuance of our views. That will mean that you can easily discount them as too familiar. Or you could give them too much weight because they strike a chord in your thinking or irritate you because you begin to seek not the threat of debate, but approval for yourself. These will be your problems though. David and I will always be your friends and we will always seek and speak what we think is true and we hope best for you. To the extent that gives you a bedrock in trying circumstances, we are here."

"You see, my friend," I said with a smile. "That is why I am such a blest man. She can speak with such sympathetic frankness that I come for her counsel daily."

"I cannot but confirm your words" Alexander responded. I did not need them spoken to know your reaction, but having heard them so kindly expressed, you have given me a valued gift. I thank you both. Now, let us examine issues.

"I have spent my first months in office like a judge caught between two great lummoxes pounding each other to their own mutual destruction. They represent the small-minded victor who, in a rapacious vacuum, attempts to assemble all the spoils and claim them for his own, and the embittered loser using surrogates to preserve his interests as if there were no price to loss. Until we are certain that the British will agree to end this war and thereby recognize our independence, we can do little toward reconstituting the individual states and beginning to build an association of the whole. For the British, it is a self-fulfilling prophecy that we will fail, but we cannot begin to prove them wrong until we have a treaty.

"With the signing of such a treaty, let me project what I consider the basis on which we should restructure from colony to state. In the treaty, we will define those whom we can consider as enemies and from whom we can confiscate property. As a government, we will have to protect the interests of all others who, through real or contrived grievance, are additionally accused of being the enemy. That will require defined acts of pardon. At the same time, we must agree on those who are the aggrieved and are due compensation, what is owed for the service of the military, and how we will compensate for that service. I am directing studies on these issues so that we are prepared to act appropriately."

"I think these things are basic and honorable for a free government," I said.

"We have the state constitution, upon which you had specific impact, and it is accepted as the structure of operational government and the definition of law and rights. It must be accepted without modification as a beginning. There will be plenty of time to amend it where practice identifies weaknesses. At that point, I would feel the state government fully functional and it will be my responsibility, and that of the assembly, to appoint those who will make it operational."

"Presbyterians would call that 'decently and in order'." I quipped.

"Here is where I look for your observations and suggestions. According to our constitution, the chief magistrate has specific, therefore limited authority, but he does have substantial influence in his office. It will be my words that will frame for the assembly the direction of our victorious state. I will captain the ship, and although

I will hold that position within defined terms of office, my influence can be significant and in itself defining. As the first man in just this particular position, I feel a great responsibility to get it right. What are the forces that I must put in the first position on which to build the most worthy structure for the people of North Carolina?"

"I am overwhelmed with the task, as I see are you," Rachel admitted, "but I consider that we cannot be modest and demure. You are not in this position, Alexander, by accident. You are particularly trained and imminently capable. We will give you what we can and are grateful to be considered resources for the task," she added with her usual elegance. "I will say before my husband, education is a primary goal. The constitution hints at the first position for education but you must force it to reality because I am afraid that ignorance is more pervasive in our people than learning. Education must not be the plaything of the elite. Education must define this nation."

"I would hope that you would not only confirm that there will be no state religion but that there will be protection for the expression of Christian beliefs," I added next. "The Church of England still has powerful friends and members in eastern North Carolina. I believe that they have muted their presence during the war but may attempt to have some position of primacy for their denomination with individual states. That cannot be."

"David, I can appreciate your concern, particularly now that the Presbyterian Church has attained such influence." It seemed to be a veiled criticism but he went further. "I am concerned that the Protestant denominations, those that are numerically largest, may attempt two coups in the face of the unstable present. First, that under the guise of keeping the Church of England at bay, they may seek to legislate against it to their benefit. Second, over time I've become concerned that the dissenter denominations, those small and close-knit like the Moravian and Quakers in our region, will be singled out for political persecution. I will be on guard on these points, as I will seek Christian value equitably distributed. I think in a truly free society, religion will always lurk as a means for the unprincipled to seek dominance through deception. Religion can be a costume for the fox invading any barn."

"I can accept your concerns as of real value but beware that in an attempt to protect the dissenter, you do not encourage the advance of theological heresy. The line is small but distinct."

I shifted the subject. "It seems to me that the courts also need attention, beyond the structure that has been established within the new constitution. At least here we have the real value of our own English law as a foundation," I observed. "But notably we have been in the midst of the rebellion of frontier people as manifest in the Regulators. Where settlement is sparse or where settlement is in direct contact with aboriginal people, there is always the tendency for might to overwhelm legal form."

"You have struck another of my concerns that seems to me to

be neglected: law and order," proposed Alexander. "I myself must admit that given power, I used the law to gain personal wealth. Others have used it to gain personal power. We must proclaim the law as inviolate – not a stagnant rule but a living expression of community. You might use the word covenant here, equally applied and equally applicable. This principal I must attribute to my Princeton education and my legal experience."

We were in agreement. "Now I also think that the structure of public transport, our roads and waterways, must be singled out for attention," he said. "We cannot function as a union of states, if we cannot interlace our transport, communication, and commerce. And we must establish a viable internal exchange if we expect a vibrant economy that can compete eventually with the other great nations of the world."

"In this area," I admitted, "I am afraid that you will have to seek counsel from another source. Rachel and I stumble in the field of economics but I find comfort in your ideas. Alexander, I fear that we are not a source of original thought for you in terms of inspiration. You are a man of lofty ideals and practical ability. The combination is what our state needs at this time. Some would say you have a political turn. I think that we can give you a very honest sounding board from time to time and it is exciting for us to feel so well connected with a friend who will have such positive influence on the future of our country. I would ask you to trust yourself. At the same time, I would urge you to be sensitive to your place in God's plan. We have a chance to initiate a great and robust nation and you are in a position to influence decisions that will shape the future. Don't neglect to appreciate this opportunity in the context of the cosmic purpose of God. Pray for sensitivity and demonstrate compassion. I have heard you say, more than once, 'the government is the people,' but remember that the people without the centering harmony of a relationship with God, are little more than a mob."

Rachel excused herself to some demanding chores in the kitchen and, as she left the door to the room ajar, Alexander and I were soon inundated with some of our rowdy children. "Whoa there, children – a little respect. Your friend, whom you admired so in his uniform, is now the Governor of North Carolina. You cannot jump on him as if he were one of your academy boys."

"If you are Governor, do you have a new uniform, Uncle Alexander?" asked Patsy with eyes fixed on her hero.

"No, Patsy. There is no uniform for my new office and I am afraid few other compensations either," he responded, which confused her and Patsy never stopped when she was confused.

"What are compensations and can you wear them," she wondered.

"There you see, Patsy, we have been talking grown up talk all afternoon, and I must remember to speak to my audience in terms they can understand. Compensation is just a big word that means to get something for what you give."

"You mean like I give Daddy a flower and he gives me a kiss?" she wondered.

Alexander laughed. "A fair comparison, my dear, although stuffy old men in the Assembly would never see it so."

After dinner, the older children were allowed to sit quietly with us and so we talked as concisely as possible. I wanted the children to be exposed to more complicated ideas although I knew full well that much of what we said was beyond their grasp. At one point, Alex noted that there would come a time when the world of adult ideas would be theirs and that would prove the test of how wise we had been at giving their new country an intelligent beginning.

Alexander rode off after breakfast and after he had given a short visit, and a few encouraging remarks, to the academy students. He was going on to Salem to spend two nights at the tavern in learned discussion with those German merchants, and to attend their Sunday worship and singstunde. Then he would be on to a session of Surry court. At least once a year he would come to us. He valued, with good reason, the confidence of his family and we were like an extension of that family, albeit dressed in a parson's clothes.

CHAPTER THIRTEEN **1782–1786** Medicine and Healing

During our conversation, Alexander had advised us that he and his new brother-in-law, Thomas Henderson, had been developing plans at the court house to formally create the town to be called Martinville. They believed that the court house would be a natural center of growth and they had surveyed lots. I think that Alexander had entertained such plans as early as his move from Salisbury to his land up on the Dan. He and Henderson had acquired some of the confiscated land of Edmond Fanning. The first court was in a home owned by Robert Lindsey near Deep River. By 1781 the court was in a new log building on land surrounded by Henderson and Martin. That was the court house that gave its name to the battle and was the assembling point for Americans on Greene's order.

In 1785, the legislature authorized the location of a town called Martinville on 100 acres of land of Henderson and Martin. Alexander told us that with all these interests concentrated in Guilford, he had been reluctant to accept the added task of President of the Senate. He certainly had no idea that Burke would be taken prisoner, or that he would then be elected Governor himself. He had been propelled by circumstance to rapid advancement in office at the state level and had to distance himself from his county plans. Simultaneously citizens from the northern half of the county prepared petitions asking for a division. These shifting political circumstances ended with the plantation Alexander had built for his mother, "Danbury," located in the new county of Rockingham that was authorized by the legislature on his recommendation in 1786. His residence near Martinville remained his official home and he remained a senator from Guilford.

A constant complaint from people living in the northern part of Guilford had been that the court house was too far south and it was difficult for them to carry on public business. The division gave those to the north their own court house. In the new Guilford County, thus reduced in size, the court house location was still not in the center of the county. Now, however, it was an established fact that a great battle had been fought adjacent to Guilford Court House, so it would be confusing to speak of another location by that name. The established public identity of the location was more important than its proximity to a central point. So everything was left in Guilford as it had been. The court house and gaol, and later the rebuilt jail, were of inferior construction. The first thing the court did was to get the main building up off the ground onto wooden blocks.

As part of the agreement to donate the land for a county town, Henderson and Martin had retained one lot in Martinville where Battle Street and Greene Street intersected. The town increased rapidly to include several hundred souls. Hance Hamilton, Robert Lindsey, Robert McNairy, the Whittingtons and Bevills, lived at Martinville. Lindsey operated a store. Henderson, before becoming Clerk of Court in Rockingham County, had moved the store house of James Buchanan over to join the court house to hold the court records. The composite of these several structures made the court house look like it had been created by a committee, each with their separate plans. There was no church, so except for the existence of the court house, this was little more than a cross roads community. The houses around New Garden Meeting house to the west and Martinville to the north, were the nearest settlements to our farm. Many of our students over the years came from Martinville or were housed there by families during the school year.

Right after the war, large portions of every court were occupied with questions of confiscated land. Without any compunction, Whigs declared their neighbors as Tories and sought to claim their holdings. There was enough land that the state declared subject to confiscation, that one would think the buzzards would have been satisfied to pick clean. In our county alone, there was almost 6,000 acres of land that had belonged to Henry McCullock, out of the old Granville Tract, which was declared confiscated and which the court sold. Down in Randolph, where the Tories had been more heavily concentrated, many families were left destitute by confiscation.

Those first euphoric months of victory seemed to spiral into uncontrolled greed. People who had been declaring "death to tyrants" were raging tyrannically against the weakest, most unprotected of their neighbors. I had been naively concerned that I would not have the words to help my congregations to recover their Christian beliefs, after they had been through the devastation of war. Now I looked out on my people and saw among them the face of the most unforgiving evil I ever expected within the walls of a church. Judgment had suddenly become theirs and they would wield it with shameless disregard. I realized that I had been equal to the task of pacification of belligerents within the context of war, but the power of impassioned greed seemed beyond me, probably because it came from inside as well as outside my congregations. There was no "they." It was "us," who had become the tyrants.

Over and over again in this time of tribulation, I climbed those pulpit steps at Buffalo and Alamance and surveyed those faces and I tried to speak sincerely to those who would hear. "For Presbyterians, judgment has always been the stumbling block. We have a history of attempting to ever tighten the lid on judgment so that we could contain it within a phrase, a covenant, a creed, and be certain of what was right. But judgment is a tool of the Almighty and it is always dangerous in human hands. Humans covet judgment as an instrument of control. We are never equipt with enough knowledge to be able to apply equitable judgment. We can attempt to do so and must, within the supposed equality of a court, but it is always a struggle. That is an essential lesson of the Old Testament. That is why Jesus, the Christ, in the New Testament, gave the emphasis to love, a quality shared by God and humans. Love is at the core of what God frames for human community.

"We cannot, we should not, disclaim our heritage but we must always be aware that in our covenants and our creeds, we should be seeking to truly do the will of God and not use those documents to freeze our actions in our own prejudices." I caught my own hypocrisy as I spoke. That is why I knew it was God speaking, through me. "It is through education that God can lift up the prophet, the preacher, the believer, yes, even the saint. By education we mean learning but also we mean concentrated spiritual study, prayer, and interactive communion."

I tried so hard, I prayed so fervently. Rachel and I were distraught often during this period, over the hard, inflexibility within our communities. We always concluded, that it was not the journey for the Christian that was most important but ultimately, it was the promise of eventual redemption that we found in Christ. It was difficult, however, because we had our own roots in those dour teachings of wrath as judgment and the certainty of the idea of the chosen. We had all that tradition. Ours was not a clear, unfettered image of God's will for His people. Prophets of the Bible spoke as they heard God's voice, not by interpreting what they thought God might intend to be saying. We had to remember that God, who was at work in the prophet, was also at work in the believer, who was hearing the prophet.

My efforts seemed to me to crash like a crystal upon a marble floor – noisy, shattering, scattering, then loudly silent. I was buoyed during the week by the eagerness of my students. I saw in these evolving minds the hope of greater enlightenment in their lives. I could imagine all the possibilities of our moment in history, but all around me, I saw the Biblical story of the rejection of God's purpose by His people. I had to wonder if it was in us to surrender something of self to achieve a new hope of a better human age. Was it in me?

One of the commonalities, shared by almost the entire congregation at Buffalo as well as Alamance, was that they also had roots in the Scottish period of enlightenment. Accepting that, I often wondered why did they not transport shades of that enlightenment with them to the frontier? Scotland was one of the most forbidding soils of Europe but there, in the same unforgiving place of Knox and the Covenanters, had taken root the university emphasis on critical thought, tolerance of different views, and free inquiry. Why had not more of that been transported with these Scots-Irish to the American frontier? I remembered a Quaker named Boone in Bucks County who called us a "pernicious and pugnacious people" and that is all I could see around me. My prayers and lengthy deliberations did little to ease my apprehensions. Could such people as we, bathed in the blood of revolution, subsequently calm our lust into a tolerance of different views? I concluded it would take a process and it needed God to assemble an array of men of incredible critical thought.

Rachel and I watched as more of our family and neighbors sought new locations over the mountains in the western lands. As Governor, Alexander Martin had carried on a struggle for equitable cession of the western portion of the state to the federal government so that it could become a state. He had several conditions, however, on which he refused to compromise and there were forces, individual and government, that made this cession one of the defining birth pains of the nation. As he explained it in detail to me, Martin first wanted to be sure that men who had served in the army with the promise of payment in the form of bounty land in the western territories, were in fact honored with such grants. Second, he considered the existing treaties, made with the Indian Tribes in the area, had the effect of legal contracts between governments and should be honored in order to preserve the sanctity of law. A new country must honor its treaties. The problem he faced was that so many white squatters had already invaded the treaty lands, including veterans who were just taking their bounty rewards without title. The Indians wondered if the white man's government could be trusted to be honorable. Leaders arose among the early over-the-mountain settlements and proclaimed the State of Franklin. As one of the last acts of his term of office, Martin had to issue a Manifesto declaring the new state illegal and void, and its leaders in contempt. Governor Caswell, succeeding Martin, had no such scruples concerning the legality of the Indian claims and eventually the land was ceded to the government and became Tennessee. The final issue for Martin was that as compensation for cession, the government should assume the North Carolina state debt for the cost of the revolution. That was eventually settled with the assumption of the debts of all the states by the federal government.

Each time Alexander had visited, we spent hours in discussion concerning these issues that arose as part of the consequences of independence. As graduates of Princeton, we had been shaped in our thinking by the ideas of men like John Witherspoon. We never anticipated that we would be placed in the position of influencing the application of those ideas to the formation of a new nation, although in retrospect, we could see that those teachers may have had such visions.

As a young man, Alexander had been marked for the clergy by his family but he had rejected it for the law. It was his brother, Thomas, who had become a priest of the Church of England after leaving Princeton. Nonetheless, Alexander had been nurtured under the Old School theology of Francis Alison at New London Academy and the New School theology of Witherspoon at Princeton, and both men shared the certainty that political philosophy was part of moral philosophy. Their assertion was that political philosophy had its basis in morality, which was founded on the law of nature, which was the law of God.

I always heard Alexander avow that civil society implied a compact, and I would counter that he was affirming the value of a covenant. He framed his compact as when men agree among themselves to live in society and therefore give over to a person or council the right to decide controversies arising among themselves, to compel within law obedience in such decisions, and to direct the whole body toward the common good. In this order he would constitute a polity.

It was from the teaching of Alison that he said he first

understood the separation of the powers of government into the three classes of legislative, executive and federative, functioning with a common matrix of law. I knew that Alexander, as the executive officer of the state, would see the state constitution we had approved in 1776 as that legal matrix, and he would seek to stabilize the powers of the legislative and executive within the standards of the common good. It was precisely what he declared to the Legislature in 1783 after becoming Governor. In the euphoria that accompanied word of the signing of the Treaty of Paris, he said, "Let the laws henceforth be our sovereign; when stamped with prudence and wisdom, let them be riveted and held sacred next to those of Deity. ... Happy will be the people, and happy the administration when all concerned contribute to this great end." Then he, like me at Buffalo and Alamance, stepped into the reality of victory. The political reality was the fine line between hope, effort and the common good, and their shadow-side of greed, corruption and self interest.

I often think about my involvement in medicine as an avocation. It goes with the territory. As I said earlier, it was not uncommon for ministers, in lightly settled areas of the frontier, to take on ancillary tasks connected with life and death because the preacher was often the most educated person and thus always imagined to have special abilities. If they then had reasonable success in those tasks, they were confirmed as professionals. That was true in my case and I became a self-trained doctor. It was also true that I became more commonly called Doctor than Preacher or Teacher. Somehow that title was not as austere or overwhelming as the one and more respectful, coming from children, than the other.

My experience with Lord Cornwallis' doctor, Robert Jackson, at the time of the Guilford battle, confirmed my interest in medicine and me, personally, in my capabilities to the task. Jackson had assumed immediately that I was a qualified doctor and I performed right along side him in the intense hours after the battle. It was a case of confirmation by one's peers under the most extreme of circumstances.

Before Dr Jackson left with the Highlanders some days later, he presented me with a walking stick as a symbol of his regard, and although I rarely used it in my younger years, I kept it in sight as my talisman. Years later, I found in a Philadelphia book store a book concerning emergency surgery that he wrote and I added it to my medical library. Yes, my medical library was an important aspect of my practice. Since I had not received a medical education, I was often presented with cases about which I had no experience or training. I was expected to be familiar with every medical situation; in fact, people depended on me to be so. I depended on my library to provide directions or diagnoses and treatments for whatever the calling. I knew that several of my classmates from Princeton had become doctors and I developed a regular correspondence with them as consultants.

One of my more sensational experiences, early in my medical career, one which my children delighted in hearing me tell, occurred late one night when I was returning from a visit to a sick neighborhood child.   It was a dark overcast night and I was unconcerned until I became aware I was being stalked by a pack of wolves. They were close enough that their brilliant eyes shone in a cluster. I realized that I had asafetida in my medical bag which I had given in a small dose to the child to alleviate her digestive problems and had prescribed that the mother hang a bag around the child's neck to ease her asthma. It was well known that asafetida was very attractive to wolves. Suddenly the wolves raised a glorious howl and the eyes came running toward me. I had no switch or stick to ward them off and knew better than to try to get down to find one, so I pulled the bridle off the horse, and using it as a whip rode full speed for home, closing the gate in time to ward off the trailing wolves.

A few years after the war, a more fortuitous event affecting my early practice was the arrival of Dr. Jacob Woodside, a product of the College of Philadelphia. He was a distant cousin of Rachel's, his family having come first to Maine from Ulster. He boarded with us and I encouraged him that there was a large demand for a doctor, for which I had tried to be a substitute and would gladly relinquish to him. In order to introduce him to the community, I made it a practice to attend him on his patient calls whenever possible. He obtained a fine open spider phaeton which served us well in good weather. In rain, it was quite dangerous, especially on our deeply rutted roads. We had a personal exchange of services – I giving him directions and introductions, and he adding to my instruction in many areas of medicine. Our roles were sometimes confusing to the patients and we had to allow for a certain flexibility in our manner.

Elizabeth McAdoo, a member of the Buffalo congregation, was having a bowel problem and we arrived at the McAdoo home together. Mrs. McAdoo was a large woman who came into the room after Jacob and I had been ushered in. She was immediately taken aback seeing both of us on call, but recovered sweetly and headed for the rather large chair which she used exclusively. Her approach was an expansive waddle, using her cane as balance. She circled gradually before the chair, placed the cane before her with both hands pressed flat on the hilt and began a slow descent. Midway, gravity took over and she collapsed in one massive plop, her skirt billowing out in a combination of air and loose flesh accompanied with a loud and sustained fart. With perfect aplomb she looked up at me and pronounced, "Pastor Caldwell, as you have heard, it is not my spirit that needs help today, so perhaps you should leave and let the doctor attend me."

Woodside was a handsome man and I recognized that female patients seemed to brighten perceptibly on seeing him enter their room. Well over six feet, he would stoop to enter, then straighten up again once within as if he were a rising sun dispelling the shadow of illness. He had intense dark eyes and a smile of perfect whiteness. In his company, I was never the doctor but the dark perception of depressive judgment. Patients usually believed that they would have time enough to seek my benediction, but at the moment, they preferred the prospect of the doctor's cure.

In his eleventh month with us, he went out on a call alone on a very stormy night. In route, his carriage slid into a deep rut in one of the poorer roads and upset and he was thrown clear, only to strike head first into a stone. When he did not arrive at his destination, the family on whom he intended to call sent out a younger son who found him in the road. The phaeton was overturned nearby with the horse in place and the young man was able to right the carriage and struggled to get Jacob up into it, whereupon he brought him back to our house. Jacob never regained consciousness but lingered under Rachel's tender attention until the next morning. The children were uncommonly distressed because they had almost thought of him as a contemporary and many had made him the image of what they intended to be when they grew up. It was a shock to us all and we grieved as his family and buried him in our churchyard.

Jacob left few assets but I assisted the court in collecting his accounts. He had already given me several books on particular subjects for study. When the court placed his books, instruments and medical supplies at auction, there was little interest and I bought the lot. His phaeton was, I thought, pretentious for an austere Presbyterian minister but others bid the price up beyond my means anyway and the merchant, John Hoskins, acquired it. I made do with my plain four-wheeled carriage. Because I used it almost exclusively in my medical practice, the county did not tax me for the value of the carriage as they ordinarily would such a luxury.

In this way I gained the core of my medical library and the

official tools to be more comprehensive as a doctor. My library which had originally been equipped for my ministerial duties but had been kindly disposed of by Lord Cornwallis, now also became the doctor's office and my replacement library became multi-faceted.

Malaria and dysentery were very common diseases of the army but they also were known during the summer in our area. Malaria was a fever that affected the whole body in a series of spasms, fits, flashes, and laborious breathing. Frequently it might deteriorate into delirium, and derangement. When it was found early, the immediate treatment involved the application of bark and emetics. Bark did not help with dysentery but here commonly I used blistering, cathartics, opium, ipecachuana, snake root, camomile flower and wine. To treat dropsy, I recommended exercise, wine, stimulating liquors, highly seasoned foods, and blisters.

From the Moravians at Salem I was able to get supplies of most medicine and my correspondent friends were kind enough to supply my needs for less common remedies. Bark was the most difficult to keep in supply because it came almost exclusively from an evergreen tree grown in South America between Venezuela, Peru and Bolivia. From this bark it was possible to extrude quinine

Typhus, typhoid fever and yellow fever were all diseases found in endemic or epidemic form, meaning they were spread by the bite of rat fleas or by lice in clothing next to the skin or in the hair. Typhoid fever was our most common example. Rancid water or spring freshets that left dead fish exposed in fields, brought on the contagion. Symptoms began with loss of energy and throbbing headaches. After some days the pulse would drop and dry tongue, delirium and a series of putrid symptoms developed. Blood letting was important at the beginning of the disease but was used cautiously as the disease developed. A vomit was recommended because it would squeeze all the glands and shake out of the nervous system all the contaminating poisons. When the fever was finally fixed, I used mercury. It subdued all manner of contagions and all infections.

Smallpox was a feared disease that was a scourge of any army and came to our neighborhood after the passing of two armies. Inoculation was used in both the American and British army to great perfection. I remember discussing with Alexander Martin our inoculations that were periodically required at Princeton and he said he was inoculated a second time in Baltimore when he marched his regiment north to join Washington in the first year of the war. I used inoculations any time there was a threat of some outside contagion entering the neighborhood.

My friend Benjamin Rush was a renowned exponent of heavy bleeding, considering it to relieve as a purgative. I treated many common illnesses such as smallpox, pneumonia and pleurisy with a heavy bleed followed by a dose of mercury for the inflamation. I used bark as a tonic for a weak pulse.

I was not prepared to do serious surgery at my home so I usually sent such cases to the Moravians. When presented with extended and debilitating illness, often part of the aging process, I prescribed visits to a mineral spring for the curative waters and fresher air. North of the Haw River there was a spa operated by an energetic Scotsman, John Lennox, and for a while by one of my former students, Archibald D. Murphey. Later, Rockingham Springs, south of the Dan River, was available and popular.

I always considered myself fortunate in having very good health other than a case of malarial fever that I suffered after I returned home following the Guilford battle. I attributed that to the very bad night air and the general exposure in the elements to which I was not accustomed. It was Rachel who gave me the hovering care that brought about my complete recovery. This was a time when she had to supervise the recovery of the farm immediately after the British had devastated everything they could get their hands on.

CHAPTER FOURTEEN **1787** Andrew Jackson

"Andrew, I never met your dear mother but I have heard my sister speak of her often and I recall that Nancy was with her when she died." Rachel was speaking with a tall young man in Henderson and Searcy's store at Martinville. When he had overheard her addressed as "Mrs. Caldwell," he had introduced himself as "Andrew Jackson from the Waxhaws" and Rachel had known him immediately. He was a very slender lad with a shock of blond hair, a large jaw, and animated eyes. He had a confidant presence and spoke with an easy conversational tone.

"You must also know that it was the nursing by your sister that hastened my recovery from the plague after she brought me home to the Waxhaws. I was captured by British dragoons near home along with about 40 others about a month after your battle here at Guilford. I had been up delivering news to my aunt's family on the movements of Cornwallis. They spoke often of you at that time but we did not meet."

"Yes, of course," I said. "I remember Nancy referred to that visit and she was very concerned then that you might be captured as you served as a courier of information for our army."

"We were taken to a prison ship off Charles Town and kept under foul conditions until I came down with plague along with most of the rest. Your sister accompanied my mother and another lady and they came to bring us home. For mother, it was too great an exposure and she died of the plague herself and we had to bury her there in Charles Town. I was brought home almost a skeleton, and I recovered only through the care and consideration of your sister. She will always be my dearest friend."

"She considers you part of her family, Andrew, and we shall honor that relationship. You must visit us at the farm. It is just down the road and David will be delighted to show you his academy. The children will be fascinated to see you. They are enamored to speak with young men with "soldier's tales" to tell. Will you come to Buffalo Church this Sunday and return home with us for the afternoon meal?"

The visit was arranged and Rachel was excited when she told us at the table that night about her meeting with young Andrew Jackson. As she passed around a bowl of potatoes she began, "he is such a fine young man, David, and Nancy says that the dearest wish of his mother was that he become a Presbyterian minister. I believe that he is determined on the law but he says he wants to meet you."

"Mother, did he know Uncle William?" asked Alexander.

"Oh, no, son. He was a small child when William died. Why do you have such an interest in your Richardson uncle?" Her question was left unanswered but expressed again her concern about a morbid fascination of the boy.

"Samuel, Andrew is just your age. He has seen considerable tragedy and I am afraid a good bit of brutal treatment in his life. He will be interested that you have already been licensed to preach by the

Presbytery." Rachel was proud of the progress of our oldest son's following so closely on my footsteps.

Rachel and all the children waited outside before the service until Andrew rode up on a fine horse and they could welcome him and bring him inside. When I looked out from the pulpit I saw him sitting there with my family. The people at Buffalo greeted this visitor with enthusiasm. Several had already met him at Martinville where he had found quarters above Henderson's store. The young ladies of the congregation blushed sweetly at his courtesy. I noted several mothers measuring his qualities closely.

When we arrived home, we found that a crowd of the academy boys waited to see this young soldier. Our children had obviously spread the rumor that he was a special hero, so they all wanted to hear from him. We sat outside while Rachel and the cooks finished preparations for the Sunday meal. The students who lived in the academy quarters took their meals in the large class room at the same time the family was served in the house. That required the participation of all the female slaves, even the younger girls. The kitchen, a separate building now, was a hive of activity for each meal but especially for this Sunday banquet. Ordinarily we tried not to burden the slaves with too many extra guests, and then on some Sundays Rachel and I would be invited to a meal at a member's home. So we always had to count heads before church and have the cooking planned according to the calculated total.

As we sat in the yard, the students and younger children were given the preference in conversation with Andrew. He spoke of his experiences in the army, how his education in the classical academy had been interrupted by all the activity after Cornwallis and the British had returned to South Carolina. His easy speaking voice was steady, without being in any way boastful. Andy said he had attached himself "like a shadow" to William Richardson Davie, an American cavalry officer who had been raised by our late brother-in-law, William Richardson. After Andrew was captured by dragoons, a British officer had commanded him to clean his boots. He had told the officer that he was a prisoner of war and could not be commanded to do such tasks. The officer had drawn his sword and only by throwing his arm up above his head had Andrew protected himself from the blow which had cut his arm to the bone and left him with a deep scar on his forehead. The boys were mesmerized, unable to speak or breath. Andrew was a god. The scars were a talisman of bravery.

"I have recently been reading law with Colonel John Stokes, a fine lawyer and a true hero of the revolution," Andrew said for my information. "In battle in the Waxhaws, very near my home, he was cut down by the British and sabered so many times that his hand was cut completely off. When asked if he requested quarter, he boldly refused and was run through again, but he survived. He has a silver knob in place of his hand and when he pounds it in the court room, it has a dramatic effect." There was a chorus of "Ah!"

Around the table, it was the time for the older children to talk with Andrew. "May I call you Andy?" Samuel asked.

"Everyone does except Aunt Nancy," he responded.

"I understand that you and John McNairy are friends. John and I grew up together."

"Yes, I met John when we were reading law with Mr. Spruce Macay in Salisbury."

"I guessed that you would have sought out Macay," I said. "He was at Princeton with your friend Davie."

"Yes, and they were both very proud that you too had been a Princeton man. I understand that several of the Presbyterian ministers in the Carolinas attended Princeton."

Alexander wanted to know if it was true that Andy had once intended to be a Presbyterian minister. "Would you have gone to Princeton?"

"In the first place," he replied, "it was my mother who 'intended' that I go into the ministry. It had a certain attraction for me but I never felt any particular calling."

"You are so brave," confessed Patsy, who had listened intently to every word out of Andrew's mouth. "Why don't you be a soldier?" We laughed, to her embarrassment, but Andrew spoke to her with a serious answer.

"Patsy, the life of a soldier is not a happy one. It is hard to have a family because you are away from home so much. I confess that I like to fight but I do not like the feeling of hurting another person. If my country ever needed me to fight, I would hurry to serve but I hope to be better now at verbal battles."

Thomas thought that men who had been in battle could understand the hardships of life. "Don't you consider yourself a better man for your experiences, Andy?"

"Better is certainly not the term I would dare to use, but I believe I have a deepened appreciation for the uncertainty of life. I no longer see myself as indestructible. We are given a time and a circumstance and we should try to make the most of it before it is gone." I was struck by the poise with which Andrew addressed us. There was no youthful reticence about describing inner feelings with adults and no deprecation of his exploits before peers.

There was constant chatter. It did not get too serious because the children had so few experiences that they could associate with Andrew's. His father was dead before he was born and his mother sacrificed all her life for him and his brothers. He had worked early and studied hard, and when the time came, even as a young boy, he had suffered the life of a soldier. I thought how all our children had known a stable family life, and except for the shared deprivations of a few months of war, they had never suffered. We had each other and even the presence of all the boys who had been my students had given them the feeling of many contemporaries with whom they could develop relationships. In contrast with Andrew, they had been raised with stability and security. They had shared with him similar foundations in the Christian faith, but by comparison my children appeared naive, even immature. Would they always appear so? Andrew was confident and motivated but he also seemed to yearn for security and love, as if they had not always been stable elements in the structure of his life.

After the meal, Rachel and I invited Andrew and Samuel to go into my study so that we could talk yet more seriously. Both boys seemed to be flattered by the opportunity. Andrew was not overawed with his elders and initiated the conversation, turning to me after we were seated.

"Pastor Caldwell, in your sermon today you raised the issue of the common good. In the church in which I was raised, I heard a great emphasis on God's purpose for his chosen people." He spoke deliberately, as if each phrase laid out a thought building on the previous statement. "My experience in war has taught me that people are motivated if they feel that the outcome of their efforts will be mutual benefits that they will share. The worst results seem to come when motivated people begin to fear that they cannot trust their community, the people around them, but must themselves look out for their personal interests. Their attitude is, 'If I don't protect myself, who will?' I hear the message of the church saying that God is operating outside the whole community – with His chosen. I believe that I fear those who think only of themselves as much as I fear those who somehow think that they are singled out as chosen. How do we justify either with the concept of the common good?"

The question had come to me and I knew that Rachel could provide as insightful an answer as could I, but I was also aware that I was giving an answer to the question in front of my son whom I had been training specifically in theology. Andrew would not respect my answer if I attempted to defuse the question lightly. Rachel would not let me be ponderous. Samuel would expect me to hold to the values he felt I had given him. I had a narrow platform. I was rubbing the nub of the chair arm as if finely polishing it.

"Andrew, I find myself each Sunday, at either of my churches, looking out at people who have had to take the theology that they have absorbed in their life experience and fit it, apply it, with what a common crisis like war has done to their lives. These same people are faced with the unique experience now of living within law as part of the structure of their own government. We call that democracy and it is new in the world and confusing to the uninformed. Yes, our people are the uninformed. Their experience is to distrust government and law because the law has always been applied from far away. They have had to suffer the law without ever having influence upon it. Their simple recourse, therefore, was to wish to be left alone – to get as far away from the reach of the law as possible. Of course, life can allow only a few hermits." I gave a wry smile. I was sure he understood that I spoke of the Scots–Irish in my comments.

"From our pulpits, we have preached that as people of the book, we have been given a structure for the lives we live. We raise up preachers to lead us with insight along paths we identify as righteous. We as Christians have the Christ as our living example and we have the Holy Spirit as our daily companion in the journey of the faith. We Presbyterians, out of our life experiences in the Reformed faith on the soil of Scotland and Ireland, have refined a structure of covenants and confessions, wherein our fathers have interpreted the will of God through the teaching of Jesus and through the intercession of the Holy Spirit. We have gone further. We believe that our God, the Creator of all things, omnipotent and omniscient, knows all things to the end of time and has a plan which already knows those who are chosen for salvation.

"What then, you ask, is the common good? If in the end, all is predestined, then how can we all benefit from the common good.? Why should we try, if it is pre-ordained?" There was a pause for him to consider this perspective.

"My answer is to say first that God is! All that we know as power, creation, life and death is in God and it is through His son, Jesus Christ, that we know that the expression of that totality is Love. When I read how early fathers of the church interpreted that faith, I see it as a struggle, but I see in their struggle degrees of enlightenment for our age. I do not see predestination as a limitation on human aspiration but a human attempt to confirm the totality of God. That is the faith that I preach."

"That helps me with your theological perspective," he acknowledged, "but what about the relationship to the civil community?"

"In the civil community, I am aware that all people do not share my faith, confirm my denomination, even profess my God. History tells us that order has commonly been applied by the strongest survivor and has been maintained by subjugation of spirit and will. Christ has told Christians that only love can be the ultimate conqueror – that love that turns the cheek, that respects what belongs to others, that seeks good in the face of evil, that cares for the weak and feeds the starving and protects the innocent. In the end, only that love can survive. If the Christian faith is an anomaly, if it is a superficial panacea, how truly we Christians are to be pitied. How pathetic are we. But we believe, and in our belief, we are empowered. In our empowerment we must find the mechanism, the mold, through which we can influence community, not always believers or common believers, to function as a state or nation. I believe that we find it in the common good. That is where I was today, trying to lead a particular flock to recognize the common good as Christians. In the infinite fear that I may be approaching pontificating, and will bring down the wrath of my wife, I will stop there. Do I bring any insight to your question?"

"You do indeed but I will 'suck upon the bones' a while to truly get the flavor of your thoughts."

"Well put," said Rachel. "I will remember to 'suck upon the bones' of some of his sermons next time he becomes overly profound. Andrew, I tell you most frankly that David and I have been so troubled with the depth of the bitterness and retribution awakened by the war. In a time when we think people should be almost gleeful about the future opportunities in this vast land, we seem to be blinded by the need for revenge. We are most sensitive to it within the church family. If civic virtue is to be built on moral law, how can such people be trusted as advocates of the moral law? We pray fervently that the Holy Spirit will be more obvious among us."

"Mother, how can you express such doubt? We have a covenant relationship with God. In our victory we have the certain faith that the purpose that God visions for us will see fulfillment. There will be times of testing, but in the end the will of God will be done," announced Samuel with the certainty of youth.

In the course of several months, we had other such sessions with Andrew Jackson in our home. He liked to come among the students. I think that in some terms he hungered for the time when he had been a student of classics where the task had been to learn words, sentence structure, and declination. Having returned to that touchstone, he would enter my library where he could find the challenge of applied thought. I found him to be an adult who was intentionally unready to surrender the exuberance or curiosity of youth.

I heard that he, McNairy and some of the Searcys were fond of drinking bouts often ending with a wake-up call to the citizens of Martinville. The three had learned to be hard drinkers under the tutelage of Colonel Stokes. Such rumors did nothing to enhance Andrew's professional reputation when he was admitted to the bar of justice on the circuit in Guilford, Randolph, Surry and Rockingham. I felt something less of him for it, believing that he had the capacity to rise beyond such material self-indulgence. I was more tolerant than my sons, who considered him a bounder of the first order and had dealings with him only when he came to see Rachel and me. It was a matter of some redemption that he had been active in organizing the first celebration of the anniversary of the Guilford battle with speeches, horse-racing, and a cock fight. I suspect that a large part of his celebration was motivated by the fact that March 15th was also his birthday. He called to me that day, "Rev. Caldwell, do you not think it appropriate that we should celebrate our hard won liberty?"

"I do indeed, Andrew," I replied, "and it seems proper that we do it with youthful vigor and enthusiasm. In the process don't forget those who are not here to frolic with you. Freedom came at a great price and it will not be sustained without sacrifice." Of all the young people, I suspect Jackson had the most objective appreciation of what liberty demanded of self.

In the spring, John McNairy received appointment as judge of the Superior Court of the newly designated Mero District of the western territory. Selecting Andrew Jackson as his court prosecutor and Bennett Searcy as clerk of court, and with a few others of their cronies, these next generation frontiersmen crossed over the mountains.

There was no one at play in the barn yard when I got home, a strange lack of activity that seemed uncharacteristic. I tied my horse but did not remove the saddle immediately, seeking instead to find why there was such quiet. The students must have been at study I concluded, so I went first toward the house. Samuel met me just inside the door. "Father, you are at home. I am so glad. There has been a terrible accident. Mother is in with Edmund," he said motioning with his head toward our downstairs bedroom.

I walked in and Rachel jumped to her feet as if launched. "Thank God. Oh, David, we did not know how to get news to you." She was trembling. On the bed with eyes closed lay Edmund. A white cloth was wrapped round his head and he appeared flushed.

"What is it, Rachel?" I asked. "Has the boy been hurt?"

"Sit down." she said, as if to prepare the explanation. "It happened yesterday, in the mid–afternoon. The students were at exercise and I was back in the kitchen preparing the supper menu. Edmund was out playing with the older boys. You know how he insists on tagging along with them instead of playing with children his own age. I did not know at the time, but they had a game going behind the academy building. They had created a hay stack under the second story window and had somehow attached a rope on the roof so that they could swing out and drop into the hay. At first, they were careful not to let Edmund try, but some way, no one seems to have been watching and he got the rope. He tripped as he tried to swing and instead fell straight down, head first. The back of his head struck a large field rock. We feared that his neck was broken. The boys came for me immediately, afraid to move him. I got a board and we brought him here keeping him as straight as we could. We put him on the bed and installed the board beneath the mattress. Samuel rode all the way to New Garden and Doctor Kepley came in about an hour. Oh David," she sighed. "We needed you so. His head was bleeding profusely and we cleaned the wound as well as possible and I found the compound that I have seen you use to staunch bleeding. Doctor Kepley felt certain the boy's neck was not broken but we still made a kind of collar to keep it straight in case it had been twisted violently. Examination of the wound, however, was more complicated. The doctor felt that the blow had been severe enough to crack the skull, which had serious implications but we would not know until the swelling was reduced and he was again conscious."

As she began to speak of the details of the injury, I started my own examination. Edmund seemed to be in a deep coma. His breathing was regular and Rachel said there was no temperature. I examined the rest of his body closely until I was satisfied that there were no other injuries that were unobserved so far. For the next several hours, I searched my limited medical library for any information about skull fractures and damage to the brain. I had made Rachel understand that this was an accident and in no way the result of her neglect and she had performed precisely as she should with the patient. I would deal with the older boys later but would let them spend some time now managing guilt as their real punishment.

Edmund began to stir on his own on the third day, and by the fourth, he was awake and complaining of an aching head and sore neck. He remembered nothing of the game that had created the accident but I did not think that unusual. By the end of the week, he was up and about but uninterested in playing outdoors. Dr. Kepley came several times, for which we were truly grateful. I appreciated his diagnosis at each visit and we concurred on the progress of the patient. By the third week, however, the wound continued unhealed and open and began to ooze matter which appeared as a fluid. No further treatment was prescribed but the wound remained as an open sore refusing to heal. We had to dress the wound at least daily and wrap Edmund's head. Eventually, Rachel made him a kind of skull cap to wear and we laughingly called him "our Rabbi." Edmund was no longer the aspiring boy rushing after older boys, eager to grow up faster. He was an average student without any animation or imagination. He became self-absorbed and in spite of the efforts of the whole family, he was progressively more withdrawn over time.

Rachel and I talked often at night about Edmund and the effect the accident had on him. I did not share with her my dark, sometimes despondent, concerns that somehow this might be a demonstration of judgment on me, perhaps because of some arrogance that I had displayed at the meeting of the Assembly or for my willingness to excuse the actions of the Regulators in my congregation. Each time I had processed these thoughts, I had prayed profoundly. I found peace but still I did not share those morose thoughts with Rachel.

CHAPTER FIFTEEN **1787** Governor Martin

After Alex Martin concluded his last year term as governor, he stood for election again to the Senate from Guilford. Charles Bruce and James Gallaway had served in that seat while he had been in the Governor's office. In 1785 on his return to the Senate, Martin was elected again as the President, in effect going from the first office in the state back to the second. It was in this session that the county was divided. In the new county of Rockingham, the northern half of the old county, Alexander had almost unchallenged political control. His brother-in-law, Thomas Henderson, became the Clerk of Court and his cousin, James Hunter, Sheriff. His family home, Danbury, was almost in the center of the county. Alexander, however, kept his residence at Martinville and considered Guilford his home county. To some in Guilford, this appeared to be overreaching and his detractors increased. In early spring of 1787, Alex paid another visit. Although cloaked in the same warm friendship, this time his stop also had the particularly tactical flavor of a politician with important constituents. As was his usual practice, he visited with the students in their class and spoke to them about the important events of the day. He did not dwell particularly on his activities but gave them a general history lesson and some thoughts on how a country should be governed. He was going to be making a trip to Philadelphia soon and when he returned he promised to come again and tell them about the changes that were about to be made to our government. In this way he prepared me for what might be the concerns that had led him here at this particular time.

Before Rachel had joined us, Alexander asked if I would come alone the following week to see him at Martinville as he had something to discuss only with me. It was a peculiar request which he might have made of me any Sunday when he had been at Buffalo when I preached. He seemed uneasy and I attributed it to guilt in not asking Rachel to join us. Before Rachel came in with tea, I agreed to meet him then.

"I am sure that you have both seen that politics is waxing hot locally these days and I want to concentrate on that, but first I must tell you some special news. There is to be a federal convention in May in Philadelphia called to consider a revision of our plan of government. Perhaps you have already heard. I have been chosen by the Assembly as one of the five delegates to represent North Carolina and I will be leaving soon."

Rachel quickly responded. "Congratulations, Alexander. We were not ignorant of the intended convention and I had told David I had hoped you would be a representative."

"Yes, that is how it has come to be and I take it as a considerable honor. My political instincts, however, alert me to the reality that what transpires at Philadelphia may not be held in automatic favor by my friends in North Carolina."

"Alexander, you know that we are really babes when it comes to political issues," I inserted as a qualifier.

"I knew you would say that, David, but just as I have countered such disclaimers before, I know of no one who has a more natural grasp on the local attitudes than do you and Rachel. People trust you instinctively with their inner feelings because they need to have your confirmation to underpin their ignorance.

"Whatever government we conclude at a federal level will be approached skeptically by people in our region. It may be favorably accepted in the East because it will improve the economic security of Eastern businesses. For our people nearer the frontier, it will appear to have few obvious advantages and government will be far removed which makes it always suspect to them."

I said I thought that was "a balanced assessment."

Alexander continued. "We need to depend on people like you two to give this proposal of government a fair consideration – even to the point of taking a risk that it will not be immediately so beneficial."

I wondered, "why should we have to risk something we see as without benefit, Alexander? Why can it not be created as a government that benefits everyone? Is that naive?"

"No, I don't think so, and in form I think the government will be of balanced benefit. My question in the beginning is, will people who are far removed from the workings of this government see why a national government must have vested power in order to be considered authentic in the eyes of the other countries of the world, and why it must have economic resources sufficient to administer uniform policy? These are complicated but necessary issues and I know full well that when our Scots-Irish and the others of the frontier see complicated issues on another man's plate, we are inclined to say, 'not my concern.' The whole matter of surrendering some personal independence for the common good, what Dr. Witherspoon used to call the creation of a civil society, will be the morsel of this government concoction that will be hardest for them to swallow."

"To use your metaphor, Alexander, I am fearful that is where I have a tendency to get choked." I said that with a smile as I thought that he was being too trivial with that metaphor. "On the one hand, I have said repeatedly that my frame of reference tends to be the covenant. I see respectable men sitting together and agreeing to exchange a reasonable level of unfettered independence for basic guarantees of inalienable rights. Beyond that, the details of structure, I tend to leave to the authorities. Over all, I am very suspicious of the sovereign power in a government. I see the necessity of a head of state but only with the significant power vested in the people through a legislative process. I do not have your strong feelings about the sanctity of the law. I am willing to concede on that point to your knowledge as a lawyer. At the same time, I appreciate the need to sacrifice to the common good with the protection of the law."

"It seems to me that is not more or less than we were demanding in assenting to this revolution in the first place," observed Rachel.

We had reached a consensus in our little company of friends but I sensed that we had avoided the details where the devil lurked.

"I wanted you two to particularly understand where I stood approaching this national deliberation. You will be interested in knowing the other members of the North Carolina delegation. William R. Davie, Richard Dobbs Spaight, and Hugh Williamson are all supporters of a strong central government. William Blount is less so but he has strong economic interests and all four are from the East. Blount has interests in the West but I will be the only member living in and representing the frontier. I will be representing what is rapidly becoming the most populous part of the state against an entrenched majority of delegates with strong ties to commerce. Governor Caswell and Willie Jones were originally included in the delegation but declined and were replaced with Blount and Williamson so you can see that we started with a much more balanced group. I anticipate that some states, perhaps Virginia or New Jersey, will place consensus plans of government on the table but we have little chance of formulating such agreement in a single plan with the range of interests in our North Carolina delegation. I believe that I will frequently find myself in more natural agreement with delegates from other states, but I must be careful not to alienate my fellow delegates enough to find myself isolated and inconsequential in relation to our state vote. I can say these things to you as I can to my family but to few others. That is why I need you to be open with your opinions. The circumstances, the make-up of our delegation, and the strong feeling toward a powerful central government, will be pulling me from my roots and you must help to pull me back."

"We won't be there to do that nor will your family," I said. "You will have to go it alone but we are confidant that you will represent our interests and will make your choices through your own intelligence and on that we are well satisfied." He faced the most difficult challenge of his life but he had eagerly sought to influence the direction this new country would pursue, and if this convention succeeded, it would create a unique government.

"I am not faint-hearted in my approach to this convention, I assure you. Actually, I look forward to the debate," he acknowledged. "Although public debate is not my strength, I believe that the numerous small discussions, committee sessions, and meetings in the members' rooms, will be where I can exert significant influence. Most delegates will be merchants or the landed class. I will be one of the few who represent the majority of small farmers whose support, in numbers, will be necessary for ratification. Through my Princeton connections and my credibility as a former governor of one of the bigger states, I will be listened to by merchants and planters. They will be looking for my opinion as a practical reality. It will do them no good to create a form of government so weighted toward the moneyed class that it will not be approved by the people. I think my input will be important but I also recognize that I will not be able to easily deliver the vote of the frontier no matter what form finally is presented for a vote. Do you see the thin edge on which I perceive to operate?"

"Yes, I do, Alexander, but remember that no one there will have any more experience than do you. They may all put on airs of self-confidence but they are illusions. Give other people room to maneuver. Don't press for decisions too early. Let them see that you are willing to consider good reasoning but hold fast to what you have expressed as your fundamental objectives. You have the capacity to prevail."

We walked down to the site where I was expanding my mill on the small branch south of the house. "We have a steady run here but not rushing water. I may have to adjust to seasonal dry spells that will limit when I can operate the mill but I believe that it will be sufficient for my purposes and profitable. We have many mouths to feed on our own place and more students every year."

"I marvel at your capacity to succeed in so many worthy endeavors, David. You are pastor to two congregations and doctor to a wide neighborhood. I believe you are the most noted and respected teacher in the state. You have a large and growing family and you are a very good farmer and a trained carpenter. Now you will become a miller to the community. Do you have still more ambitions in the back of your mind?"

I gave a self-effacing chuckle but it was sincere. "To some trades I have been called, Alexander, and to others I have been impressed by the need. I am fortunate that I seem to have been gifted for a homestead and God has used me for a larger purpose. I am not unmindful, however, that skill at too many things produces no master.

I am in regular prayer with my God. I correspond routinely with Dr. Benjamin Rush. Rachel is my constant partner with matters of the family. I served a good apprenticeship as a carpenter and my neighbors are good advisors in farming. I try to keep my body fit to perform the tasks to be done but I am not reluctant to seeking good aid and advice. I think I have struck a worthy balance."

Having deliberated at such an encompassing level at our home, I was astonished the following week when I visited Alexander at Martinville and was delivered an unexpected confession.

"I am to be a father," he said as if the words could not get out of his mouth fast enough. "Does life not present us with bizarre fortune?"

I was startled. "Under what circumstances? I have never heard you mention any amorous liaison and I assume this is the result of a liaison."

"I hold myself entirely responsible for the circumstances. A few years ago, a young woman, Elizabeth Strong, bought a place north of the Dan from 'Danbury.' My mother particularly welcomed her into the community where her sister and brother-in-law had located during the war. She had several children and had been married to Thomas Strong who was a long hunter. Just after the war, he had gone hunting, 'over the mountain' as they call it, in the fall and was never heard of again. She had no means to declare herself a widow. We became attracted to each other, I will not go into the details but she is to have my child in the summer. I don't expect you to excuse or bless the circumstance but I felt it important to tell you before it was general news. I do not expect her to keep it a secret."

"I see. Then you are not seeking a way to make her your wife."

"No. It is not my wish and she has made no demands. Elizabeth intends to raise the child herself and I will of course provide for expenses."

"A child is more than expenses, Alexander," I said with a touch of critique.

"I know that. My mother is beside herself. On the one hand she has wished for years for me to make a 'successful' marriage, something 'appropriate to my position,' but this is an embarrassment to her. I have never been drawn to the idea of a family, nor am I in love with Elizabeth. We are at peace with the arrangement and intend it to be so but I wanted to tell you and Rachel, as you are my spiritual advisors."

Again I could not immediately answer. "I gather that it is not advice that you ask of me now. It is done and you and Elizabeth have made your choices. It is not an acceptable choice in the eyes of the church, but in these uncertain times, it is not an unheard of circumstance. I must say, by way of criticism, that 'in your position' I think your actions demonstrate a level of irresponsibility that I did not expect from you. I do not mean to imply that I think less of you for it, but it does not demonstrate a good moral leadership. But I will say no more. You are our dear friend and you will remain so."

"One more request to presume on that friendship," he said. "I hesitate to leave for Philadelphia not being certain that Elizabeth is in good health and that we have little to fear at this time concerning the birth of the child. I have brought her here in the carriage and she is waiting upstairs. Would you agree to see her as a doctor and examine her general health?"

"She is here?" I asked completely surprised. I hadn't seen this coming though I suppose that it was a natural progression. "Alexander, she is not my patient and I will not be able to serve her during this birth. I will be glad to meet her, and to the extent that my examination as a doctor will place your mind at greater ease, I will examine her."

Alex went out and returned in just a short time with a woman I judged to be in her mid–30s. She was tall and pretty, mature in bearing and carried herself with poise. She was wearing a yellow dress with a small white flower print. "Dr. Caldwell, we presume upon you under awkward circumstances and I am very grateful for your consideration," she said immediately without introduction. Formality would have seemed out of place and pretentious and her comment eased the atmosphere.

"Mrs. Strong, I am pleased to meet you as a patient and as the Governor's friend. Shall we agree that there is no presumption in that?"

We talked together for a while to further ease any tension, then Alexander left the room and I proceeded with a general examination followed by a specific pelvic examination. Fortunately, I routinely carried my small medical bag whenever I left the house and that was sufficient to the purpose since I found no complications. "I find, Madame, no reason to believe that you will have anything but a normal term pregnancy, and barring any future mishap, you should deliver a normal child. You are in good health. I understand from Alexander that you have had other children so you know what to expect. I do believe at your age, that you should not perform any heavy house or farm work particularly involving lifting or extended hours in the heat of the sun, until you deliver. Otherwise, I prescribe good food and plenty of it. Do you have family to help you with your housework and will someone, an adult, be routinely available to you in case of emergencies?"

"My sister and her husband are nearby and their oldest daughter, who is near seventeen, has come to stay with me until the baby comes. My own children are younger but they are usually responsible in their actions. I think that Alexander has told you that his mother is very upset at the prospect of this child and I do not, in any way, wish to be beholden to her before it is born. I hope she will become adjusted after the birth and will ultimately take more than a general interest in the baby. That will have to be her choice. I do not intend to maneuver her into feelings that do not come naturally."

I found her a woman of good judgment, although in this case, she and Alexander both appear to have acted out of character. Now, however, she was prepared to add another child to her family and allow others to accept whatever relationship with which they felt comfortable. I could respect her attitude without condoning her actions. I had been invited for my friendship and professional skills and I felt no compunction to add my judgment.

Alexander seemed satisfied with the encounter. He commented further about his departure for Philadelphia and said he hoped to be back before the arrival of the child. I noted his very fine carriage which stood outside. He had always been on horseback when he came to our place but he and Prince would use the carriage for the trip north and it had been a fortunate conveyance for Elizabeth in her condition.

Rachel's reaction to the events at Martinville was surprise equal to my own with just a touch of shock appropriate to a woman. "He should have told us both. I think less of him for it. Some men can disappoint at the most unusual times," she added and I made no attempt to have her expand on her meaning. "What is she like?" I was forced then to detail every word of our conversation although I did not disclose any details of my medical examination.

I preached the next Sunday at Alamance and took my text again on the continued need for healing in our community. The opportunism that had surfaced with such vengeance after '81, seemed to have run its course. There was no more land to be confiscated. The courts were now burdened with challenges to some of the earlier confiscations and some old Tories were recovering the land they had earlier lost. Some of the feuds would not heal in a single generation but the level of toleration was acceptable by frontier standards.

My text was the message to the Romans in the twelfth chapter of Paul's letter, verses 3–5:

> In virtue of the gift that God in his grace has given me I say to everyone among you: do not be conceited or think too highly of yourself; but think your way to a sober estimate based on the measure of faith that God has dealt to each of you. For just as in a single human body there are many limbs and organs, all with different functions, so all of us, united with Christ, form one body, serving individually as limbs and organs to one another.

I made use of the text as I would the two sides of a coin, applying it first to the victory we had shared and the right we had acquired to govern ourselves. This could only be viewed as God's grace. It was the measure of faith that God had given to each of us. I continued in that vein for some moments, confirming that they had progressed beyond the euphoria that had come with the end of the Revolution. "Cheers of victory have the effect of exciting the ego and filling us with the illusion that we have done the impossible. But the ego is soon like a balloon, losing lift and floating down to earth. We look around and see God has wrought a new thing. Our world has been transformed. The material has been taken from us and we build on a new spirit not of our making. We say to ourselves, 'God has done this,' and then we seek to discern, to what purpose? What is the one body He expects us to be?"

That was my line of thought as I continued to try to guide

them into a comfortable grasp of their identity as a community. I felt an impassioned delight in the faces that showed reconciliation in the words that I spilled out before them. I had lost the ownership of the phrases I spoke as if they passed through me in transit. I was fulfilled as the instrument, aware that God filled me with the truth and finally, it was they who professed.

But I could not leave them without the means to build on their victory. I turned over the coin and laid before them the task beyond community and I called it citizenship. Here I was less certain that I could be the conduit for insight. When Paul spoke of the parts of the body working in harmony, could I, with slick assurance, speak of the sovereign states functioning in union as part of the whole as a metaphor for the will of God? We had broken covenant with a king and a parliament that had aborted their covenant with us. With whom would we make a new covenant? Were we only about to exchange Caesars?

Then I explained to them that debates would soon be met and deliberation involving representatives from all the states would soon take place. "Pray for God's presence. Pray that the Holy Spirit will guide the debate. Pray that modern prophets will indeed come among us." Now, the same faces that had been aglow with a grasp of their purpose in community, looked back at me as mirrors of my own uncertainty. Had I, in a single sermon, taken them to the summit of the mountain only to dash them again on the rocks of uncertainty below? I had taken the risk because I was confidant that God would bridge the doubt and restore our insight.

These were simple people, ill-informed. Had it not been demonstrated that they could be roused to accomplish extraordinary ends? My concern was to be able to arouse them and me to perceive a nation, and to become firm in what they would want of that government, and what they might be willing to give up to have a national consensus. In two weeks, I would have them again and I would expect of myself greater clarity for our journey.

CHAPTER SIXTEEN **1787** Constitutional Convention

There were few interactions between our people and our immediate neighbors to the west, the New Garden Quakers. The animosity that had risen in Pennsylvania had been transferred south and was compounded when Quakers had refused to become combatants in what fell locally to being mostly a Presbyterian war. Incidents produced by these conflicting responses to war were repeated as folk tales until unseen impediments became hard and fast between the communities. Necessity penetrated the barrier, while not removing it, and within each community raised certain morale issues of significance.

The corn crop came that year with an unprecedented abundance that fell on Quaker and Presbyterian alike. The labor force on any single farm was unequal to the task and resulted in a quaint custom, the 'frolic.' Heaps of corn were piled in the open space where the students played. Five piles from that many farms had been deposited and allowed to flow into a single oblong, irregular mound. The labor forces arrived from the five farms participating, black and white, free and slave, and two of the white families approached God as Quaker and three as Presbyterians. Without instruction, the blacks settled at one end of the mound of corn and the whites at the other, Christians randomly mixed. Children played together at the side – hobnob. A slave dealer who also lived nearby, Stephen Holland, had a coffle of slaves he was taking south for sale and he brought them over to help shuck. The Coffin family lived at New Garden and the Hiatts just outside that community. The McQuistons were our immediate neighbors and the Wileys were part of my Alamance Church membership.

A 'frolic' was a social event that made play of work. As each group arrived in our yard, the level of chatter rose perceptibly until it reached a plateau of sound. There were crocks of fruit drinks located on various tables. Families had brought food in their wagons that was taken to the kitchen, and enough chairs for those who would husk corn and to use at dinner time. The conversation among the adult whites centered throughout the evening on the Philadelphia Convention.

"I think that because it is being held in the Quaker city," offered one of the McQuiston men, "those politicians think they have to hold a Quaker service. Why, they have gone behind closed doors. They won't let anyone else in and appear to me to be waiting for the spirit to move them." That was the kind of remark needed to ignite the spark at such a 'frolic' – innocent, light-hearted and bound to be followed by serious comments.

There were no regular reports of the progress of the convention. Those that appeared in the northern papers came from rumors built of pieces of information leaked by individuals. "I read that two plans are under consideration, one proposed by New Jersey and one by Virginia," said Robert Wiley. "Little states are afraid that they will be under-represented and big states fear that the small states will act in unison to give maximum value to their vote."

William Coffin had no hesitation in raising the issue of slavery as a critical stumbling block. "We are of course opposed to slavery and we pray that such an immoral practice will be forbidden in a government of free men." There were some moments of heavy breathing.

"Slavery is the single issue that I believe all at the convention must understand could block a union," said McQuiston. "You approach it as a moral issue. As an economic issue, I can see in this very evening the conditions that might be brought together to end the practice but they are not yet here. My son in Georgia could not operate a large plantation as he does now without slaves. No virgin government can accommodate all those positions into a common law. That is why this is a test of states."

"I must comment," I added, "that my fear is that with such a corrupting cross-current as slavery, these delegates will attempt to impose a strong central authority. That in turn may be able to decree systems and institutions that will so erode our freedoms that we will long for a king and master as did the people of Israel."

"Thou should remember, brother," said William, "that the sin of Israel was turning against God. I fear that. It is the jeopardy among these learned spokesmen that they will be so motivated by the potential of human endeavor that they will reject the infinite voice of God." He continued. "Brother Caldwell, you understand that we Quakers will look first at the national law protecting dissent and the free expression of religion. That is our sticking point."

"Yes, I have come to accept the integrity of dissent within the faith. I believe that in recent centuries, Protestants have forgotten that to the Roman church we were the people of dissent. It cannot behoove us, as established structures of faith, to now reject dissent in a general concern about heresy. I am fearful, my friend, that it will be this liberation of thought now so enticing to many in leadership, that will invite Jews, Moslems, deists, even non-believers into our country as participants in our experiment. We are a Christian people and we must guard against those who would deny the Christian faith."

There was little argument. No one knew enough of the facts to carry the debate. Each could only speak from their own prejudices and try to shape their fears so others hearing would absorb those fears into their own. So the evening progressed.

As the sun fell, drifting down into the tree line, torches were lit to allow the last ears to be shucked and the pile of corn to be divided and loaded into the separate wagons. Then the whites, taking up their chairs, went in to supper. The blacks, free and slave, remained outside and both white and blacks were served from the same busy kitchen. As we went in, I had caught sight of Coffin's young son, Levi, hanging back as if to defer to the entrance of his elders. I nodded to Samuel to "invite him to come in with you," for they were near the same age.

Samuel whispered, "I have, but he is interested to speak to some of the slaves in Holland's crew."

Seated during supper, Rachel sought out Priscilla Coffin to

inquire concerning the school at New Garden "You teach both boys and girls in your school, I understand."

"We do, Mistress Caldwell, but I believe that our school is much different from the one that you and Dr. Caldwell hold," responded Priscilla. She was a woman of plain tastes, as were all Quaker women, but she had a sparkling look in her eyes that seemed to animate all her features. "It is very basic. I think we limit it too much to necessary, practical knowledge, and miss the opportunity to train our children to greater imagination. Oh yes. We do teach our boys and girls together. Again it is a practical rationale. We only have to pay for a single teacher. Actually, William and I need our children much of the crop year, so they go seldom. William was once a very respected teacher, so he works with our children in the evening and I think they are better trained."

"We call ours a classical school, as you know, and much of the learning is in classical Greek and Latin. It is intended as more advanced than a field school. I don't mean to sound demeaning in that description, just clarifying." Rachel feared that she had appeared to belittle other schools.

"No. No. I understand that your school comes from your Presbyterian tradition of training toward a theological education. In Pennsylvania we were well acquainted with the Presbyterian log colleges."

"That is our model," admitted Rachel, "but we don't call it that. Wouldn't that sound pretentious on such a frontier?" They laughed together.

"Why, indeed is our education not more a source of inclusion, William," I posed to her husband.

"I'll tell you why," butted in John Hiatt. "Quakers do not seek inclusion. We train our own and shun those who wander from our midst. We strike those who marry outside our church from our membership. We don't want education to get in the way and further erode our faith."

"Can your faith be so easily eroded that you must govern marriage and restrict education as preservation?" I asked. "Pardon me. I should not make such a criticism of a fellow Christian and a guest in my own home."

William was diplomatic. "You are right, Dr. Caldwell, and such is a continuous debate within our Quaker fellowship."

We had gone too close to the edge and brushed against a nerve. Most of us had come to the frontier in company with families of our own denomination. We had found safety through our faith and we guarded it from "erosion" fearing a weakening of the bonds on which we had depended. In each denomination, we used orthodoxy as our identity instead of seeing it as the roots of the faith that we all professed.

Sometimes I had to remind myself that my academy was intended as more than a field school. Boys who were entrusted to me were believed by their parents to have more than average prospects.

Some had already demonstrated above average talents and my function was to prepare them to advance. So I did not tolerate with indifference the fool or the malcontent. I did not attempt to govern my students with fear, although I believed myself strict. One of my assistants once told me I was "indulgent to a fault." Perhaps I appeared so but I was determined never to be unkind. I had a respect for a student's person. If I had lacked that, how could I expect to mold that person toward some advancement. In return, I never experienced a lack of respect from them. They came to call me, "Dr. Caldwell or Dr. C." to my face and that was a sobriquet that I appreciated. It accepted me as other than preacher.

Teaching Greek and Latin can produce miraculous tribulations in translation. At times a classical author would find himself translated in absurd nonsense. I always tried to react with mild reproof to such misadventures, sometimes with just a little scorching sarcasm. At times I would cry scornfully to the other students' delight, "Murther dherrig!" (Do you perhaps understand Irish?)

"Archie" Murphey was one of my best students and I made him an assistant for a year. He reported one day that Tom McGee, one of the older students who had never given us any problem before, had an altercation with our old goat, Billie. The goat was allowed to graze free most days and provide a general service of keeping down the otherwise unfettered growth of bushes and weeds around the edges of the court. I was unaware that Billie had an interest in learning but this day he had found a Greek dictionary that Tom had left behind on a bench. Before Tom was aware, Billie had devoured α through ϵ. Tom ran to rescue the book crying out, "you damned barnyard bitch." Aside from the fact that he had the wrong gender, Tom had committed a punishable offense and on Friday evening, at our weekly assembly, he had to answer for swearing. Archie, as monitor, had inscribed his wording precisely. After the others had defended their lesser misdeeds, all eyes turned on Tom to stand in his own defense.

Having explained the circumstances, he blurted out, "they are a damned creature; and I can prove it by scripture."

I bit my lip but with a stern face responded, "Tommy, Tommy, I don't question your Bible knowledge but there are a number of smaller boys here and you should set a better example before them." The shame and embarrassment was enough punishment, I was certain. Tom never again transgressed but accepted his responsibility as a senior boy. He is today a lawyer of exceptional reputation.

I found with my congregations that in most cases, the mere public marking of a transgression was usually enough to result in reform. The public acknowledgment that the preacher knew, usually corrected the offense.

Through late July and into August of 1787, we expected to receive some post from the north with a summary of the findings of the convention. I lamented the fact that I had not asked Alexander Martin to write me such a summary but was a little disappointed that, after preparing us for his attendance at the convention, he had not thought of writing us anyway. On September 8th, like the chariot of some eastern potentate, his dusty carriage, with Prince seated tall in a great leather coat, whip in hand, swung into our court yard. A cloud of debris mounted into the sky. Students cheered the arrival. Everyone came running through the nearest available door.

Prince jumped down, and with appropriate flourish, opened the carriage door and announced, "Governor Martin."

There was applause and Alexander doffed his hat and acknowledged the greeting appropriately. We were all filled with excitement, everyone smiling with welcome. Most there would never in their lives expect to travel as far as had he since last he was here and none to a gathering such as he had just been a delegate. We all sensed that this was a memorable moment, but at the time, no one was quite certain why.

Inside, when Rachel and I were alone with him for the first time, he declaimed with vigor, "I have a son!"

Rachel kissed him and rushed to the breakfront to take out glasses and her best decanter. "This may not be the fancy brandy you are used to being served in the great houses of Philadelphia, but it is the best to be had in a Presbyterian house in Guilford County." With that she swept round in a flourish offering us each a glass. "His name?" she asked. "His name?"

"We will call him Alexander," he replied a little awkwardly, knowing that he would refuse for the time to give him the family name of Martin.

"To Alexander," I toasted. "May he become the worthy politician his father is and a professing Christian."

Alexander laughed. "Now that toast has a message in it."

"Only in the best spirit my friend and with our sincere best wishes. I trust Elizabeth is recovering well after the delivery."

"She is."

"Then, to Elizabeth. May she reap the love of a fine son to make soft the burden of her years."

"That smacks of an Irish tavern toast, David," said Rachel, "but I shall not enquire where you heard it."

We chatted comfortably over several brandies. Alex concentrated first on the social news of Philadelphia for Rachel's benefit. He had many conversations with General Washington. Much of the work of proposal and compromise had taken place in the hotels, away from the actual convened meetings. There had been marked civility, and with few exceptions, good will. He felt that the Princeton education he shared with ten of the delegates, his service as a state Governor and a member of the legislature, and his service under General Washington, had all given him an advantage of connections only a few others could approach.

I knew that it had been Alexander and his younger brother, Thomas, who had persuaded old James Madison to send his Virginia namesake to Princeton. "What about Madison? You must have been thick as thieves."

"That is strange. We were certainly friendly. I felt, however, that James was always trying to appropriate me rather than convince me on issues. I was in no way beholden to him or he to me. I think our friendship was useful but Virginia men are accustomed to treat their North Carolina neighbors as if they were vassals. It may sound petty, but having a Virginia Plan, well organized as it may have been, did not make them arbiters of the convention. I did have dealings with Madison, however, which may directly involve you, but before we get to that, let me detail for you some of the decisions of the convention.

"I left premature to the adjournment and signing of the new constitution. Davie had already left when I got news of the birth of Alexander and I thought that the important decisions had been voted upon and the final document was safe for approval. I may regret later not having my name on this constitution or I may be very glad in the end that it is not. I did arrange before departure to have a dozen printed copies sent to me of the final document so that I could distribute it to key people."

"You sound somewhat ambivalent about the finished product, Alexander. Are you unhappy with it or do you question its adoption by the states?"

"No, I am committed to the constitution. I believe it to be the work of good men and I believe an expression of free deliberation. As a form of governing states, it will be unique in the world. It is a perfection of the union of federated states.

"David, you said before my departure, that you had a particular interest in a Christian covenant. Much debate, formal and informal, was on the fear of a theocracy and therefore the need to clearly separate church and state. That has been done, not with a strong statement but by the establishing a civil government. Religion is concerned to the extent that there will be no religious test as a qualification for any office in the United States."

He was looking into my eyes as he stopped, understanding that I would have to process such a definition. "You mean to say that there is no affirmation of the Christian faith in the entire document?"

"Yes," he said, "but this was the result of considerable debate and it was not an attempt to reject faith or to weaken faith. Our conclusion was that if we were to keep religion separate from government, we should not speak of it any more than necessary in a civil document establishing government. The civil authority should, on the other hand, have no way to insert itself into the practice of religion. I understand that this may be far from what you expected when you expressed your primary concerns to me previously, but I can only say that I tried very objectively to represent your thinking in this debate. I believe it was well heard. I am also satisfied that the way the issue was dealt with was a wise decision."

"Your wise decision of men may not be the will of God." I wanted to firmly stave off his attempt to patronize my issue. I was angry but determined to be composed.

"The constitution establishes three branches of government,

if you will. Within the legislative there are to be two bodies as a compromise that would satisfy the need to protect the small states against over-representation by the large, and protecting the large from inflating unrealistically the power of the smaller states. A House of Representatives has its membership determined by population, one member as a minimum and another for each additional 30,000 people. There was a compromise here in counting slaves, but let me get to that in a minute."

I was having difficulty concentrating on what he was saying now, so angry was I about his comments on religion. Rachel could see I was fuming and Alexander saw my unhappiness. She said, "Alexander, should we talk through your comments about religious content first, before we detail the type of government?"

"I know you are both dissatisfied with me at this point but I think we can only have a reasonable discussion about your religious concerns, if you have a feeling for the entire document. This is difficult because you have not had that document to study and you have to listen to me, but I wanted to place all this before you as soon as I could and I am risking your tolerance in doing so. I believed that only the two of you were well enough informed and deeply enough rooted, to start this process of examination, giving a tolerant ear to the whole before putting too fine a point on one aspect of the whole."

"All right," I said. "That is fair and I will just have to suppress my emotions and hear you out."

"Good. Now, the second branch within the legislature is the

Senate and there each state will elect two members regardless of the population of the state. In the House of Representatives, all revenue bills will originate and the house will act on all Presidential vetoes, more on that later. The Senate will be a more powerful body because each Senator will represent his whole state. The Representative will, however, be more reflective of public opinion as it breaks down on local concerns.

"The chief executive will be called a President. He will be chosen by a vote of electors appointed from each state equal in number to the combined total of that state's Senators and Representatives. The method of appointing the electors will be up to the individual state. A Vice-President will be elected in like manner. The President will be the Commander-in-Chief of the Army and Navy and, in times of war, of the militia. He can make treaties, and with the advise and consent of the Senate, appoint Ambassadors and judges of the Supreme Court.

"The Supreme Court will be vested with the judicial power of the United States along with inferior courts as Congress sees fit to establish them. That gives you a brief summary of the government design. Now, let me say something about the broad questions that seemed to drive the discussion and define this constitution. Do you have questions here?"

"Your description of the executive is abbreviated showing only his control of the military and ceremonial responsibilities. Does that represent the true limitations on his power or are there subtle details that give to him implied powers beyond the government?" I asked.

"There were those delegates who wanted a much stronger President, who would take enumerated powers away from the legislature and the states. By placing the revenue powers in the House of Representatives, the control of the veto power of the President, and the impeachment power over the President, however, the majority sought to circumscribe that office in such a way as to prevent any assumption of powers beyond those assigned. There is no way to be certain that at some future date the people will not abrogate this constitution by the surrender of powers. The time will surely come when it will be tested."

"On the subject of slavery, Alexander," postured Rachel. "I assume that the states retain their right to ownership of slaves within their borders."

"Slavery is the issue wherein the entire convention could have floundered, and I think why it was wise to debate in private. A national policy on the ownership of slaves would have divided the states irrevocably into at least two camps and we would have had no chance at a single union. That was clear on the first day. For a while we could proceed around the issue, put it off until other progress had been made. Ultimately, it came to be debated as it related to counting slaves as part of population in determining the size of state delegations in Congress. The slave states claimed slaves represented part of the population just as free blacks were part of the population in non-slave states. The non-slave states would have none of it. The compromise worked out in committee, counted slaves as three-fifths of all other people and excluded Indians as non-taxed persons."

I raised my eye brows and turned obviously to Rachel. "There you have it. The best minds in the country have defined a slave as three fifths of a person. Oh, for a Solomon to raise a sword and begin the division." Rachel smiled, a look of toleration.

"If there is any part of this constitution that I am not proud of, David, it is this one. It is only institutionally deferring this problem for another generation because we were not wise enough to decide it for ourselves. I will allow, however, that it was more desirable to form a union even if half a loaf on the question of slavery was the price.

"I will defer my conclusion about your constitution until I have read it and absorbed the finer print," I concluded. "You should know, however, that if anyone but you had given me this report, I would have come away deeply disappointed. I have been preparing my congregations to accept a new form of national government but I do not think this is the one I had in mind."

"It does seem that such a government is good form," observed Rachel, "but I don't get the feeling that the average citizen can feel a security in the words. It may satisfy the lawyers, no offence, but I do not see the citizen, the free man, in it."

"Perhaps, that is exactly the point of my uneasiness," I added. "I could not frame it at first. Where, Alexander, are the guarantees for the people in this document? I have been like an echo about my covenants but that is what I am looking for here. You delegates have laid before me, or before the people, a well crafted form of government but what do the governed receive beyond the assurance that the form appears more democratic?"

Alexander took a deep breath, as if he was about to expose a confidence. "This is what I was referring to when you asked about James Madison. I did not forget your covenant and there were many there, not just Presbyterians or Princeton men, who shared the conclusion that this constitution must contain a guarantee of the basic rights of the people. I talked into the late hours with these people and Madison and I were closely allied. In the end, the majority feared that debate over such a list of guarantees would destroy the consensus we had achieved. My own belief is that having surprised ourselves, that we could put slavery behind us with a three-fifths compromise, the majority thought it had better take what we had and not overstep our unity. It is a weak man's compromise but it carried and we anticipated that it would.

"Our minority, those who thought a guarantee of citizen rights should be part of the constitution, continued to meet and developed several strategies. We all thought that in the individual state ratification conventions there would be demands for these rights in varied forms. Each of us was pledged to work in favor of such positions while pledging to remain firm for ratification of the constitution. We did not anticipate that we would have to sacrifice the one for the other.

"Madison and I, along with just a few other like minds, developed a specific strategy that involved Virginia and North Carolina directly with some alternate states, dependent on how the early state conventions voted on ratification. Ratification of nine states would establish this constitution between the states. If we could reach at least eight states in ratification and have key states still in debate, one of those states could refuse ratification unless there was a certification of citizen rights attached to the document. The others who then had already approved the constitution, would have to agree to such amendments as the price of a nine-state majority. That will be problematic because there will be states that will refuse to ratify until there are nine. If more states wait on the fence, more will have to carry the issue of these civil rights. Otherwise the ratification may be defeated out of hand.

"Now we consider North Carolina. All our delegates, even though Davie and I are not signers, agree strongly in favor of ratification of the constitution. That is unequivocal. Only I, however, feel strongly about these citizen rights. Some even oppose them in principal. We must find a strong cadre in North Carolina who will advocate the inclusion of these rights as a prerequisite for ratification and see that they are elected as delegates. Can I count on your support?"

I paused before I answered. "Alexander, you have my support. You are my politician. But I think you are asking me to become involved in a new level of political tactical maneuver that I am not sure is suitable for a Presbyterian minister. I must wait until I have read and studied the finished product. I have a more pacified reaction to this new government after I hear you speak so fervently concerning a guarantee of citizen rights. I can translate that comfortably to my belief in a covenant of balanced values. Please see that we get a copy of the Constitution as soon as it arrives."

"Forgive me for my political tactics, David and Rachel. I am so used to weeks of intense political give and take, that I used the same tactics to influence you. Let's agree that I have this day given you my preview of the debate and document agreed to in Philadelphia. It should be no more than a preparation, a synopsis, of the document itself which you will soon be able to analyze yourselves. After you have done that, we will talk about the debate that will be specific here and in our state and how we might influence it to the highest purpose. Agreed?"

"Yes, of course, and now let me bring you before my students because they are begging to hear from you. They are getting the finest history, political, and civil lessons that any academy is able to offer. I hope they know that."

CHAPTER SEVENTEEN **1788–1789** Ratification

Alexander was good as his word and two weeks later he sent Prince over with a copy of the Philadelphia Constitution. I call it the 'Philadelphia' Constitution because my immediate reaction upon reading it was disappointment and the initial conviction was that we could not accept such a constitution. I held no real objection to the form of government proposed. I could see the logical compromises that had surrounded the conflicts between different size states and I could see the rationale that surrounded the compromise on slavery. My disappointment remained in the absence of a feeling that this was a covenant between government and the governed. What the government was and who would be responsible for what function, appeared to have been covered. But where was the definition of what the people got – what basic rights were they guaranteed under this constitution?

In the afternoon class, I admit I was distracted – unable to keep my mind on the exercise of Latin grammar. In the morning we ordinarily spent time reading from an important Latin text. Today it was Catilina from C. Sallustii Crispi concerning Bellum Catilinarium. We had been working in this text for several weeks and, as usual, the boys found interest in the subject of war but that did not seem to carry over to any proficiency in their language skills. I spent the first hour of the morning having them read in turns in the Latin believing that the feel of Latin as a language lifted their skills of pronunciation and removed the sometimes thick colloquialism in their speech. It amazed me how "lazy lipped" some of these farm boys could be and there was always a give and take in their use of their own English language. In a single term, the class would reach an acceptable level of literate speech by natural competitiveness among their peers. Then they would return home for holidays or the summer and come back as perfect rustics. My measure, as a teacher, was that they recovered acceptable form more quickly each time and therein I knew we were making progress. Language, literature, Latin, were never intended by me to make them socially superior. I wanted them to learn to be able to associate beyond their immediate family or neighborhood and they needed the skills of communication. That did not mean that when they were home, they had to appear somehow superior to their siblings. A learned man is courteous to everyone and bears a level of natural sensitivity that allows him to give every other person the feeling of hearing and being heard.

After an hour of reading in Latin, we turned to translating what we had been reading. It was here that the material with which I had to work became conspicuously raw. I always reminded myself that this was an exercise in memory skills which even the most inept student could improve upon. Translation is thus ever intimidating because we naturally respond with visceral fear when memory fails– the lump, the paralyzing chill. So, unless I knew their ignorance to be the product of lack of attention, my method was to share their struggle. I tried to find the logic in the error they made, then pleasantly expose them to the proper solution. I was strict but I wanted them to learn in a competitive environment where they came to seek understanding as much as I. We succeeded together, not because I exercised them into rote repetition of words and ideas, but where we all perfected a skill that was our own. In practice, I believe that my methods succeeded more often than they failed and I lived long enough that I was blessed to be able to make that calculation with certainty.

By afternoon, the sample copy of the Constitution had arrived and I had finished a first and second read. That had taken over a section of my mind, and so our Latin grammar exercise tended to the disjointed. The boys recognized I was not totally focused, and as was natural when they caught the feel of less attentive supervision, they were disorderly. We were reviewing syntax. I went over the first principles: every sentence consists of a noun and verb, every nominative has its own verb implied or understood, every finite verb has its own nominative implied or understood, and every adjective has its own substantive implied or understood. "Now let's consider the construction of the six cases." Then I assigned a boy to take each one of the cases.

John Lindsey took the first: every verb of the finite mood, expressed or understood, agrees with its nominative, expressed or understood, in number and persons. Then with ease he presented the examples: "puer legit, the boy reads; homines aiunt, they say; Romani coeperunt, the Roman made haste."

Then James Paisley had no trouble with the second case: "every genitive is governed by a substantive, expressed or understood. Examples are: liber fratris, the book of my brother; est officium patris, it is the duty of a father."

Samuel Finley surely saw that I was inattentive as he began, "the dative of acquisitive to which anything is acquired or from which it is taken, is joined by any noun or verb expressed or understood, as: dedi Petro, I gave it to Peter; cui dedisti, to whom did you give it; Petro, to Peter; non est solvendo syn taxeos, he is not able to pay the sin tax." A smothered laugh began at the back of the room and spread. Finley sat down and the laugh grew.

"How much sin tax did Peter pay?" called a nameless voice.

"All right, I heard. You boys have me at a disadvantage this afternoon. I have just received from our friend Governor Martin, a copy of that Constitution that he told you he had been part of writing in Philadelphia. I carry it in my pocket and I have read it already several times. I am distracted by its content."

"Let us see it, Dr. C., please."

I took it out of my pocket and held it up and they seemed to be impressed at such a paper. "It is an important document that will have a lasting impact on your young lives when it is finished."

"Finished? I thought it was finished in Philadelphia."

"No. This is the document that these important men were delegated to write for us, the people of all the states. In convention, they were able to debate the issues that concerned the individual states and then to design a government form that they thought best suited a large federation of states. They debated and put form to ideas. This is that form, this document. They have returned it to the individual states and each state will now have a convention to consider what has been written and decide where and if it needs to be modified. It is also possible that individual states will decide not to accept this constitution. If they do not, they will not be part of the United States. In that case they will refuse to 'ratify.' That may be a new word for you and it means to accept or agree to something. Our state Assembly, and remember that Governor Martin is president of the Senate in that Assembly, will now set up that convention for North Carolina. So we will have the opportunity to express our opinions of this Constitution through the delegates that we send to its sessions."

"Who will we send from Guilford?"

"I really don't know but they will have to represent many different opinions."

"Do you mean that there will be people who do not like this constitution, Dr. C?"

"There will be those who do not want it at all. There will be others who have questions about certain things that are in the constitution and some things that have been left out. This is a process, boys. It is why we believe that this country will be so different from most other countries in the world. The people have a part in deciding how it will be organized and then will have a voice in how it will be governed."

I could see that some of the students were trying to lead me away from the lesson so I cut off this discussion and returned to syntax, but in the next few weeks, I was surprised that many of the students were sincerely interested in this convention process and I thought it wise to keep them informed. So much did they appear to gain by our discussions that I decided to make discussion of events in the world part of our curriculum. That led me to including more history and political and government issues in my classes. Independence meant that my boys were going to become leaders in more fields than education and theology.

As the students were exposed to a wider scope of study, I was drawn further into the political development that was energizing a new nation. I couldn't blame my absorption on the students because I knew the night that we received that copy from Alexander, that I would seek to have my say. After supper, instead of going into my study I waited for Rachel to oversee the cleanup of the kitchen and we went in together to talk about the Constitution.

"Does it disturb you so much?" she asked sympathetically. She had read it once herself already.

"Disturbed is not quite my feeling. I guess I am not

comfortable with the result. I suppose it is like patriotism. I want to believe that there has never been anything better coming from the minds of men and that in this Constitution I can see the hand of God. But that is not what I feel. I can't find God in it. I don't feel that I can stand before my congregations and urge them that this is the course that God has intended for us. It is eloquent enough but it does not convey the comfort and reassurance that people struggling for survival can recognize. Lawyers may like it and merchants but it does not seem to me to be a document coming from, and finding relevance in, the people."

"You seem to have had a more specific image of what you expected than I thought," she began. "I found a great deal of reassurance in what Alexander presented as a summary of the document, and in my first reading I think his summary for us was very accurate. I share with you a disappointment that there is not more of an expression of rooting this government in the traditions of Christianity, but I have seen reason in what Alexander said. By leaving out such affirmations, we confirm that there is no union of church and state. I believe that it must never appear that the one has jurisdiction over the other."

"Would it have been so threatening to affirm God as the source of our free course to independence? Should we not have been more specific in saying that there will be no state religion? By saying nothing in our constitution, do we not invite the infidel into our midst? It is not satisfying.

"And look how it begins, Rachel. 'We the people of the United States...' This document is not the product of the people any more than it gives voice to their basic concerns. It is too disingenuous even in its presentation."

"I do not want to be the sounding board upon which you work up a contempt of this constitution," she said. "Think for yourself what you should do. It is a matter of earnest prayer. This is the work of wise and representative men. You have said so yourself. If the devil was in their midst, then you must offer yourself to be one of God's instruments to destroy it or make it right. Why don't we pray here a while?"

And so we did and my soul was eased. I was calmed. Certainly the devil had been at work, and was at any such human endeavor where men become enamored of their own importance and accept the temptation to grasp for their own will. God is not finished. This constitution is a noble effort. God will direct the hand of His people to make it more perfect. I was satisfied that my task was to make myself more available to the process. I didn't know what that meant beyond the fact that from the pulpits, I must be informative and help my people to feel secure in the events they were observing.

At the end of the year, the November Assembly took on the task of calling the meeting of the Ratification Convention which was to be held at Hillsborough on July 21, 1788. Alexander was again elected president of the Senate and he was the only member of the Constitutional Convention in the Senate; Davie and Spaight were elected to the Commons. Two weeks into the session, the Assembly met in joint conference and the Ratification Convention was considered. Negative attitudes were in the ascendency and the joint session decided this was to be the most democratic convention yet planned in the state. Anyone eligible to vote for the lower house of the Legislature (that meant all freemen, twenty-one years old, who had lived in the state for a year and paid taxes) were eligible to vote at the voting places in their county on the last Friday and Saturday of March. Each county would elect five delegates and any freeholder in the state was eligible. I considered this news was particularly good because it meant that to an extent as reasonable as possible, the people were going to be allowed to have a voice in this decision. I urged both congregations that they must plan to vote so that this was their choice.

To my astonishment, a delegation of freeholders, most of whom came from my two churches, waited on me and insisted that I must stand as a delegate. I reacted with sincere surprise because I had only fleetingly thought about this possibility. The broad qualifications for delegates had also made it possible for ministers of the Gospel to be elected to the convention.

William Wiley allowed that, "You have done more study and given more thought to this convention than any other man in North

Carolina. Yours is a voice which must be heard."

"That is a great complement, but remember that Alexander Martin was a delegate to the Philadelphia convention and he is the person most informed about this Constitution and he is your friend."

Wiley answered as if already prepared for my response. "We know and respect Governor Martin, but in this case, it is our feeling that he has had his say about the Constitution already and now we need to hear from others."

Eventually, I allowed myself to be placed in nomination along with Governor Martin and about a dozen others. The campaign that followed was like none ever had been before in public elections in the state. Speeches were being made on all occasions where there was a small gathering. The Assembly had arranged for 1500 copies of the Constitution to be printed and distributed widely.

By spring the campaign was so rowdy that I was sorry I had agreed to be nominated. Some places on some days were awash with liquor, and fear became the weapon of both those who favored the Constitution and those who did not. My students were exposed to the seamy side of public debate and it became harder every day for me to speak of God's hand in the actions of a responsible electorate. I did not make any speeches as others did, but then again, I continued to have a weekly pulpit where I tried to preach the truth and guide the faithful.

Alexander and I had one conversation during this period

meeting at Martinville during court week. "Are we to compete for votes, David?" he inquired with a wry smile.

"I hope not. Both our voices need to be heard on this topic. I am satisfied that your constitution will be ratified but I also hope we will influence a few changes that may improve upon the structure."

Alexander became serious. "This election has become too raucous. It is no platform for information and I have no idea what we will see for results. I hope we will have enough delegates elected with good will in their hearts to preform the serious task before them. I am afraid now that we may have such a destructive experience that civilian government will cease to be civil. People need to speak their minds but in the end they must reason responsibly and respectfully together."

"I hope you do not become too pessimistic, Alexander. I understand that you were very nearly elected Governor at the Assembly but they turned to that paragon of past deeds, Samuel Johnston."

"It is true and he is a very capable man, even if he does represent the entrenched power of the East. I do expect at some point to become a candidate again for Governor, but I am afraid that ratification may turn over every one's apple cart and politicians may be so maligned, that we will never again be allowed to serve. I really wish that I could just skip the whole thing. From a political standpoint, I might preserve better electability."

The election results could not have been anticipated by any one. Alexander was defeated and I was elected. More amazing still, the other four delegates of Guilford were all members of my congregations: John Anderson, Daniel Gillespie, William Gowdy, and John Hamilton. Guilford was to be represented by a Presbyterian minister and four of his flock. Had there ever been such a delegation?

Thirty framers of the Philadelphia Convention who had been nominated had been elected as delegates to the ratification conventions of their states. Only one, Alexander Martin, had not. Of the five North Carolina delegates to the Philadelphia convention, four were elected, all as in favor of the Constitution. Only Alexander Martin had not been elected. I could not rejoice because I could not see what good had come of all this. "Had Alexander's forebodings come to pass? Then I thought, is this what he wanted all along and had he been politician enough to make it happen? Who in my congregation, had succeeded in such a Machiavellian maneuver – electing five from the same church?"

The trip to Hillsborough was not hard and it was close enough that I could return home to preach each of the three Sundays covered by the Convention. It was natural that our 'Presbyterian' delegation for Guilford met at Alamance Church and rode east together. The delegates assembled in Hillsborough in what had been the Church of England on Tryon Street, half way up the hill from the Eno River. It was the 21st of July, a hot time of year to hold a convention but the site often had a good breeze up from the river.

"How do we approach our responsibility, William?" I posed to William Gowdy on the way. He had been a member of both houses of the state Legislature and I expected him to have better that average political astuteness.

"I think we should make as much noise as possible so that we can be heard on some of the issues that we feel are important," he responded.

"You sound like you spoil for a fight, William. I thought that we would look on this as an opportunity to give positive influence to the organization of this country," I said, surprised by his tone.

"You are about to see a powerful eastern majority at work. They will try to sweep this convention with the power of their political will. This time, they will be surprised. The opinion in North Carolina is against this Constitution and these larger delegations have seen many men elected who are not politicians. They are going to make the politicians work to have their way. I have only read reports of a few of the other state conventions but it seems to me they have been reflections of their state legislatures. They have, so far, all approved of ratification and only a few have questioned the lack of any declaration of citizen rights. I believe this convention is going to be a debate of the people about their concerns."

Daniel Gillespie was troubled by Gowdy's attitude. "I am not here to be a stumbling block. I want to see the people's will prevail but I do not want to create some internal battle between sections of the state or classes of people."

"I am afraid of this new central government," allowed John Hamilton. "The more that government can be centered in the state, the happier I will be, but I can recognize that if our country is going to be able to protect itself in war and in economics and compete with strong nations, we must have some centralized power."

John Anderson only added, "I don't understand what a president is going to be like."

We rode along for a while without further talk until we came to the top of a rise and from the shade of some very large trees, we looked across acres of meadow. "Could we stop here for a rest," I suggested. "And while we are at it, might we have a Presbyterian prayer as we approach our task?"

After dismounting and tethering our mounts, I gathered my friends in prayer and we all knelt beneath the trees. I prayed for our best selves. I declared that I knew that God was present and we knew that people had delegated a task to us and we represented them. But we also had to understand that we were God's instrument at this time. I talked about our ancestors who had fought and died for our covenants and for our creeds. I recalled what we had all seen on the battlefield around the courthouse a few short years before. I reminded them and myself that our actions would define the kind of world in which our children would raise their children. I kept them on their knees until their backs screamed for relief. It never hurts for the body to feel what the mind ponders. Then I pronounced a blessing on our work.

News on everyone's lips upon our arrival was that New Hampshire and Virginia had ratified and that made nine states that had approved the Constitution. That was enough to declare the Constitution adopted and the United States created. Only New York, North Carolina and Rhode Island were yet to be heard from and New York was to vote in five days. I met young Davie and asked him about his mother. Then I inquired, "William, what is your reading of the news? I see our purpose rather circumscribed now by the action of others."

He had an indulgent look on his face, a look I had seen him use before when speaking to children or servants. "I believe you're right. I left the convention early, but I was convinced that the work we had done was so thorough and well constructed that it would be impossible to defeat."

"You don't think we can make improvements?

"Of course we must let people be heard but I don't see significant improvement as indicated."

The pocket debates held throughout Hillsborough the night before the Convention was called into session centered on the direction of debate. Would we be stirring up a lot of wind in the heat of summer to no special purpose? The clear majority of delegates, however, were opposed to the Constitution. We were hearing ourselves referred to as anti-federalists because we were opposed to the federal structure as set out in the Constitution. There were no organizational meetings, no caucuses of political affiliation. There was a concentration of the anti-federalism represented from Rockingham, Surry, Mecklenburg, Rowan and our Guilford; and the most adroit among us were Willie Jones and Samuel Spencer. On the side favorable to the document, the debate was led by Davie and James Iredell.

At one point, James Gallaway, whom I had known for years, approached me and he said he had been in discussion with Willie Jones. Gallaway was a Scots merchant who had established an outpost of a Glasgow merchant house on the Dan River at the site of the old Sauratown Indian village. Before the war began, most of the Scots merchants in America were considered to be firm Tories and had been closed out of their trade with the non-export, non-import laws. Gallaway, with greater foresight than most, had become an active member of the Committee of Safety for Guilford County and proved himself to be a true friend of independence. Now he was a delegate from Rockingham County and a close lieutenant of Willie Jones. "Willie wants you to open the debate tomorrow against the constitution," said Gallaway. "It is our opinion that no single person at this convention holds more respect than you, and your words cannot be discounted out of hand as perversely political."

"James, I will take that as a compliment, knowing Scots to be cautious with their compliments. I must tell you I do not oppose this Constitution as a principle. I believe it will be the Constitution of the United States and that North Carolina will be one of those states in that union. I am disappointed in it and I would hope this convention would define and make proposals to improve upon it. With those qualifications, I will be glad to open the debate on behalf of those who have misgivings. I guess that will officially qualify me as an anti-federalist."

James seemed pleased. "It does. You are now officially to be categorized as 'in our camp.' I believe that within that group, the majority will accept this Constitution as the price we will pay to be part of this union of states. I think a more accurate interpretation of attitudes would be that we fear the excesses of a strong central government and seek to preserve the local powers of the state."

"Then I can be comfortable in that camp." We talked on about what we expected to transpire on the first day and who we thought might respond to my remarks. William R. Davie seemed the best guess and James knew of his relationship to me through my sister-in-law. "Perhaps," thought Gallaway, "that might soften the edge of his tongue."

Soon after debate was opened the next morning, Willie Jones rose and stunned all the observers by moving that the Constitution had been an item of debate for too long. Everyone here knew how they intended to vote and for the sake of economy, of cost to the state, we should have an immediate vote and be done with it. The assembly momentarily froze and Tom Person immediately seconded. The tactic placed the Federalists in the position of seeing the ratification rejected without debate and North Carolina placed as not just unsatisfied, but in opposition to the other states. The message would be unsettling and would leave the Union a chain with a missing link. It would mean the fulfilment of the British taunt since the Treaty of Paris, "the Americans will never agree on a single government."

With a calm, extemporaneous voice, James Iredell rose to point out the potentially very embarrassing impression that this action would communicate to our sister states who had fought at our side to rid ourselves of a king. With dispatch, Willie Jones had made his point, established the potential power the anti–Federalists had to shape the convention and so, with Person's acceptance, he withdrew his motion.

After some testy procedural questions, as the July heat rose gradually to possess the atmosphere, I was recognized to open debate. I had in my hand a copy of the North Carolina Constitution of 1775, and I raised it to remind the delegates that I was among those who had met in Halifax in the cold and foreboding winter of 1776 to create a government of the people. "We met in a spirit of compact. Those of you who know me know that I am a Presbyterian minister and that eleven years ago I spoke at length urging that we look to the covenants of the Scottish church as a form suited to such a document of government. I placed before that body an example of those covenants and urged they be studied as we proceeded. You see, a covenant supposes that reasonable persons with varying interests can sit before each other and exchange guarantees to protect those basic interests; then they can agree to a form of government comfortable to all, representing the interests of all."

Again I raised the example of the North Carolina Constitution. "Look at what was wrought. There is no fancy preamble, no words to rally support. The heading is 'A Declaration of Rights' and there follows twenty-five rights, interests, that were to be guaranteed in this document. Only then did this document speak of 'The Constitution, or Form of Government' with a patriotic preamble to remind us what we have been through together."

I laid down the North Carolina Constitution deliberately as if it were somehow a sacred text. Then with equal deliberation, I picked up the Philadelphia Constitution. "I have studied this proposed national Constitution which is designed to be the foundation for a federal union. Nowhere, nowhere, do I find a compact. Nowhere do I see the rights of the governed enumerated and thus nowhere protected." I paused and scanned the room. My congregation was hot. There was no breeze. Most jaws were rigid.

"I am satisfied that a plausible effort has been made to create balance in a representative government. I am not lawyer enough to

297

understand the efficacy of a supreme court. I do not know what a president is although I understand the value of a head of state. But nowhere do I find the comfort and reassurance of my rights, my personal rights, guaranteed. If I am to place my security in the hands of this government, is it enough to assume good faith and judgment?

"In my concern, I turn again to the preamble, the first words of this document and I read, 'We, the people.'" I repeated, deliberately, " 'we, the people.' There is a design, a twist to these words that gives me pause. By what right do representatives of the different states assume to sit as we, the people? They are representatives of state legislatures where they themselves have been elected by some of the people. That phrase, used as it has been in this document, is all we have been given to secure our concerns. My friends, it is not adequate."

As I sat, Davie rose and was recognized. He cleared his throat, as if announcing himself with a trumpet flourish. "My fellow delegates," he began. Then he cast himself in the roll of having been a molder of this proposed Constitution, and noted that all the state delegates had considered the states to be the rock on which this Constitution was constructed. The people found their security in the legislative branch where in the House of Representatives, the members were immediately elected by the people, and in the Senate, which represented the sovereignty of the states. By their choices, the people protected their rights and interests and by their equal representation, the states rights were protected. He spoke with much gravity in defense of this deliberative work. It began to sound like Philadelphia had been a modern-day Olympus. "We spoke for the people." It began to sound like "we are the people." His points were crafted with clarity but then delivered with a flaunting certainty. Bodies sweated and wilted into postures of surrender. All the vigor of expectation was rung from delegates and their energy shut down. Davie's style was one of such personal rectitude that there was no consciousness of the needs of others. That was no way to sway this body of listless deliberation.

Iredell seems to have been far more tactful. In the next days, the document was examined by section and paragraph. Iredell not only clearly interpreted the articles, he related them individually to the whole and pointed out particularly those concerning the rights of the states. It was clear that there would be a Bill of Rights proposed, and I assisted a small committee in drawing up such a list. It was not intended to be offered in motion, but circulated so that at the appropriate moment, when the bill was proposed, preliminary thought would already have considered the most fundamental rights that ought to be included.

The one other issue upon which I was determined to be heard was a clause more precisely defining this document as placed on the underpinning of the Christian faith and on our protection against the immigration into the United State of Jews and Pagans of every kind.

The expression of my concern was countered by my old Princeton friend Samuel Spencer, who was by the way, a fellow anti–Federalist. I pointed out that I had been responsible for the inclusion in the North Carolina State Constitution of the article that discouraged the access of Jews, Pagans, Moslems, and Deists from participation in the process of government, and I thought that should be carried over in some way to the Federal Constitution. Spencer's challenge to my issue was balanced and fair and I must admit, satisfied my concern, although I would still have preferred a stronger affirmation of the Christian faith. Samuel concluded that, "do you suppose that the people would chose men without regard to their character? The Gentleman is concerned that this article might let in the most vicious characters to office. I ask, what test could shield us from them? On the other hand such a prohibition might certainly exclude from office conscientious and truly religious persons who might serve well the cause of the people."

It was Spencer, who in another debate with Davie, provided for me the words organized in such a way that I could affirm them to my congregations as the character of this constitution. He said, "when individuals enter into society, they give up some rights to secure the rest. There are certain human rights that ought not to be given up, and which ought to in some manner be secured. With respect to these great essential rights, no latitude ought to be left. They are the most essential gifts of the great Creator, and therefore ought not to be destroyed, but ought to be secured. They ought to be secured to individuals in consideration of the other rights which they give up to support society." I copied down those words and afterwards told Spencer of my admiration and unity with his views.

On the 30th, after all the articles had been individually debated, it was Willie Jones who moved to have the previous question put so that he might introduce a resolution stipulating certain amendments to be added before adoption of the proposed document by the state. To support his proposal he asked to read a letter given to him by James Madison that had been received by Madison from Thomas Jefferson, in Paris, while Virginia was debating this constitution. In the letter, Jefferson said that he wished that nine states would adopt the constitution, not because it deserved ratification, but in order to preserve the union. But he wished that the other four states would reject it, that there might be the certainty of obtaining amendments.

More electoral maneuvers over the next couple of days led to the inevitable result. By a vote of 184 to 84, North Carolina decided to refuse to ratify the Philadelphia Constitution. This fell short of rejection but left the state outside the United States as a "sovereign" entity. Also contained in their action was wording similar to that which the anti-Federalists had failed to carry in Virginia. The refusal to approve was declared in effect until after a Declaration of Rights and amendments had been added to the document. Davie likened the action to "a beggarly bankrupt addressing an opulent company of merchants, and arrogantly telling them, 'I wish to be in copartnership with you, but the terms must be such as I please.'"

I must admit that I was pensive on the ride home. On the one hand I felt that we had acted honorably and that we had properly carried the issue of a Bill of Rights, which was as close as I was going to get to a covenant. In the process I had come to accept the basic Constitution and the form of government as worthy of the support of reasonable men, and without misgivings particularly to the question of civil rights, I could recommend it to the people of Buffalo and Alamance. My mood, however, reflected an anxiety in my inner spirit. I perceived that I had allowed my deepest personal prejudices to influence the role I had allowed myself to play at the Convention. As a man of the cloth, I had taken it upon myself to try to reveal the face of God in the actions of His people. I had let myself become the judge of who should be a citizen and who should be limited by civil law. I had decided my flock had to hear this from me, instead of declaring the decisions as God's will. Even if I were the instrument of God's purpose at this Convention, I could not sanctify my words to others. That could come only from God's revelation to them.

I had not been at home in the atmosphere of political debate. The give and take of debate laid upon the grid of individual self–interest did not wear well with me. Gowdy felt that he "had his say" and he seemed satisfied. The others had not participated directly in the debate but had observed the process as agreeable.

In three months' time, at the regular meeting of the Assembly,

Alex Martin was again chosen Speaker of the Senate. Nothing had changed and everything had changed. North Carolina and "the pigmy state" of Rhode Island, out of all the original colonies, stood outside of the United States. For all intents and purposes, it was an independent country. But to make sure no one assumed it as such, the legislature saw that all its actions paralleled those of the United States so it could not be interpreted as out of step. Most of the actions of the Legislature concerned local bills, except for the calling of another ratification convention with the purpose of getting on board the ship of state. Sentiment in North Carolina had rapidly gone over to the Federalist side. Realizing it had acted on principle and come up empty, popular opinion feared that it was risking exclusion from the promise of nationhood.

The arrangement agreed to by the Assembly was that a second convention should meet, concurrent with the next regular meeting of the Legislature, on November 2nd at Fayetteville. Once more, each county would elect five delegates at the same time they voted on their members of the Assembly. Martin was not elected to the Guilford delegation to the Convention, again made up of members of my congregations. I was most reluctant following my previous experience but convinced myself that I had a continuing responsibility.

Between this Assembly and the next, James Madison had proposed his own Bill of Rights, which the new Federal Congress approved in March. North Carolina's concerns had been made moot.

As if to send a further announcement of the demands of popular assembly, a month later, revolution broke out in France.

Where Hillsborough had opened my eyes to the dynamics of a political assembly, Fayetteville demonstrated for me the intensity of political organization. With Alex absent, the Senate elected William Caswell as its President. Three days later, Caswell had a stroke and died. Then the Assembly re-elected Samuel Johnston as Governor, and Charles Johnson to succeed Caswell. On the 16th, sufficient progress at organization having been accomplished by the Assembly, the Ratification Convention was convened. What might have been a perfunctory approval of the national Constitution as modified with a Bill of Rights, deteriorated into debate over more particular amendments to limit the power of the government. In the end, by a vote of 195 to 77, North Carolina approved the Constitution of the United States.

During that debate, I became aware that very active political "lobbying", as they called it, was anticipating further organizational debate in the Assembly. When it re-convened, Alex Martin's name was often being mentioned. At first, I could not follow why since he was not here. Then it became clear that political surrogates were here on his behalf.

A week after the convention ended, the legislature took up the issue of the election of the two Senators who would now be necessary to represent the state in the national government. The two houses put forth a list of eleven nominees, all but one of whom had been delegates to the Convention. The investiture of Johnston as Governor had been delayed, and as one among the nominees, he was elected to the Senate. Now there was an open Governor's office again. This time, among the nominees was Alexander Martin, and after a difficult and protracted campaign by his friends, he was elected. He was about to leave his home for a meeting with Rachel and me, when a delegation dispatched by the legislature waited upon him and from there conducted him back to Fayetteville for his investiture.

It was a few weeks before we saw him again and he could admit with greater candor the influence he had been able to exert on events. "I can assure you," he began, "that I chose my actions with an eye to preserving my reputation, as a man and with the electorate. As God is my witness, I was never false to any man. I decided, when I returned from Philadelphia that it would be almost impossible for me to be both committed to the Constitution that I had helped draw up, and to delay its ratification as Madison had suggested. After my meetings with you and others whose influence I found dependable, I began to wish that I could remove myself from the debate, at the same time knowing that I was bound to stand up for my actions. The people of Guilford solved my dilemma. They sent you instead. I knew there was no better advocate for the issue of a Bill of Rights than you, although I did not share your concerns about the religious test in the document. I was justified in my trust. You accomplished what very well might have proved my undoing.

"When the legislature met, I was an acceptable alternative of all sides when my name was placed in nomination for Governor. I was not even there. The action was carried by my friends. Having avoided the divisive debate, I had set no enemies against me. Except for old wounds, there were no complaints to be raised against me. It may seem to you that I have been duplicitous, but I tell you truly, I made a political decision that turned out to have been more astute than I had any right to expect."

I was still going through the process of evaluation of what I had just been told when Rachel responded. "Alex, you may have gained your success at the expense of some level of trust – a certain loss of simplicity. You have matured from our friend to our political friend. We can now see you in your roll of elected official working within the restraints of the law and the political process. I don't think I can ever again be as open with you in my inner self. I cannot say for David. I have no intention of being cruel."

"That does say it well for me but that does not restrict our friendship," I added. "The process of life is the aging of innocence. In this situation, I became a judge with a window on your world. I don't know that I would be comfortable if you were suddenly in a parallel position in mine. We understand each other as we project ourselves to be and friendship comes with feeling comfortable with that relationship. It is only God who knows us better than we know ourselves. Therefore I marvel at your skills. I am astonished at an insight into the mechanism of civil government. I think I can make better judgments as a citizen. I find I have no reason to fear that. I see it as my responsibility."

In the spring of 1791, North Carolina was entertaining the new President in his progress across the eastern part of the state. When I saw the Governor at the spring court in Martinville, he seemed pleased to tell me that Washington had suggested a meeting that would include a tour of the battleground in Guilford on his return north. He had heard of the President's interest from William Blount and he was making further inquiries. "He was entertained with handsome ceremony in old Tryon's Palace in New Bern at the start of his southern tour. Now he will be returning to Mount Vernon after a very arduous circuit. I assume his route will be through Charlotte and then Salisbury and then possibly to Salem. He has not ordinarily allowed himself to be entertained in individual homes during his tour, as he says he does not want to burden individual citizens with the maintenance of the President."

I said I was amused by such a reluctance given the examples of English kings and their historic 'progresses' across their island.

"Oh, I think you are correct. He certainly does not want to raise that specter," he allowed. "But there is wisdom in meeting physically with the people – letting them see that a President is one of them and not a king. I know first hand what a charismatic force this man is. There was a time when I would have followed him over a cliff if he had commanded. I sincerely believe that he has determined it to be his responsibility to create the single image of what a President should be. He will mold the office as noble and paternal and he will be the standard." Alex agreed to keep us informed of any plans developed for the President's visit.

In the summer, Rachel said she had noticed that our son, Edmund, was becoming combative. He was nine and had spent his life on the farm. At times he had participated in some of my class exercises, but because his attitude was that of indifference, he was a distraction. It was easier for me in the evening after supper to sit with him for a few hours and instruct him. He was good at memory tasks but was frustratingly unable to develop or comprehend the interaction of any thoughts. Thus, in Latin he could learn vocabulary rapidly and any rules of grammar. He was unable to convert such knowledge into any structure of composition or the translation of any idea. I found it sometimes infuriating as we would progress so effortlessly up to a particular stage of the lesson and then find nothing. If I did not know better, I would be certain that he was mocking me, testing my humor.

My son had his fall when he was almost seven and he lived with the open wound in his skull that seemed to close very slowly. Then, before the President's visit we noted the wound had sealed at last. That may have happened earlier but it was then that we first noticed it and we rejoiced that this unpleasantness might be over.

Rachel said that he had become very upset with the young

slave, Cecil, who had found him playing at the mill near the dam. When he warned Edmund that he could be caught in the wheel, our son had raised a rock and run after the boy through the yard until one of the older students caught him and restrained him. When Rachel got there he was in a fury, his eyes red with rage, almost incoherent. Only the hold of the older boy kept him from what she was certain would have been harm to the Negro or himself. She took him inside and literally had to ask the boy to restrain him for about an hour before she felt confident that she could manage him.

"What are we going to do, David?" she wondered.

"We will have to watch him day and night for a while until we are satisfied that this is only a passing spell."

That night we talked further and I suggested that this task of supervision was in reality the assignment of a jailer and it was too unpleasant a job to ask any of our children to take on. Having said that, I modified myself saying, "but until we know what is wrong and how restricted we have to be, it really only should be our children who can be expected to be firm enough and kind enough."

"John is the eldest at home, almost twenty-one, and certainly strong enough," said Rachael, "but I am afraid that he is just in the flower of his life and placing a burden on him now might make him despise his brother. Perhaps we should make it a task jointly of John and the twins. They are fourteen and both sturdy boys. If John could act as the senior in this case, perhaps he might see it as a responsibility and challenge. Tom and David will love the opportunity to boss

Edmund around, but we will have to work with them so as not to create more unpleasantness than we already have. Oh, David, it is not a welcome prospect but we have to see that Edmund has the care he needs. He is our unfortunate one."

Rachel and I were invited to dine with President Washington at the Governor's house in Martinville on June 2nd. The Governor had met the General the previous afternoon at the tavern in Salem where he had been staying. They had spent a pleasant evening in the town and a private time after dinner to review the events since they had last seen each other in Philadelphia. They rose at 4 o'clock and, rode east to reach the court house in time for the mid-day meal. They were greeted by a crowd of the curious, including most of my students, whom I had allowed to attend under the supervision of my sons, Samuel and Alexander. Both were home for the event. Of course my other children all went along and Rachel and I stayed with Edmund. The local greeting was very cordial, the attitude of the crowd being awe in the presence of the President and the great hero of the Revolution. Flags flew in abundance, including many locally made in imitation of the design of the new national flag. Several of the flags were relics that had been in use at the battle. Washington spoke briefly but made it clear that he wished to view the ground that made up the battlefield privately, as a general who had not been present. He asked those who had taken part in the battle to lift their hats and many did. Then he praised their struggle and sacrifice and that of the families who had been in the midst of the fighting. Then he said they had nothing to fear from the new Federal government because it had been created on their behalf to represent their wishes. "We who serve in this government serve your interests. It is up to you to see that we do!"

From the approach up the New Garden Road, Washington was shown the first, second and third lines of defense all the way to the court house. He followed the positioning of each unit, British and American. He easily observed where the dead had laid, by the mounds that were their graves. He walked the fence line along which the first militia units had been breached. He walked through the wooded area encompassing the second line. His party broke out of those woods on the edge of that amphitheater behind which stood Greene's seasoned regulars on the hill. He could imagine the vision of General Webster who had to advance against that sight in Cornwallis' absence. There was the position of the two forces in such close and crucial combat that Cornwallis had ordered his gunners to fire point blank into the mix. In addition to the Governor, the President's party included Captain Charles Caldwell, the commander of the light infantry unit that was escorting the President since he had come back into the state; Colonel James Martin, the Governor's brother and commander of the regional militia at the battle; the Governor's secretary and nephew, Thomas Rogers; and Thomas McQuiston, whose lands were part of the battle. Having already studied the battle with General Nathanael Greene before the general's death, the President was an authority on the strategy Greene applied.

Charles Caldwell was a young man who had not fought in the battle, but who heard it re-fought here ten years later by these heroes of the war. As they moved across the contour of this hallowed land, now returned to the farming uses to which it had originally been put, they were shadowed by locals in the distance behind trees. The President was not getting his lone view of the battlefield but people were respecting his need for space. The observers were mostly men and boys, who just wanted to be near the great general. It was a day that was retold for years by aging men who must have appeared to be the spirits of the frontiersmen and redcoats who had once fought there.

That evening at Alex's home, Rachel and I arrived to find the little village awash in people there to catch still another glimpse of the great man. His traveling carriage stood near the front door, along with Governor Martin's slightly smaller vehicle. We were greeted by a Negro man dressed in a black suit and many observers recognized us as we went in. The governor's house was far from pretentious but it was the largest at Martinville. It was log-framed with a large central rock wall anchored by the central chimney. We were greeted at the door by the Governor's mother, whom I already knew, and directed into the main room

On entry, we were introduced to President Washington and to Captain Caldwell, which created a rather confused situation since the President thought we must be related to the Captain. The other guests included Ruth Martin, the wife of Colonel James; Thomas and

Ann Henderson, the Governor's sister; Thomas Rogers, and Tom McQuiston and his wife. It was an intimate evening. Most of the guests were relations of the Governor. One of the early discussions worked out the relationship of Charles Caldwell to me as second cousins, he of the Cane Creek, Virginia branch of the family.

"Mister President," said Alex, "my very close friend, Dr. Caldwell here, was not in the battle. At the time, he had a price on his head and was spending nights under the stars hiding on creek banks."

Washington said, "I presume that as a Presbyterian minister, you were perceived by Cornwallis as a perfect instigator of rebellion, Doctor Caldwell. Did you suffer under the circumstances, Mrs. Caldwell?"

"Cornwallis took over our farm and kept me and my five little children in the smoke house for several nights. It was a minor price to pay but David's library, papers, and sermons were burned, which we did regret."

The President was especially solicitous of old Mrs. Martin. He observed that she was a revered matriarch and demanded attention. "Mrs. Martin, how were you affected by the fighting?"

"It is polite of you to be concerned, sir. I was at our home up on the Dan River. It is rather remote and Alexander had it built for us just as the war started so we could be out of the way of the fighting. In '81, I am afraid that in spite of my son's precautions, the fighting came very close. But Mr. President, are you aware that just months after the battle, Alexander became Governor for the first time when that rascal, Fanning, took Governor Burke prisoner?"

"Yes indeed, I am. At the time, the news came slowly and then was somewhat overshadowed in Virginia by the attempt of Tarleton to capture Governor Thomas Jefferson at Richmond. These were actions that showed desperation, but at the time, we feared a complete breakdown of civil government." Washington turned toward the Governor and raising a glass said, "Governor I want to praise you for what you accomplished under the most dismal of circumstances. It seemed to me that you were the government of North Carolina in your person, all other officials having been captured or otherwise occupied. The night before last at Salem, I heard those modest people praise your attempts to convene the state Assembly on two occasions at Salem. And the night Governor Burke walked into the room like a ghost, must have been unnerving."

"Startling certainly," replied Martin. "I must admit, I was never happier to see anyone in my life. I handed back control of the government like a hot pot of stew and that is about what it was at the time." There was a hearty laugh around.

Later in the conversation, it was the Governor who initiated comment about the events at Germantown that brought Martin's resignation from Washington's army. It was an awkward moment about an event I was sure several there knew in detail but had seldom heard discussed. Alex guided the conversation saying, "It is difficult to consider that it has been fifteen years since I served under you that terrible day at Germantown. The smoke and fog and the death of

Nash still haunt my dreams."

Washington remembered, "I learned that day never to expect victory until you control the field or the standard of your enemy. We were so familiar with that town. I finally had all the right men in the right positions of command. Then we had the fog and we were left to rely on sounds. The blind firing of some of my men on others was interpreted as the signal of the general assault, and we were firing on our own. That damnable house, a stone fort, with Yankee cannon-shot lobbed over from one side onto our men advancing on the other."

Alexander replied, as everyone was drawn in as a listener to the two, "The bloody chaos on the battlefield was followed by accusation and recrimination as I had never seen men heap on other men before. I survived only to be pilloried and I concluded I could not pay the price. When I arrived home, I thought my life had ended."

"He was," broke in Mrs. Martin, "a man drained of purpose. I feared he would surely die."

"War destroys men in many ways," said Washington as he turned with some intensity to speak face to face with the Governor. "You represent here today, an example of fortitude found in few men, who can be so tortured by the vagaries of conflict yet reclaim their capacity and redirect it into success. I salute your success and respect what you have accomplished in laying the ground for this state to take its productive place in the union." Alexander was so overwhelmed that I do not believe that he heard the applause. I could not help seeing in the words of the President, the personal redemption of my friend.

Conversation at the table was more convivial, allowing the women to blush at flatteries and the men to make overblown references to President Washington's guidance in the war as Commander-in-Chief. It was pronounced as only appropriate that he now be the Commander-in-Chief of the United States. Such praise was always followed by a formal toast about which the President grew visibly weary.

I thought it appropriate to encourage the President to express his feelings concerning his reconnoiter of the battlefield with Captain Caldwell. "I believe you had some of the local participants in our great battle to guide you over our sacred field this afternoon, Mr. President. Will you honor us with your impressions?" I had already been told that during the tour, at that moment in the role of "General" Washington, he had made several comments unfavorable to the deployment of militia by General Greene and I was perhaps baiting the great man. Our local militia had been much maligned by General Greene after the battle and it would assuage their feelings if Washington might somehow make their actions more legitimate. I was ready to help such comments along if they were not immediately forthcoming.

"Pastor Caldwell," began the President as if prepared for a similar question, "I am aware that a number of your congregants were part of the Guilford militia whom Greene tactically placed as his first line of defense. You may also be aware that I consider Greene to have been my friend and my most capable general. That said, I was frank today to express to Captain Caldwell, and those who accompanied me, that I believed I would take exception with the practice of using local militia in a front line disbursement while placing my more experienced line units in a third position. I know that Dan Morgan was successful with such a deployment at Cowpens and Greene had good reason to imitate that very recent success. Given the known unreliability of militia in general, no disparagement intended, I have always preferred to keep militia, and some cavalry, as a reserve to be used once the more experienced troops have established the character of the battle. The general and I simply had a tactical difference of opinion."

"I believe you know, Mr. President," began Governor Martin, "that my brother, Colonel James Martin, commanded the Guilford militia, and he had hoped for a much more tenacious stand by his men behind the rail fence. He has been much galled, however, by the implied blame that General Greene places on the somewhat predictable reaction of these citizen soldiers up against trained Europeans. It is a rather sensitive subject at our table at Danbury."

The President chuckled. "I can imagine, Governor, and I can imagine, Mrs. Martin, that it is difficult for you to see your son's command criticized."

"It is, Mr. President, but I have learned, as my sons are more deeply involved in military command and in politics, that criticism is part of the competition for advancement of both position and reputation in those professions."

"Adroitly observed, Madame. Neither are positions for the thin-skinned." Everyone chuckled, but the Governor wondered at the possibility of a concealed reference to his military service.

I had been reluctant to enter a debate of strategy, but since the President had acknowledged the involvement of members of Buffalo and Alamance in the militia, I took the chance that I might speak with acceptable deference. " I was not involved in the battle directly but I do have a closer knowledge than most of the character and the motivation of the men of the Guilford militia. Mr. President, they are somewhat better than subsistence farmers. Their roots, in most cases, go back to the tyranny of British persecution, political and religious, in Ireland and Scotland. In Pennsylvania, they had nurtured little regard for Quakers, which opinion has not been changed by the refusal of the Friends in Guilford to fight, leaving the burden largely upon them. They have also learned in Ireland and Scotland, and in a few generations in the colonies, to be suspicious of wealthy Americans whose abundance has been known to come often from speculation and exploitation.

"I have an idea that when those frontier sons of Ulster stood behind that 'passable poor' rail fence, and listened to a portly, Pawtucket Quaker, with his bright uniform and New England accent demand from them three firings and then an orderly retreat, there was more than a little resentment. When they saw the bright uniforms and billowing bright flags of the British within the hour marching toward them to the tune of bagpipes, many might have justifiably asked, 'who is this that wants us to get off three shots, and why?' Now, old Dan Morgan was one of them you understand, and I have no doubt that he knew how to ask at Cowpens and left no doubt that he understood the risk he was asking them to burden. I know it sounds like I am trying desperately to justify the actions of my neighbors, but I am certain these are no cowards and I know they hated the British with all the fury of any soldiers in your army.

"I am inclined to offer the opinion that I come to the same conclusion as you sir, that General Greene made a tactical error in the way he deployed the militia. He himself was unsuccessful in motivating untrained farm boys to absorb the initial charge of the largest, best trained professional army in the Colonies. That seems to me to have been a task beyond his skill."

The President had been more than tolerant in hearing my tirade and I blanched at my own prejudice in defense of my people. What I said though, I believed, based on conversations I had after the battle and since, as I have been able to talk with those militiamen.

"Your defense is certainly sincere, Pastor Caldwell, and I find much merit in the insight of your argument. Even the best General can find himself, in any given circumstance, unequal to the task of motivating men to perform with meritorious bravery. I will say of Greene, however, that no man I know planed campaigns with more deliberation, commanded in battle with greater tactical leadership, and suffered the hardships inflicted on his army by elements and the enemy with greater empathy, than did Nathanael Greene."

It was the Governor who rose immediately to toast, "to General Nathanael Greene!"

The dining room would have seemed particularly small to the President when compared with the banquet size of his own at Mount Vernon. Still, it accommodated us well. Prince, dressed in a fine yellow suit, was in charge of the staff which served with ease and a degree of precision that contradicted the frontier setting. The room was ablaze in candle light. Venison and wild turkey were featured.

At one point during the meal, the President became serious and asked the opinion of the public, in the west of the state, about the enactment of an excise tax on manufactured whiskey. He held up his glass. "You produce here a brandy of particular quality which has long been appreciated. As a Virginia planter, I know how we have made it a staple on our tables. My Treasury Secretary, Mr. Hamilton, advises me that even as a domestic product it must be taxed in order to generate the means to support the government in every one's interest. Now Hamilton is a money man and he does not always give balanced consideration to all aspects of a debatable issue. What say you, gentlemen?"

I knew Rachel chafed at the paternal structure with which the President qualified his question, aware she could have answered with equal insight. I picked it up quickly. "Mr. President, as a clergyman and doctor, I cannot praise unequivocally the value of whiskey in our population but I do know that for many of our poor farmers, it is the only product that they can produce, with which they can acquire their meager hard currency. If they are to be able to benefit economically in a free society, they must be able to depend on some method to capture capital. Cheap land becomes expensive, and unless we intend to always have an increasing wave of subsistence farmers scratching on the edge of our westward expansion, we have to allow them to acquire some capital."

"My word," said Washington. "Coming from a pastor and doctor. Are you, sir, also an economist?"

"In no way, I assure you, but I have seen generations in Pennsylvania, Virginia, and North Carolina, of the landless poor drawn by cheaper land. They scratch there way out of a position of fragile survival into a farmstead that is the platform upon which their children build a respectable plantation, capable of securing the families of their children. The price of our federal government cannot be the burden we place on the back of our poorest citizens."

Alexander commented, "You can see, Mr. President, why Dr. Caldwell is my most valued advisor and confidant."

"I think you make your point very graphically, Sir," he said to me. "I agree that we can press our frontier poor too far but we cannot tolerate a rebellion like you had here with the Regulators in advance of the Revolution. The Federal government must represent their interests fairly, but our citizens must also obey the law."

"That is what Governor Tryon said to me, Mr. President," I

ventured. Did I go too far? At least he had asked. Tryon had opened fire. The test of this centralized power of the new government might come sooner than we thought.

The President began his final stage of his southern tour the next day. The Governor had intended to escort him out of the state in style and had Captain Caldwell mount the Light Horse as a personal guard. Washington begged to have none of it. He was a citizen President, not king or prince. He had visited his people now in all the thirteen states and he was going home. He had shown them what a President was.

The ordination of our eldest son, Samuel Craighead, in February of 1792, was a satisfying event for our family. I had found him to be a good student and I think he had set his mind on being a minister even as a small child. He became a Licentiate of Orange Presbytery at nineteen and spent much of the time, before his ordination five years later, in the Mecklenburg area where the Craighead name was so highly regarded. His mentor was James Hall, a minister in Iredell County. Samuel was tall and well made. His expression was accommodating, but he was very determined in his beliefs. He would hear out any other argument but was rarely swayed and was very tenacious. I heard him say more than once among the family that he was the son of a learned preacher, and the grandson into the sixth generation, of influential preachers. He believed that many generations of Presbyterian blood should make him a reliable authority. In the family, we smiled at his certainty but we knew that if that carried over too much to his ministry, he would become overbearing to a congregation. He balanced those characteristics with a very pleasant manner that his people came to trust and love. While he was yet a Licentiate, he held a revival where upwards of 70 young people were admitted to the Lord's Table in a single day.

It was Rev. Hall who encouraged the congregation at Sugar Creek to call him as their minister and persuaded him to accept. When his grandfather, Alexander Craighead, led his entire congregation from Cub Creek in the Virginia valley away from the danger of Indian war parties in 1765 and settled them on the Rocky River in North Carolina, Sugaw Creek had been part of that colony. So Samuel was picking up the stream of the faith that his fiery grandfather had put down.

Within a year of Samuel's installation at Sugaw Creek, our second son, Alexander, was also ordained and called to preach at Rocky River and Poplar Tent in Mecklenburg. Rachel was gratified that her two sons had taken up the work of her father, whom they had not even known. God's hand was satisfyingly manifest. Of the two boys, Alexander was the scholar, one of the best students I ever taught. When he was in a class in Greek, he automatically thought in Greek. The same was true when we worked on Latin, to the extent that, he took on the attitude of a Roman or a Greek. He could sense the source of an idea which was being spoken about, while others in the class struggled only in the translation of words. He was not as self-assured as Samuel, although his manner was contagious as it drew converts. He could be called "handsome," although he never seemed to consider how he was perceived by others.

At the time of his ordination, Alexander had already been smitten by the charms of Sarah Davidson, the daughter of John Davidson, the master of the iron industry in that region of the state. They were married at "Rural Hill" considered the finest home yet constructed in North Carolina. Could it have been more glorious than to stand beside a minister son, gaze upon another minister son who was the groom next to a beautiful bride, surrounded by the most honored society of the area interspersed with your family and close friends, and to pronounce these two married? As parents, Rachel and I had certainly prayed and planned for our children to find fulfilling lives and supportive marriages, but was this not too good?

The reception table and tent laid out on the wide, perfectly groomed lawn at "Rural Hill" was trimmed in green and white bows connected with draping streamers – also green and white. It was June and the summer had not gripped the Piedmont. Tables covered in linen cloths were beset with food in pyramids. Barrels of the best local wine and brandy were offered freely in a slightly secluded grove of trees. Our children met their children and Craigheads socialized with Alexanders and Davidsons and Davies and Caldwells. There was no dancing and the 'blue stockings' among us cast dramatic frowns upon those who tasted wine or brandy. There was enough judgment, hypocrisy, and contradiction to freeze the moment but we did not dwell on the dichotomy. I find that people rarely do when they celebrate.

I don't remember precisely now at which meeting of Orange Presbytery I first was asked, "what think you of this 'Age of Reason'?." I remember I made no connection until they added, "you have surely heard of the writings of Tom Paine." The Tom Paine I remembered was the author of the pamphlet "Common Sense" that all of us read as a rational justification for our revolution in 1776. I soon began to perceive how pernicious was his "common sense." By the end of the very year he published his thoughts, I was urged to be satisfied with including, "all persons shall be at liberty to exercise their own mode of worship," as the only reference to religion in writing our North Carolina Constitution. I was concerned about this Trojan Horse that left the Almighty everywhere, and nowhere. I insisted on the inclusion of Articles XXXI and XXXII partly out of concern that the Protestant religion must be the spirit under which we are to be governed, and the suspicion that it was the intent of Deists and infidels to purge that very spirit.

Tom Paine would tell you that "the bravest achievements were always accomplished in the non-age of a nation," when the enemy of the people was across a sea. I came to understand in the South that when war finally came 'round, it was civil war, where honor and bravery and greed have no sides. In our victory, we had destroyed our alter-ego. There was little joy after the celebration. Our struggle was that we had to live with the brother we had tried to destroy – who had tried to destroy us. We were as suspicious of a new central government far removed as we had been of the offensive government, far removed, that we had been emboldened to throw off. And where indeed was the Almighty hand? That was the struggle, like lead weights, that I had to drag up the steps to every pulpit on Sunday.

Oh, I knew of Thomas Paine all right, and he was in Paris, party to a revolution that had swept out the government that had been partner to our independence. France, where liberty was due to come, "when the neck of the last king was strangled by the bowels of the last priest." France, where purging the state had to include tearing out the church and where the word of God had perished. As the head of King Louis had rolled, across America societies of Atheism sprang up in the French style.

For my son, Samuel, the Infidel Crisis, as it was characterized in Mecklenburg, threatened to take over his church and literally divide it. He was accused of being an enemy of truth and a hypocrite, a term used fluently to describe anyone who professed to be governed by the fixed principles of justice or honor. But he was defined by the openness with which he heard the accusers and calmly undercut their excesses, "like the sunshine and showers of April."

The extended continuity of my academy gave me a reputation as an influence on the establishment of the University of North Carolina. Often when we were together with Governor Martin, we speculated on the actions that would be necessary to begin such a school in the state. I think that he must have made it a rule to bring it up in conversation every time he was with a Princeton graduate who had taken up residence in the state – he believed in it so earnestly. Of course Davie considered himself the diviner of all things social and academic that would raise the standards of the state, but Martin and I were familiar with the raw potential that education might capture even among the poor farmers. We did not imagine an institution of class identification that would be producing a social elite. Just before his inauguration in 1790, we considered the subject again.

"Is it time," he asked, "to broach again the idea of a state university? I am surprised that no other state has yet been first, but I think that if it comes from me, a westerner representing those poor farmers instead of one of the Eastern merchants, it might gain broad enough support to get approval. The East will not be able to hold back support just because we suggested the university, and we could convince just enough of the western assemblymen to gain a majority."

"What can I do?" I responded eagerly. "I will canvas the Presbytery and our Princeton friends."

"We need to do all of that, but I think we really need to present the idea as a popular aspiration." He began testing his ideas. "Even our poorest farmers want a better future for their children. Those who push west will still have to deal first with the elements, the dangers of survival; but many now are ready to build on what they have been able to acquire. They want to end the cycle of moving each generation to survive on cheaper land. If our state is to prosper, we need to provide them with the prospect of opportunity where they have a place."

I was struck by that line of thought because I had been concerned of late. "I find the attitude of all young people to have a natural restlessness, but more and more I see older people who seem to be surrendering to their surroundings as the best they can get. I have wondered how we could inspire them to believe in their communities and to commit to the opportunities they can influence directly. Constant complaints become the platform to sit upon and do nothing. Believe me, I know that is the aspiration that brought many of our Scots-Irish to this frontier. 'Let me get away from people, and governments, and taxes and leave me alone,' is like a chant."

The Governor's efforts were critical to the creation of the university, but it was Davie who put forth the university bill. It was politic that neither party tried to take ownership of the legislation, although its critics did attack it as being elitist. The valuable gift of land by Benjamin Smith gave the bill substance and was parlayed politically into justification for the funding legislation introduced by a letter signed by Martin, not as Governor but as president of the board of trustees of the university.

No sooner had the university been voted, Old East constructed, the faculty put in place, and the first students entered, than the 'Infidel Issue' was raised by the first professor, Dr. David Ker. He was a Presbyterian minister from Fayetteville, born in Ireland and educated at Trinity College, Dublin. He was an exponent of Paine's Age of Reason and considered the love of virtue as nothing more than superstition. He held with Paine, that all religion was a contrivance designed to make captive the mind of man. He found the ministry of Jesus to contradict the history of Jesus as constructed by the Church. This form of Deism was well rooted before Joseph Caldwell was selected as the first President of the University. Another graduate of Princeton, but no relation to me, he found at his arrival that religion was "so little in vogue and in such a state of depression, that it affords no prospect sufficient to tempt people here to undertake its cause." He found that in the eastern part of the state, all it took to gain respectability was to renounce religion. Even William R. Davie, raised and educated under the learned tutelage of my late brother-in-law, Rev. Richardson, became known as a Deist – Davie the fashionable.

I found myself assailed all around. In the ministry, it was by Presbyterian clergy who considered themselves Deists or Universalists. When my encouragement of a state university, which would complement the training I had been providing for years in my academy, nurtured the disciples of the Age of Reason in the academic world, my classical academy was defined as a tool of deception where the continued study of ancient languages held back exposure to the study of science as the future of mankind.

At Buffalo and Alamance, I was never to face a frontal challenge from Deism as did my son, Samuel, at Rocky River. I admired Samuel's fortitude for his faith. He wasn't wrathful but stood firm like a rock. I held, as did he, that we were people of the Book, nurtured in our creeds, and true to the covenant we had instituted with God and man. My approach remained that of a teacher, in the pulpit and in the classroom. I taught the Book. At Buffalo I was used to defending the inspiration of the Bible against those who would make it tablets of stone. To do that, I always had to be proficient in my scholarship. I was repeatedly tested by those who would make the Bible theirs in ownership, and I preached to them that they must live the message the Bible offered. At Alamance, I was more likely to be called upon to find the conformation of God's purpose to their actions. They were not as inclined to turn inward to seek faith as they were inspired as a flame. It was Alamance where I would have feared more the threat of Deism that acknowledged God as creator and saw no need for structure or community. The advantage I had over the position that Samuel had to face, was that at both my churches, I had been their shepherd for so long – for most, all their lives. My churches could not conceive of a temptation to stray.

CHAPTER NINETEEN **1795** Philadelphia

Martha, our 'Patsy,' was naturally a special child in our eyes. She was our only girl in a house full of eight boys. Of course she was spoiled. In addition to her numerous brothers, she had several score of young male academy students – first to follow, then to pester, then to be pursued by. She was the match for the whole lot. She could routinely out-smart and out-perform any boy and make them know it. As a young girl, Patsy could appear coquettish, but she preferred the role of the scholar. Like all the children, she had a longish face and just the hint of dimples. Her eyes were green. Her nose was perfectly proportioned and her cheeks were fairly high and tinted with a natural blush. Her hair was the color of corn tassels. Like her mother, she bore herself with dignity even as a child. She was always very pretty.

Patsy was her mother's shadow, attentive to every task. She learned to be intensely proficient and would explode in irritation when her own work was not up to her standards. When she succeeded, she could hardly contain herself and she demanded to be recognized for her accomplishment. She could not attend my classical academy for boys but I trained her in the evening using standards equal to my other students. That training did not conflict with the attention I was giving to Edmund because I was teaching him on a much more restricted level.

As a youngster, we attributed her excessive reactions to her competitiveness with her brothers and the natural favors she always got as the girl. In her teens, we began to be concerned. Her first extravagant behavior of note was the day of President Washington's arrival at Martinville. As the crowd built and there was music and loud voices, she began to be agitated. She began to shout and jump around in a strange dance. Her face became flushed and her eyes seemed unfocused. She was with her brothers and just as they became concerned, probably embarrassed, the President arrived and everyone went into paroxysms of joy. They diverted their attention. When they next noticed, Patsy had collapsed into a crowd of observers as if she were drunk. The older brothers picked her up and rounded up the little ones and brought her straight home in the wagon. By the time they arrived, she was calmed and angry that they had taken her away from the celebration. She would not tell us what had happened as if she didn't really know. The boys had been so caught up in the excitement that we only got partial descriptions from them but we knew that it had been some kind of event, perhaps a seizure. Our fear was confirmed at Alexander's wedding.

Patsy and Sarah Davidson's two younger sisters, Margaret and Elizabeth, were to attend the bride. Patsy had been acting peculiarly before we left home to go to Mecklenburg and she appeared in deep melancholy all the way. The evening before the wedding, she could hardly sleep and the next day she was so agitated that Rachel had to dress her. Just before the ceremony, she began to make a soft hum and fortunately Rachel was near enough to come to her. She lapsed into catalepsy before the wedding party. I was out of sight with Alexander and was not told the reason for the delay. The wedding proceeded as Rachel cared for our daughter and only afterward did I get to examine Patsy as she was recovering her consciousness.

I suspected serious consequences from these incidents and wrote to my friend, Dr. Benjamin Rush, describing our experiences with Patsy. In the meantime, as young people will, thinking themselves indestructible, Patsy welcomed into her circle the attentive overtures of the Reverend Sam McAdoo. Sam had been one of my students and his family attended at Alamance. He was a licentiate of Orange Presbytery and considered an appropriate catch. For nearly a year Sam and Patsy carried on a rather structured courtship, almost always connected with some church function. Sam was tall and red-headed with a bright personality and intensity in the pulpit. Rachel and I confessed our mutual suspicion that there appeared not much passion in the relationship, but laughed that after all they had been raised as Presbyterians. We knew that the spells of melancholy that alternated with her interest in the courtship were an unhappy pretext to a marriage.

I had no sooner heard from Rush that he feared some sort of cataleptic condition, than all our attempts to discount the inevitable evaporated. Patsy had two days of deep gloom. She had no interest in any activity. She would sit by herself for long periods, then suddenly busy herself with insignificant matters. A napkin she was folding seemed to grow in importance and she could not make it respond to some fold or position. She began to tear at it and then make a sound that quickly built to a rage. She began to scream, and although Rachel went immediately to calm her, she thrashed at her mother. As I hurried to the room, I took Tom by the arm and pulled him along with me. The three of us were finally able to get Patsy into a chair where we could better control her. She raged steadily for at least twenty minutes before showing signs of calming. Finally, I was able, with a patient spoon, to get her to take some valerian, which seemed to calm her. Dr. Rush, in his letter, had suggested the use of mercury pills and bleeding depending on the severity of the incident. He had also said that in the hysterical female, such madness was often brought on by love, jealousy, or grief. Patsy had begun to plan her wedding, but again this did not seem to be an overly passionate courtship that might unbalance her judgment.

With the help of the other boys (not the students, because we did not want to start any kind of rumor that might be heard in the community) we were able to keep Patsy restrained. As the afternoon wore on, however, we needed to have relief and couldn't bring ourselves to tie her to the chair. So, following Rush's direction, I dosed her with two mercury pills, and after another hour, bled her to the limit of about two pints. I took another pint in the evening and during the night she seemed eased. The next day she suffered some mild salivation and soreness in her mouth and she had a complete evacuation of her bowels.

"Rachel, I am poorly prepared to care for her. I am called

Doctor, but you certainly know that my training comes from observation with only a few doctors, and what I have been able to consume from books. I have attended no medical school. I have no experience with this sort of situation. I could not appropriately care for such a case in another family, but I am particularly helpless in my own. I will feel such guilt if what I use to treat my daughter makes her worse or is even fatal. I am profoundly lost."

"You are profoundly concerned, as should be a father. I know you are using the best judgment available to you and there is no better judgment nearby."

"Do you think that the Quakers, or the Moravians at Salem, might be able to do something?"

"I would not rule it out but let us care for her here for now. She seems eased. Perhaps you should write Rush again and give him the specifics of this attack and see what he recommends."

The reply from Rush suggested that I bring Patsy to Philadelphia so that he might examine her and treat her there for a time. I could observe and prepare myself if she did require care for a longer period of her life. That prospect had been avoided in our household, but now it had been said, and Rachel and I began to consider such an alternative.

Alexander Martin came to our aid at this point. In 1793, completing his second limit of three one-year terms as Governor, he had been elected the junior Senator of North Carolina in the Federal Legislature. In October each year, he would be ride to Philadelphia for another session and in 1795 Patsy and I joined him in his carriage. It was a fortuitous arrangement for a trip which would have been difficult under any other circumstances.

Patsy had been familiar with Alexander all her life and he was extremely solicitous of her every need. It was a relief to me because he was willing to talk to her about many subjects, and when she was engaged in conversation, she was distracted from pain and from wanderings into the obscure. Alexander became adept at seeing the things that could upset her and his conversational diversions helped me. At the inns, where we sought accommodations in route, he would always see to her comfort before turning to his own. Prince too was a help and Patsy liked talking with him. At one point, she asked to ride up with Prince for part of the way. When we reached Philadelphia, we went directly to Rush's home, although it was the 6th of November, and Alexander was already late for the opening of the Senate session.

At first we stayed at the Rush's Philadelphia house and Patsy occupied the room that had been used by Rush's mother's. After about a week we moved out to their little country retreat called "Sydenham Hut," about two and a half miles outside the city, where we could be a little independent. On many days we would go into town. Patsy would stay at the house and I would accompany Rush on his visits with patients or go to the hospital where I followed him with interest. After he had been made consulting physician at the Pennsylvania Hospital, it became one of the most highly regarded sites in Philadelphia for visiting dignitaries.

Each day, he arrived at the hospital punctually and went immediately to the third floor where his medical students awaited him. He went first to the women's ward, which was large, very clean and lighted with tall windows. Black patients were found in the ward with whites. During his tour, a profound silence and decorum were maintained as he moved, stopping at each bedside, flanked by the attending physician. He reviewed the patient's progress and the regimen of medicines. In the more complicated cases, he addressed the young physicians, pointed out the nature of the case, the tendency he expected, and the treatment he had prescribed.

The men's ward was on the second floor and here he went through the same sequence except that he dropped the courtly manner he had observed with the female patients. With the men, he found many cases to be chronic and he imputed them to "drinking spirituous liquors," and frequently reminded them of their failings. Then we walked down to the basement where the lunatics were housed in cells. There was a long hall off of which doors opened onto the individual rooms. Each door had a hole through which food could be dispensed. The doors were heavily bolted. Opposite the door was a window with a large iron grate to prevent the breaking of the glass. Some of the patients had beds and some fresh straw. Some were fierce and raving, nearly naked; some were singing and dancing and others in despair; some were dumb, not opening their mouths while others talked incessantly. I was quite depressed by the surroundings except for the fact that everything was being done for these poor souls and it was remarkably neat and clean.

"My methods," he said later to me privately, "are the source of much public controversy among the medical professionals and the public in general. You know that many people still consider that insanity is God's way of punishing evildoers."

"Benjamin, you are asking that of a minister. I am afraid that in the countryside that is a majority opinion and I must admit the source is the weight of judgment that the church applies to their believers. I am a Presbyterian, where judgment is an important part of our message."

"I know," he replied, "and it is personally perturbing. I am an Episcopalian, estranged from my church for many reasons, and I have a Presbyterian education and my children are baptized in the Presbyterian Church. I have a deep and abiding faith in God, but as a man who deals with life and death, I am confounded by the church."

We had many such discussions that winter, which I think made us even closer in our relationship than we had been as students at Princeton. Our faith was being assailed and we wanted insight to defend it.

After Rush had finished at Princeton, he had attended the Edinburgh Medical School and came under the close influence of William Cullen, who had developed the theory that disease was caused by nervous excitement and its corresponding effect on bodily solids. He went on to the continent to study at Leyden under Boerhave who favored an all-embracing theory of disease wherein the body was a hydraulic mechanism full of pipes and pumps. In a healthy person, everything flowed freely, but if the pipes became clogged, the pumps would have to work harder to push the blood around the obstruction and that caused friction and heat or fever. His cure was to bleed his patients. Rush combined the two theories when he returned to practice in Philadelphia. Few doctors in America were trained as was Rush and few ventured into the theories of medicine. Most practiced a combination of folk medicine and used printed techniques they found in a book.

Rush held that blood letting was a universal cure for all ills, and after he became particularly interested in mental problems, that included insanity. He believed that a patient could stand to be bled of 6–8 pints of blood over several days and that the body would replace that blood supply in two days. This would have the effect of reducing hypertension. He added to that, chemical purges, which caused the patient to evacuate the toxins that led to disease. A doctor could purge the patient by vomiting, sweating, or diarrhea. "My favorite purge inducer," he told me over and over, "is calomel." It was a white, tasteless powder consisting of mercury chloride. A small dose could cause evacuation of the bowels.

In his work with the mentally ill, he came to stress both the physical and environmental basis of psychiatric disorders. He promoted what he called, "sympathetic listening," as a way of structuring treatment. He recommended that the doctor catch the patient's eye and "look him out of countenance." The doctor or caretaker should be dignified, never laugh at or with the patient, and meet them with respect. Be truthful, he suggested, and act kindly toward them in their presence. Coercion was necessary only when these approaches failed. It had long been observed that melancholy was often associated with intellectual achievement and creativity. He found Patsy's intellectual promise to be a typical characteristic of young people who suffered from extreme melancholy.

After observing her for two months, Rush recommended that she be trepanned, a process utilized since ancient times for relieving pressure on the brain. Rush had elicited some improvement with his other actions to relieve hypertension but felt that, for Patsy, trepanning might help. He emphasized that the relief from trepanning was often temporary, lasting only as long as the skull had not regrown over the opening. It would later occur to me that Edmund had been manageable for several years after the cracking of his skull, until the wound had finally healed.

I observed the operation on Patsy which involved the use of a hand drill that bore directly into the side of the skull. Patsy recovered rapidly and appeared to be very nearly as she had been before her spells. She took an interest in her own treatment and became a welcome guest in the Rush home, considering as she did, that Benjamin was her savior.

CHAPTER TWENTY **1795** Herman Husband and Farley Family

While she was recuperating, Rush, Alexander Martin, and I received information that an acquaintance of long ago, Herman Husband, had been seized by the government during the expedition associated with the Whiskey Rebellion in western Pennsylvania. What a peculiar turn of events! Martin and I had known Husband as a Sandy Creek Quaker who was one of the most effective spokesmen for the Regulators in '68. He wrote pamphlets that attempted to define their complaints against the colonial government. He was not a fighter. At the battle, he tried to gain a truce with Governor Tryon but when the firing began, he rode away. Tryon still considered him one of the instigators and he fled the state. His children remained in Randolph and on one occasion, his daughter came to me when she was sick and stayed several days.

When Senator Martin came to see me at Rush's home, he was able to provide more information about Husband since the Regulator time. "He became a voice west of the mountains in Pennsylvania for the small farmers, as he had been in North Carolina. It was his calling. I understand that at one point he had a vision of a New Jerusalem where he thought God was going to provide land and political democracy for the poor. He mapped out the heavenly city based on the Book of Ezekiel and tried to make peace with the Indians."

"I ran into him here in Philadelphia," said Rush, "when he was a state representative several years ago. Then I heard that he became something of a voice of the protesters in the Whiskey Rebellion."

"David, do you remember the conversation that we had at my house with President Washington, when he was on the last leg of his southern tour? "asked Martin. "He was concerned then about the issue as it was building against Hamilton and his excise tax on whiskey. I think that even then, he saw it as a potential rebellion against the new government."

"He was interested in the attitude on that issue on our frontier," I added.

"That's right," Martin agreed. "I think that the reference may have been made that night, about the similarity of the concern of the Regulators. The excise tax seemed another case of arousing the fears of poorer farmers when distant government threatened their meager means of producing income. We had no idea then that old Herman Husband was involved again. It does go to confirm the probability that distant governments always seem to lose tract of the problems of their marginal poor."

"The request came to me by letter from Husband," I said. "Somehow, he knew that I was in the city, staying with Rush. He was incarcerated in the prison at Walnut Street and wanted us to write letters attesting to his character and to ask you, Alexander, and Senator Bloodworth, to do the same. He said that his health was bad and he feared extended confinement."

"What do you remember about him? I think I must have

known him very little, because I am having trouble even placing his face," commented Alexander.

"I suspect you were in no position to recall much about him," I answered with a laugh. "He was one of the Regulators that pulled you and the other lawyers out of the court house in Hillsborough and whipped you." We all laughed.

"Oh, that bunch I remember as one collective face of anger. I guess I owe him something for my greedy attitude at that time."

"I always thought him headstrong and impetuous, but I believed him to be honest in his intentions although not always realistic in his aspirations."

At mid-week the three of us went to the Walnut Street Prison to meet with Herman Husband. His reaction to our arrival was that of a man who had received a revelation. He was overcome. It had been almost thirty years since I had seen him and I am sure I would have passed him on the street without recognition. He was gray and wan, waxen of skin and bereft of spirit. We talked amicably for some time about the times and the lives we had each lived since last meeting.

Then Husband turned purposefully to me and reminded me that we had attempted at Alamance to reconcile the Regulators and Governor Tryon and how helpless we had been in the face of intransigence on both sides. "You see me again, Brother Caldwell, the victim of my efforts to ameliorate."

"Herman, is that in truth the reason for your incarceration? Are you not charged with incitement rather than mitigation. I understand that it is yet again your pamphleteering that has brought you to this place," I said trying not to condemn but to base our conversation on a more pragmatic plane.

"You are correct, of course," he admitted. "I told you how I came to Somerset in western Pennsylvania some years after Alamance. I found again the same poor, desperately poor, people who were victimized by government. In Alamance we charged the British Governor and in Pennsylvania it was the government of a new, independent nation that spoke of equality and freedom of speech. Such proclamations I began to realize did not include the people with whom I was familiar. Most of them just struggled for survival. They longed to be part of this hopeful future but it was denied them seemingly at every turn. They came to me and I sought to speak for them. I opposed the Constitution because I believed that unless government was more locally focused, only the wealthy would prosper. I was crushed to see the final document and I admit that I saw it as re-empowering the forces of the Anti-Christ."

He turned toward Martin. "Alexander, you are a Senator and the Senate is not elected by the people. Are you not a House of Lords?"

Alexander was challenged but this time, unlike his guilty participation in the corruption that had ignited the Regulators, he found himself in greater agreement with Husband. "I do feel the Senate to be too aristocratic and have ever since the time of the Great Compromise. I was in Philadelphia as a delegate you know and I participated in the debate. Only compromise produced a document. The first thing I placed in motion on entering the Senate was to open the doors of that body to the public. I understand you on this particular point."

"I am fairly chastised, my friend, but the aristocracy of the Senate is only one of the fair examples of rule by privilege. It is taxation and the actions of the Hamiltonians that precipitated this so-called Whiskey Rebellion. Taxation is necessary to provide for the services of government, I understand that. At the same time taxation must be progressive. The poor must not be taxed more heavily than the rich. It must be an axiom.

"Because the western counties are so far removed from the trading markets, there is no way in which they can get their cultivated produce to market and so they produce only what they can consume. How can they produce something marketable that can be preserved in such a state as to be transported? Whiskey. It is their only means to produce cash with which to pay for their land before wealthy speculators move in a accumulate all the best. It is basic economics. I was elected to the Pennsylvania Assembly and I brought this debate to the legislature. I was discounted as a sympathizer with the French Revolution."

I wondered, "are you not yourself a well known speculator, Husband? You amassed thousands of acres of land on Sandy Creek when you were in North Carolina and it is my understanding that you have similarly been favored with thousands of acres in western

Pennsylvania."

"I have been successful but not at the expense of my neighbor. I sell favorably as often as I buy. I do not hoard. Must I be poor only in order to be sympathetic to the wronged?" he replied.

"I saw across the mountains, the possibility of a New Jerusalem," he continued. "God gave me a vision of his house created from a Confederation of States into a Federal Government as it was shown to Israel in the 43rd chapter of Ezekiel. It is there, gentlemen. And because God has spoken to me, I am called 'the Pennsylvania Madman.' Must I fear my calling to be a prophet? Is that what happens within a democratic government?

"I have not led a Whiskey Rebellion. It is a pejorative created to infer an association of drunken revelry. The tax on whiskey may be the catalyst but it is the justice of the system of taxation that has brought people into arms. Hamilton and Washington have raised the specter of fear to justify injustice.

"I am overwrought, I know," he confessed. Then after a moment, "I have never advocated armed rebellion, not on Sandy Creek, nor in Maryland, nor in Pennsylvania. I have used what talent I have with the written word to try to fairly frame the debate so that everyone could understand."

"Husband, you must realize that you can't be found holding the match and not be suspected of starting the fire," I told him. "Your written words are looked on by authority as the match. It may be unjust but surely it is understandable."

We agreed to write letters recommending his character and Martin intended to speak to Washington and to Hamilton on his behalf.

The three of us made plans to drive out, the following week, to "Farley," the new estate of Thomas Lee Shippen on the Trenton Road. Shippen was the son of Dr. William Shippen, a graduate of Princeton, like all of us. The son had married Betsy Farley, a granddaughter of William Byrd III of "Westover" and an heiress to the famous Sauratown Land, the 26,000 acres that once was part of Guilford County. I was briefly near the Sauratown just before the fight at Guilford Court House, when I was avoiding capture by Cornwallis.

We made the trip on a beautiful day in March that dangled before us the promise of the budding of spring. In spite of the fact that Drs. Shippen and Rush held a bitter grudge from the war, when Shippen commanded all of Washington's hospitals, and Rush made disparaging remarks about the general cleanliness of several bases. Professionally, however, Rush's reputation was held so high at this time around Philadelphia, particularly because of his work during typhoid epidemics, that Shippen, unable to treat his own son, had turned to Rush. Tommy Lee was handsome and tall which deceptively obscured his very poor health. He had returned from his studies in London, suffering from a debilitating combination of pulmonary consumption and painful hemorrhoids. This was Rush's day to make his regular call to bleed his patient.

We passed along a well–traveled road with which both Rush and Martin were familiar. They seemed to vie with each other in pointing out to me important locations and remarkable vistas. Rush took the opportunity to expound with two friends of varying backgrounds and professional experience, some of the deep concerns he had about the development of the country after the purging experience of revolution. "My earlier vision of a regeneration of American society brought on by the revolution, seems to me to have evaporated," he began. " I naively looked for a return to a past age of purity and piety."

I had a distinct feeling at that moment, that his words found deep and immediate harmony with concerns with which we were each wrestling. After all, we had come from the same Princeton background that had shaped our philosophical and theological opinions. Before that, Rush had been molded under Samuel Findley at Nottingham Academy, Martin under Francis Alison at New London Academy, and I under Smith at Pequa. We were the reflection of the "Log College" schools of the Presbyterians.

Rush continued to analyze the influences on our hopes for the revolution. "I had fervently seen the hand of God working toward the cause of Independence. It was a holy experiment designed to fashion an ideal society for all the world to see and emulate. Now I am surrounded by my Philadelphia neighbors who are unenthusiastic in their attitudes toward independence. I have been quoted correctly in believing that 'we have knocked up the substance of royalty, but now and then we worship the shadow'. Indeed, the other day I had much harmony with the more radical opinions of Herman Husband. The difference seemed to me to be only that he was so spiritually motivated. "

"In Philadelphia, I have observed much of what you see as a disappointment to your expectations," said Martin, "but I am here to represent a constituency that would see everything as alien. Rush, you expected an intellectual re-commitment to the free vision of the hand of God in Independence. Instead you believe you see an indifference to God that elevates self-interest in place of community. Our people, in North Carolina, have not the intellectual training to be able to think deeply about community. They have a visceral reality that always will bring them back to self-interest – me and mine. As a lawyer and by practice a politician, I must understand reality as it applies to government and mold some kind of accommodation, where they will tolerate government if it can be demonstrated that it serves them. They have simple possessions that they define as mine – my land, my family, and my crop, when it comes to government. Now where it comes to religion, there they have another set of possessions and David can speak for those. In the debate over the Constitution to govern this nation, I have been persuaded that it is important to structure the secular law separate from religion. Then the Church can define what the people see as mine in their communities. The purpose of the law in this case must be to keep inviolate the freedom of religious institutions. God is omnipotent and is present in all things. I believe we also see in the teachings of the New Testament, that the direction of Christ's message was to the hearts of the people and we must assume that from the people, He saw that the message could be taken to the leaders."

"You can imagine, Benjamin, that Alexander and I have debated many versions of this issue in recent years," I said, "before he attended the Constitutional Convention and in anticipation of my attendance at the state ratification conventions particularly. Even before that, I had been vocal, and I believe instrumental, in including in the Constitution of the state of North Carolina articles which forbade ministers from state elective offices. I further influenced the prohibition from office of anyone who denied the being of God, the truth of the Protestant religion, or the divine authority of the Old or New Testament. I had also helped mold an extensive 'Declaration of Rights' which, in my rationale, manifest a kind of covenant as was once drawn by the Presbyterian Church in Scotland. When Alexander came back from the Philadelphia convention without some sort of statement of rights for the people and no limits on non-believers, I felt he had been remiss. We debated long and hard and in that debate I believe that we came at least to appreciate each other's position. Now the news from France shines an even brighter light on the relationship between church and state."

"The two of you weave an interesting fabric in your debate and I am fascinated to hear your views set in an entirely different atmosphere from that which I see in this city," said Rush. "We may be removed far away physically from the revolution in France but it is a dramatic new illustration for this debate. During our years of passage from Colonial rule, it was the experience of the history of the church/state conflicts of England and Scotland that were ever present and that colored our Constitution. Now post-Constitution if you will, we have France to remind us of the wisdom of the separation of church and state. The French Revolution has swept away both in the frenzy of public violence unleashed.

"I too think that by the deliberate act of an inclusive guarantee of religious freedom," he continued, "and no other appropriation of religion into the constitution, we have made a more perfect document. It seems to me that we have then in this country, committed to the omnipotence of God and we have protected God's instrument, His church. Now tell me, David, speak for the church in this country. Is it prepared to carry the task of God's instrument?"

"Do you think that I would presume to speak for the church in America? No. I will use my own experience as citizen and minister, however, to show you where many individual ministers have been and where I think we may expect change. During what you have called with that benign euphemism, 'the passage from Colonial rule,' I found my pulpit called on to be many things. This may have been more a fact for Presbyterian ministers than some others, but I had to preach the gospel, justify rebellion against unresponsive authority, urge men to take up arms when other churches next door preached non-violence, and after all was over, I had to bind up the wounds and seek reconciliation. In the process, I was teacher to their children, even doctor to their bodies and spiritual advisor. Is it any wonder that I have difficulty separating church and state when it comes to government? In the course of this rebellion, all the lines that we used to think secure have been blurred. Now it is the task for men of good will to restore and then inspire. In the church just as in politics and government, the measure will be how we apply power. Some will see power as a ruler's goal. Others will see power as an instrument for public good. Some will see power as their calling and will seek to become gods."

We rolled on through the Pennsylvania countryside, crossed the Neshaminy Creek Toll Bridge, and up the knoll to Farley. We found Dr. Shippen already there. It seems that he was informed of the schedule of Dr. Rush's visits and made it a practice of being at Farley on those days. I wondered if it was professional jealousy or a concern for his son's treatment that prompted such supervision. Having been students together, Martin and Shippen had renewed their friendship since Alexander had been a Senator. I was introduced with amusement as a younger graduate, although I was the eldest of the four of us.

Elizabeth Shippen entered just as I had been introduced to her husband. She was recently a mother for the second time and literally bloomed with charm. She had large expressive eyes, a Grecian nose that set off a petite, pursed smile. I was captivated by her beauty and as she stood next to her young husband, my thought was of the promise of a national future of responsible families in secure surroundings such as these. At the moment, I found myself thinking of style which may not be the ordinary purview of a minister.

Tommy Lee made light of the purpose of our trip. "So today you bring another audience for your bleeding theater of the macabre, Dr. Rush. I dislike being the patient but I am gratified to have the company."

"I think with three doctors in attendance today, your room will be much like an auditorium," said Rush. "How have you been in the last fortnight? Have you been able to exercise at all?"

"Gentlemen, I declare my doctor to be a sadist. He prescribes daily horseback rides, of which I am at normal times very fond, to a man with a massive case of hemorrhoids. The treatment is so painful that I think his method is to divert the patient from the disease. I'm afraid my exercise has been limited to leisurely walks about the grounds with my recovering wife."

"Yes," responded Elizabeth, "it has been pleasant to be recovering together. Your suggestion, Dr. Rush, of the use of the flesh brush to bring down his frequent fevers has worked well."

It was decided that we would complete the bleed first and then enjoy a brandy as part of the recovery. The Governor remained with Elizabeth and we three doctors went up to Shippen's room for the bleeding. Rush had determined on Shippen losing six ounces of blood. I observed that they had each performed this process with frequency so the patient knew without direction the chair in which he was to sit, resting his arm and preparing for the lance. The vein was struck and Dr. Shippen held the bowl for the blood drain after which Rush used a wrap of bark to staunch the wound. We sat with the patient for about twenty minutes before he felt steady enough to proceed downstairs again to the library. Rush enquired about the dosage of opium Shippen needed at night and was told that he avoided opium because of the severe sweats he experienced. He preferred laudanum because he slept better.

Downstairs Dr. Shippen poured a brandy for each of us and we drank the patient's health. "I don't know if you are aware, Tommy, that Dr. Caldwell is a learned divine as well as the most accomplished educator in North Carolina. His congregations and academy are in the county immediately south of the county that includes your Sauratown lands."

Tommy perked up and inquired, "Are you sir perhaps familiar with that site?"

Elizabeth said quickly, "Oh yes, Tommy, the Governor has been telling me all about our fine guest and his academy. I am so impressed that you are providing on the frontier such a fine opportunity for good Christian education, Dr. Caldwell. Of course the log college schools of Pennsylvania have factored significantly in the development of the leadership in our state."

"Thank you, Elizabeth," I said. "You are kind but I hasten to say the Governor is too flattering in his description of our efforts.

They are quite modest in comparison with the rural schools around Philadelphia." I turned toward Tommy. "I am generally familiar with the Sauratown. Alexander has also told me something about it. I understand that you, Elizabeth, are an heiress through your parents, and through your Mother back to William Byrd, who first acquired such a grand plantation."

"Yes," she answered, "along with my three sisters, the land has come to us. Now my youngest sister has come of age and we are in the process of settling the estates of my late father and grandfather. Tommy has been looking after my interests."

"It has been an intriguing family adventure especially compounded by the second husband of Elizabeth's mother, a priest of the English church, who turned out to be such a rogue. Without any legal right, I am afraid he attempted to manage the estate to his own interests and the family has had to boot him out. Add to that, a half interest in that full acreage belongs to Elizabeth's cousins, one of whom lives in London and the other is a British General. You can imagine we have had the devil of a time keeping larcenist Whigs from confiscating the whole."

"How curious and convoluted has been the impact of our revolution on us all," pronounced Rush.

In June, two days before Patsy and I left Philadelphia with Alexander, we received word that Herman Husband had been released from jail and charges had been dismissed. The accompanying information was that two nights later in a Philadelphia hotel, with his wife beside him, he had died as the result of the effect of his imprisonment on his frail health.

CHAPTER TWENTY-ONE **1797–1799** Family in Disarray

Rachel agreed that Patsy's condition, added to the need to keep Edmund confined at all times, dictated that we needed a new house. We would be able to arrange the older house to the best accommodation of our two unfortunate children. A companion for Patsy could live with her and assist her varying stages of depression. We had hired Sue Collins, who had been orphaned as a young child and raised as a ward of a family at Alamance. She was unattractive but very intelligent, and she seemed to see her position caring for Patsy as a personally satisfying responsibility. She needed no larger aspiration.

Two slaves, one specifically purchased for the job, were assigned to Edmund, and they alternated staying with him at all times, locked in a room. Edmund was losing all ability to relate. He functioned in a world of his own construction – sometimes violent but more often indolent. On good days, he was a teenager physically and mentally. He took care of his own bodily functions and he knew his family and relations. Without warning, however, he could revert into a mental shell and have to be restrained, or he would drop into a sudden, deep melancholy for no visible reason. As much as possible we tried to have him with the family in normal routine but at the slightest sign of some kind of a seizure, Adam and Caleb would have to physically remove him to his room.

The new house would give us a world that was not always uncertain. The other children could have a greater degree of normalcy. The students would be more isolated from the antics that often frightened them and made them insecure. Some parents had expressed concerns about what their children might see. It was unkind, but I could not feel angry with a protective parent. In the church communities, the people of both Buffalo and Alamance treated Patsy and Edmund as their own. They were quick to excuse any outburst or peculiar actions. Patsy particularly seemed to thrive on the attention that she got from the church fellowship. She experienced among them the love that a congregation was capable of when they gave their love unconditionally.

We built the new house on the west side of the open space between the original house and the school, creating a more obvious courtyard with the three buildings. It was post and beam construction with two stories in the central block, a single story wing to one side for my office and library, and a wing on the other for a large kitchen. The kitchen entered into the dining room, and on the opposite side of the central hall was Rachel's parlor. Upstairs we had four bedrooms. Our bedroom was downstairs behind the dining room. We used local stone for the foundation and the chimneys and we had only a root cellar.

I took personal pride in applying my seldom–used skills as a carpenter to the finishing of the interior. Upstairs we used wide plank on the walls and overhead, and I made different mantel decorations for each room, simple but each unique. Downstairs I made all the wainscot, doors, and molding. In the parlor and my library, I made fine mantels and over-mantels that were indeed my masterpieces. The walls and ceiling were all plaster downstairs. I am certain there were those who gossiped about such a fine house for a minister's family, but I saw no reason I could not make use of my own skills for the pleasure of my own family. I must admit that my visit to the Shippen farm in Pennsylvania had inspired me to my shameful excesses.

The year of this building was also exciting for my students. They followed all the stages of construction, some with the intense interest that made one believe that they would surely apply this experience some time to their own lives, somewhere. Although we still referred to it as a classical school, I continued to modify the content of the curriculum to the evolving times. Alexander was generous in providing me with the most current government, and sometimes world, news and he would bring copies of popular pamphlets on political subjects. I taught largely from my personal library and rarely had books to use for general classroom exercises. In addition to some Greek and Roman classics, my students had access to Euclid's Elements of Mathematics and Martin's Natural Philosophy. I taught Moral Philosophy from a syllabus from a series of lectures by Dr. Witherspoon at Princeton.

When I thought that I recognized a particular spark of interest or aptitude in a student for a subject, I would make a specific assignment from something I might have in my library. I would work separately with the boy until I thought he had a thorough grasp of the topic and allow him to present it to the class and defend their questions. I remember Gabriel Moore, a youth from Stokes County who took an interest in the laws concerning the ownership of slaves in North Carolina. The issue was much talked about of late because of slave uprisings in the eastern Carribean islands. I had some material, and I believe that he found more through his father's family who were involved in politics. Gabriel was an impressive young man and I was pleased with his initiative. What made him memorable, however, was his captivating presence when he stood before the class making his presentation. He had complete command and his arguments were concise and sharp. I saw leadership qualities that I knew would earn him success. For a year before he went to the university, I used him as one of my assistants.

Archibald DeBow Murphey was another student from this period that I remember mostly from his voracious appetite for reading. I never could find enough for him. He was from Caswell County and came to us when he was about ten. In addition to his obvious ability to absorb knowledge, Archibald was inspired by this knowledge and could relate facts from multiple disciplines and ideas from different ages to produce illuminating conclusions. On the one hand, I saw it as a legal mind but I did not think that the structured limits of the law would be able to contain his aptitude. Ideas would leap over each other as he spoke and he listened intently to every new idea and analyzed it for content and rationality. I also kept him for a year as an assistant.

Students said of the academy that I made the scholars and Rachel the preachers. At first, that might seem peculiar, but I tried not to bring the pulpit into the classroom. If they wanted to hear me preach, they could come to church on Sunday. For them, I wanted to be the teacher. Of course my faith and my dependence upon the word of the Bible was never far from my mind and strongly influenced my philosophy. At their impressionable age, it was Rachel, whose application of the Christian life to her every day activities, struck a special cord. They were used to loving and concerned mothers, and for a few, she needed to be the substitute away from home for that attachment. For most, however, they came to appreciate that she was a Biblical scholar and teacher. They had no way of knowing that it was her roots in the Craighead family from which they were benefitting. She would sit under one of the large trees in the common area surrounded by half a dozen boys, telling stories from the Bible or explaining something of the history of the Presbyterian Church in Scotland or John Calvin in Geneva.

We traveled again to Mecklenburg County for a wedding when Samuel married Abigail Alexander, daughter of John McKnitt

Alexander. The Alexanders were another powerful Presbyterian family in Samuel's church at Hopewell. My son, along with James Wellis, minister at Providence Presbyterian and married to another of John McKnitt's daughters, were partners in their campaign against Deism and humanism in that part of the Synod. They became so dedicated to their efforts to return to religious orthodoxy that they saw danger in any deviation from creedal doctrine. They began to place pressure on local government to carry out the dictates of the church, which did not sit well with John McKnitt and his brother, Hezekiah, who were county magistrates and Elders – John at Hopewell and Hezekiah at Sugaw Creek. When those two churches decided to merge, the Elders drew up various rules of governance, most significant of which was a charge that no officer or minister of the church "intermeddle(sic) in the civil magistrate." In taking this specific stand in favor of the separation of church and state, they were rebuking the effort of Samuel and his friend, Wallis, to impose their orthodoxy on the community. Samuel learned his lesson and he and I frequently debated the subject. The controversy did not get in the way of romance for either minister. Samuel, as was his temperament, 'loved where he could not convince' and remained out of politics.

Patsy had attended the wedding with the rest of the family but the morning of the wedding, the groom had taken me aside to express his concerns about his brother, Alexander. There had been some disturbing reports that Alexander was having some problems at Rocky

River. His congregation was finding him increasingly melancholy, and in the pulpit, his previously inspiring preaching was becoming vague and wandering, leading to little purpose. He had begun to withdraw and given up all his responsibilities with the families of the church. I had kept a particular eye on Alexander during the wedding from my position as clergy and saw little of concern except that he seemed reluctant to make any conversation.

Later in the afternoon, I sat down with him myself and we had a satisfying exchange. He claimed that he and Sarah were very happy and that she was pregnant with their third child. He was not unhappy with his relationship with the church at Rocky River but they were rigid in their doctrine. Robert Archibald, who had preceded him as minister, had preached Universalism, which Alexander held as heretic and for which Archibald had been dismissed. His views remained, however, with some roots in the congregation. In matters of Psalmody in the church, there was a raging debate between those who favored the introduction of Watt's Psalms and hymns and those who didn't. He had tried to remain outside the conflict, but in doing so he seemed to have drawn the ire of both sides. I could sympathize but I saw that he was risking the loss of control over his charge. I reminded him that I had to minister over two vastly different congregations and that I believed each congregation had its own character, which had to be ministered to with different techniques. I suggested that he talk with his brother since they were physically so near but I could tell that held no interest for him. Having married into the Davidson and Alexander families, the boys had taken on the social and political alliances of the different families and that may have complicated a relationship which had never been particularly close when they were young. (That thought sounds so impersonal and I am saddened as I consider it.)

When we arrived home the next day, I took Rachel aside and gave her a synopsis of the meeting I had with Alexander and the concerns about which Samuel had spoken to me. She admitted that Alexander had seemed strange to her and she thought that Sarah had been depressed. "I jump now every time someone uses the word 'melancholy' but surely Alexander is so responsible, and he has such an intense conviction in his calling, that melancholy cannot apply to him. You don't think that he could be afflicted in any way?"

There. The words were coming out. It was inevitable. "I will tell you, Rachel, that I was disturbed by our conversation. The problems he mentioned were expressed with frustration, not with any hope that they could be overcome. On the contrary, he seemed to almost admit that instead he was being overcome – almost resigned to it as fact. I believe after my months with Rush and around Patsy, I can see when she is slipping into one of her spells and I think I can see it in others. I do not want to alarm you unduly but we have always shared openly our concerns and you should know mine particularly on this subject."

"We are so far away. I wish that we could have him over one evening and sit down together to hear him out, but that is impossible. I fret that Samuel cannot assert himself more positively. We must go to him, David."

We agreed that in the middle of the third week, we would travel back to Mecklenburg.

The letter arrived from Samuel the following Tuesday.

Dear Parents,

I write you as the swiftest way to get you this news. Last night, Alexander attempted to stab his wife, Sarah, while in some kind of manic rage. Fortunately the children were with their nurse and Sarah was able to escape to the neighbors by barring Alexander in a room where he cut himself badly about his body. Sarah was only lightly cut and there is no danger to her baby but she is terrified. Her parents have taken her and Alexander is incarcerated locally.

It is said that on Sunday he suddenly began to rant during his sermon about the presence of the devil in all he saw around him. Several people left in anger before he had to be subdued. People are said to have wept to see him in such a state and his Session had planned for a meeting on Wednesday to discuss the problems with him. I hear that he had been quite calm by the time he returned home on Sunday but he had not slept and seemed extremely agitated by morning.

I am disappointed that no one came for me immediately but am told he screamed when they suggested that to him. I don't know why he should be so set against me. I will of course work with his congregation and with the authorities here in Mecklenburg. It is too early to tell what will be done. If you decide to come now, send word ahead so that you can be met. I think that we would know more next week about what options will need to be discussed.

Your devoted son, Samuel

Rachel had opened the letter and must have swooned. One of the twins had run to the school and called me out of class. I tended to Rachel until she had recovered her composure before I realized the cause of her distress. My hand began to shake uncontrollably as I read the letter, and by the time I sank into my chair, the children were in the room, petrified.

We had to tell them what we knew and they each drew their own relationship to the events. For the youngest, it was, "will he die?" For the older ones, there was the concern that something similar was going to happen to them. They temporarily blocked that thought by pledging to take care of things if we had to go to Mecklenburg. Patsy became very quiet and that night she had one of her more severe spells of withdrawal, which clarified our course of action. It would take several days before we could arrange matters here to be away, so we decided to go on Monday and stay the week, or until we felt matters were sorted properly.

Each night Rachel and I gathered the children for a special time of prayer, which seemed to calm their concerns and focus them more securely. Later, we would discuss things ourselves and always end praying together over details of our concerns, asking for God's presence. What I now knew, gave me a more realistic and structured way to anticipate what we faced. He was our child and there was his family, and we might be facing a life for him in restraint.

The atmosphere in Mecklenburg seemed guarded but never

hostile. We stayed with Samuel and Abigail in their manse. It seemed to both of us a terrible emotional burden to place on their new marriage but they insisted that it was because this was a family tragedy, that we must stay with them. Samuel took us immediately to the jail where Alexander was confined by himself. When I approached the cell, I was startled to see that he was restrained in shackles. He was still heavily bandaged and I did an examination of his wounds and was satisfied he was getting sufficient care for those. He was, however, in a deep melancholy and he had no attention for that from anyone. Having attempted to do harm to himself once, I thought it very likely he would try to do it again. Because we were to be with him, I prevailed on the attendant that he be released from his shackles. He seemed to be only distantly aware that we were present. He took no notice of Samuel but did seem to respond particularly to Rachel. When asked, he would answer some questions but carried on a continuous dialogue with himself on religious subjects as if he were working out some theme for a text. He showed particular emotion when an idea seemed to stick or not be quite clear to him. He might raise his voice or shake a balled fist. A few times while we were there, he would shout in anger, not at us or even himself, but at something.

After half an hour, we were preparing to leave when at no apparent pretext, he suddenly bolted from the chair and ran against the wall almost head first. We all jumped up. The guard was out of the cell. Samuel and I placed ourselves between Alexander and Rachel, who seemed determined to go to him immediately. Samuel reached out to try to calm him and he and I got him seated again. "They are determined to call out the devil!" he screamed.

I put my hand on him. "Who do you mean, Alexander?"

"All those with devil tongues. And Sarah, Sarah tells them."

"You don't mean your Sarah?" I asked.

"She takes my papers and I cannot write with the noise," he cried.

This kind of nonsense went on for a while. The guards came in but I asked them to stand at the side and let us try to calm him. I did not know what extremes he was really capable of but it was clear that this was how he must have become at home with Sarah. His anger and despair would come in waves. The only name he would sometimes mention was Sarah's. He never seemed to remember the children, as if they were not present in his mind pictures. As long as we kept a hand on him, he sat like he did not want to hurt himself or others, and in that he needed only minimal discouragement. I suggested that our presence now seemed to be prolonging this outburst and we decided we should leave together and explained that to Alexander. The jailer replaced the shackles and Alexander did not say another word in our leaving.

We talked to the sheriff and the jailer. To the latter, we gave some money asking that he provide any particular needs that Alexander might have. The sheriff assured us that he would keep

Alexander away from the regular prisoners and he would continue to be seen by a doctor. Since he had been asking for more books and paper, the sheriff agreed to allow us to provide those. Rachel cried during the whole of our trip back to the manse. Our evening was spent as if someone had died.

By arrangement, we went the next evening over to the Davidson home to see Sarah and the children. The Davidson home, "Rural Hill" was an impressive structure, a bit foreboding considering the circumstances. It was well lit in anticipation of our visit and we were greeted courteously by Violet Davidson and taken into the parlor. After a greeting, John Davidson excused himself saying to me that he would appreciate some private moments with me in his library when we had concluded our visit with Sarah and his wife. With that, we understood that we would not see Sarah alone and any unpleasantries would be dealt with privately by the men.

"Sarah, I must say to you," began Rachel, "that we have prayed constantly for you and the children. What has happened is in no way your fault. Of this, we are certain. None of us can know God's plan but we must be confident that he brings us together for good. We must think first of those who cannot help themselves, the children, and then for the wronged and finally for the unfortunate afflicted."

"I will care for my children," responded Sarah with certainty and a touch of pride.

"That is as it should be," I said.

She continued. "I never did anything deliberately to harm Alexander. I loved him deeply and never thought in any other terms than to spend our lives together in the work of the Lord. At first, we had a very happy life, and when little David came, it was the fulfillment of our dearest wish. I was so proud of Alexander in his ministry. People told me he was the finest preacher they had ever heard. They loved him. We knew that there had been trouble with Reverend Archibald but it appeared that those problems had left with him. Then Alexander began to tell me of comments that he heard, that he took to be critical. They seemed unimportant to me and I told him so.

Then he began to connect what he saw as patterns of criticism. He spent more and more time in his study where he would prepare increasingly involved strategies for dealing with his issues. Everything that he produced was visibly more circuitous, more rambling. He could not seem to find a good end for his sermons. In that process, he began to neglect the baby and be ever more distant with me. I was reluctant to complain because the slightest adversity was held as against his person. He took very little interest when I became pregnant with Patsy. I was despondent because I felt abandoned."

"Well we certainly did all we could to help," said Violet Davidson in some need to make a point of justification.

"I wish we could have been nearer," said Rachel, "but I am

sure you wanted no more intervention."

"Yes, it was our marriage and I thought for some time we were just having normal problems of adjustment," said Sarah. "I knew Alexander had great responsibility and I wished to give him a secure home life."

"Tell us about the last few weeks, Sarah," I asked so we might deal better with some of the decisions we needed to make now.

Sarah changed her position in the chair so as to more directly face me. "When I told Alexander about a month ago that we were going to have a third child, he had no reaction at all. I thought that extremely strange. In the next several days, I noticed that he never mentioned it nor did he tell anyone about it. He seemed not to have heard my announcement. I was very hurt. Then a week later, he seemed one day to have stayed in his library a very long time in the morning. I knocked and went in to find him staring fixedly at some papers. He did not look up or respond when I spoke to him. I went to the window to push back a curtain and made a little noise and he sprang up with a start and cursed me for my intrusion. Then he began speaking in a loud voice about 'pestilence' and what he was saying had no relevance, as if I was not the person in the room. I was frightened and left the room quickly but then I felt such deep remorse. That night I tried to speak quietly with him. Again and again he seemed to relapse into some kind of misdirected rage. I told my parents my fears and father confronted Alexander who listened without comment. Of course Daddy thought he had straightened everything out.

"At Samuel's wedding, I think you must have seen how distant he was, how he avoided people, even family and those from his own congregation. He left the wedding by himself and walked home and I asked friends to take me home. From that day on I can say that he never again seemed normal, never present when he was in the room, talking to himself. It frightened Little David and I kept the boy away from him when I could. That was the way it was up to last Tuesday following supper.

"Ruth had taken the children to their room to play quietly before she began preparing them for bed. Alexander went to their room, I thought to say good night, but he began to yell at the nurse because the children were not ready for bed. They cowered and she was clutching them like a great protective hen. I came in and asked him why he was so upset. We had just spoken about the order in which they were being prepared for bed and he should not speak to Ruth like that. When he turned to me his face was in a fury I have never seen. His eyes seemed like milk. I feared he was possessed and ran to my room with him close behind. I have no idea when he got it, but when he threw open the door, I saw he had a knife. I was on the far side of the bed and I knew I had to get out of the door which was behind him. I spoke calmly and quietly as he began to come around the bed to my right. When he was at the foot, I tried to jump across the bed to the door and he leaped after me swinging the knife.

It caught my dress on my right side and slashed down through cutting me across my waist and buttock but I was able to get out the door and lock him in the room. Nurse Ruth had heard the commotion and had the good sense to sweep up the children and take them to the neighbors who sent for my parents. I stayed in the house and Alexander did not seem to struggle very much to get out of the room. I think he could have easily. He began making strange sounds, half groans, some cries, then some screams of rage. I believe at that time he began stabbing himself. By the time my father came and opened the door, Alexander was unconscious on the floor and badly cut."

She concluded as if exhausted in reliving the scene. We all took a breath of disbelief, not in what she said but in the appreciation that it had happened. Rachel reached over softly and clasped her hand.

The ladies took tea and I went in to speak with John Davidson. He was about six years younger than I, the product of a similar background. As a Presbyterian Elder he was prepared to show me appropriate respect. As a father, he was going to defend the interests of his daughter in all things. I accepted all that as fully reasonable. "Let me acknowledge to you, Brother Davidson, that I know my son to be afflicted. Because of the health of my daughter, I have spent much of the last year in Philadelphia with medical friends, particularly Dr. Benjamin Rush. I have studied the identification and treatment of afflictions of the mind. It is premature to determine the category of

Alexander's illness but he will have to be treated. He is not a criminal."

"I do not consider him to be a criminal, but he did attempt to murder my daughter and I must protect her security and that of her children, born and unborn. I hope you know that as well."

"I agree completely. At this time, he must be considered a risk to his family, and as a matter of fact, to himself. I have said as much to the sheriff and I understand that he must be charged under the law and the courts will make a decision as to what will be his future." With this, I think we had finished our opening statements agreeing to the stipulations.

I went on. "If the court rules that Alexander's action was that of an insane man, I would suppose that they would propose immediate treatment. Under the circumstances, I would hope that since I am a doctor and minister, they would agree to place him in my care. I am sure the court would restrain him from any contact with Sarah or the children. I would consider it to be entirely up to her if she ever wants to initiate any contact. As regretful as it is, we would not contest any actionable divorce, although I would hope she would not be precipitous about that, again because of the children."

"She should be able to decide what is precipitous," he said firmly.

"If the court sees fit, we would be able to take Alexander and give him supervised quarters and medical care. There is no way to know if he will ever be able to resume any degree of normalcy in his life. Few who are similarly afflicted do, I am sad to say."

"I do not blame you, Preacher, but I must ask if you ever had any premonition that this might happen to your son?"

"I understand the implication of your question, Davidson. In retrospect, both Rachel and I have asked the same of ourselves. We have another son, who had a broken skull when a child, who is mentally deficient now as a result. Our daughter, Patsy, whom you know, is afflicted since she reached maturity with spells of deep melancholy, for which she has been trepanned and for which she is regularly treated. She functions in a restricted context as a full member of the family. I suppose that we could have pessimistically feared that others of our family might have similar problems, but on the contrary, they all seemed bright and outgoing. You have seen that for yourself."

During the week, we continued to visit Alexander and made other arrangements with Samuel to act in his behalf in relation to the court. Sarah was very sympathetic but also terrorized, and the prospects of harm to her children made her cautious of any talk of release for her husband.

When we returned home, we made preparatory arrangements to quarter Alexander in the old house so that our patients could have some coordinated care from nurses and slave attendants. In October, a jury in Mecklenburg court found Alexander to be in a state of lunacy. Samuel, and Abigail Alexander's brother, Alexander Bean, posted the £500 bond for his release. In order to allow him to be removed from Mecklenburg County, his brothers, John and David, along with Alexander's father-in-law, John H. Davidson, put up an additional £2500 bond as his guardians. The first of November we brought Alexander home where he spent the rest of his life.

Patsy was significantly improved by her first visit to Dr. Rush. That was a particular blessing when Alexander's crisis took over much of our attention. She was also on a regimen of weekly bleeding and doses of Rush's so-called 'Blue Pills.' His mixture was Colocynth Extract, Mercurous Chloride, Jalap Resin in a fine powder, and Gamborge, all diluted with alcohol. With his recipe, I was able to make these pills and they were a standard of my practice.

Edmund, and then Alexander, were similarly dosed and bled. I varied my application of both procedures attempting to find more tolerable levels of reaction. I am inclined to think that Rush was too quick to bleed and too excessive in the amount of blood he extracted at any one time. That is a debate I need not bring up with him as he faces bitter critics in Pennsylvania and must defend his thesis constantly.

As to the use of the Blue Pill, it is unpleasant particularly for Patsy and I believe initiates some of her more violent spells of depression. At various times and to mixed degree, she has suffered from excessive salivation, sore gums, loosened teeth, irritation of her skin, and alarmingly discolored stools. Rush has insisted that this was the action of the mercury which he believed was "extracting morbid excrement from the brain to the mouth," removing what he called a visceral obstruction, or shifting the pains she felt wholly to the discomfort in her mouth. He considered all of that as acceptable results. I took issue when he added that the salivation was most effective when it elicited some degree of resentment against the patient's physician and friends. My rebuttal was that here, he was abusing their senses. I do not wish to have my daughter's bitterness directed against me in order to assist her to deal with her illness. Instead, I am more inclined to delay my prescription of the pills until the symptoms are well advanced. As a result, I believe she and Alexander learned to tolerate, and perhaps even mentally ameliorate, constipation, headaches, or weariness in order to avoid the pills. Of course Edmund had no ability to entertain such reasoning so I had to give him the pills on a schedule.

I agree with Rush's, shall we say, psychological approach to his use of mercury and bleeding as cleansers. More than once, he has illustrated his theory as similar to placing a hand–full of shot in a bottle that is lined with filth and dirt, in order to clean it. He sees the mercury as shot conveying morbid action out of the body by the mouth, thus restoring the mind to its natural attitude in the brain. I will not dispute that hypothesis. I do believe that our knowledge is not complete and we may actually be seeing some counter action that may prove ultimately harmful to the patient.

This is an unpleasant topic within the family, always overwhelmed by the grief of the afflictions of our own children and siblings. Lurking in each one of us, constantly, is the dread that we are somehow at fault or may ourselves face a similar affliction in the future. To outsiders we would surely be pitied were they to see us roar with laughter, with only our immediate family present, when Edmund, with perfect innocence, passes an explosive thunderclap–his reaction to the pills others nicknamed, 'Rush's Thunderbolts.' Of course, Patsy and Alexander were similarly victims of the Thunderbolts. Patsy would attempt to hide hers in the closing of a door or by rushing from the room. Alexander approached his embarrassment with complete concentration, never looking up or stumbling in a recitation.

It was Rachel who sank first into the despair of guilt when her only daughter became ill. She had grieved for Edmund when he was injured, but not long after Patsy showed her first serious sign of melancholia, she confessed to me a special concern.

"David, I may be the cause."

"The cause? Of what?" I asked, startled by her words.

"It will serve no one if we do not truly examine the possibility. I will say that it is a burden I cannot carry without your help, so please, let us not hide or ignore it. 'Melancholy,' is the word that everyone uses freely in the controversies of both my father and grandfather. Grandfather Thomas Craighead refused to give his wife communion after they became estranged. He never spoke to his sons, and his church removed him three years before his death. Look at my father, removed from his church in Pennsylvania because he held such views that could not be tolerated. My sister, Nancy, we know was surely innocent of the charges that she had murdered William. But she was charged and put through that terrible graveyard trial. Three years ago, we heard that my cousin, Rev. John Craighead, had to be removed from his church because of his grievous melancholy. They are mine, David, all mine. Now my daughter, my only daughter, similarly afflicted. Do I bear the curse? Is it my sin?"

What could I say. I tried to deflect her list. "Rachel, I knew your father and there was never a more brilliant man or a more learned minister. He was one of the great divines of his day. Your sister was a constant support to Richardson and it was he whom people describe as suffering from melancholia. Since his death and her remarriage, she has been with us on several occasions and we have seen no examples of distress. The others, I did not know and cannot therefore enter any intelligent facts." I realized that I should not try to discount her fears, only comment factually. What she had asked, had to be recognized as valid speculation.

"I cannot speak with certainty about your concerns, dear, but I know God to be present and to be our constant support in tribulation. There is no situation with which He will not assist us in coping. Blame cannot be at issue, given or taken. We live under the love of God in the image of Jesus Christ. Our Christ met life as it was presented, cured and cared where he could and redeemed us all. That is our certainty."

When Alexander Martin returned to the Senate for the third

session of the 5th United States Congress, Patsy and I rode again with him in his carriage to Philadelphia. It was late in November 1798, and the ride over hard frozen ground, the result of an early winter, was less than pleasant. Exceeding to her pleas and the practicality of the trip, I had stopped dosing her with the Blue Pill. She said that she would be too embarrassed to ride all that way in a closed carriage with the Governor. It was my responsibility as a parent to protect her from such personal shame.

Again we were received by Dr. Rush and his family, and although it was not intended as living quarters for winter, we stayed comfortably at the 'Sydenham Hut'. Rush observed Patsy for a week, then proceeded with the trepan. She was immediately relieved. We spent a delightful day with the Rush family on Christmas, followed by regret that we had not been at home. On the New Year, Governor Martin included us, with the Rush family, as his guests at the Indian Head Hotel. It was a sumptuous banquet and I was particularly joyful that Patsy enjoyed it with such normalcy. It seemed a glimpse of what her life might have been without the debilitating effects of her illness.

I was able to advise Rush of the details of the events that my son Alexander had been through. Unlike Patsy, he did not go through the seizures nor did he have the spells of deep depression. Instead, he tended to be a man only half inspired at all times. He had no motivation and little energy. He retreated into his books and papers – was constantly writing but rarely finished anything. When he did and I read it, I was amazed at its scholarship but dumbfounded by the incompleteness of any point or conclusion. It was as if he had inspiration, then wandered off from his pathway. Sometimes it would become entirely incoherent. I thought that it might be of use for me to have discussions with him on topics in which he seemed to be interested, but ideas that were not his own seemed to further confuse him. Sometimes he became agitated, which was surely not my intent.

Rush said he had seen such cases before and he did not recommend the use of trepanning. "I think that Alexander must just be kept from any outside pressure. He should not need to make decisions. He may never be able to be near or hear of his family. Avoid noises or anything that startles him. His life should be maintained at the most sheltered level. You have not had trouble allowing him to go with your family to church. I would ordinarily advise against it but it may be that since theology has been such a part of his life, it is soothing to him. For both of them, and in Edmund's interest as well, I think you wise to have this separate house which you can keep clean and devoted to their care. There is no need for them to be placed in any institution at this time and there may never be."

His words were confirming. It had occurred to me that God had led me to my interest in medicine so that I might have an extra capacity to care for my unfortunates. I saw the same pattern in the decision to build a second house. Rush recognized that there were no facilities in North Carolina like the Pennsylvania Hospital. His advice and continued interest made our little house a distant branch of his research. I thought I could be connected with none better.

It had been my search for instruction in medical study that had initiated this renewed friendship between two old Princeton men. That had been sustained with the mental breakdowns of my children but gradually over that time, we had spoken more and more on religious matters. Unlike many of our national leaders, Rush continued to be troubled by the likes of Tom Paine and "Common Sense." Works of such men as Volney, Hobbs, and Voltaire, and increasing interference of the French in our national politics, were no more to his liking than were the torrent of error and iniquity coming over the land like a flood from ministers of religion. I believe that Rush had been inspired by the complexity of the issue to study more his own religious beliefs and on that, I became sometimes his advisor and authority. I was gratified to have this opportunity to reciprocate for all the service he had been for me in the field of medicine.

In the privacy of his study, he told me, "I believe that Christianity is the only true and perfect religion, and to the extent that mankind will adopt its principles, they will be wise and happy." He was circling the room and his words were like a declaration.

"I am gratified that you take that position," I said. "You must know that it is much challenged in this time here and in Europe. Humanism, Deism, whatever name they give it – Islam, Judaism or other religions, are all being put forward to challenge the Christian believer. It is as if reason has opened the flood gates, and in the rush of ideas, all has been tossed into the maelstrom. Enlightenment is not an end in itself. It is like replacing our foundation by building a new house just to try out another site. It is valuable to strengthen your beliefs by shining the light of study and examination. Charlatans, however, in the guise of enlightenment, are deceiving the uninformed innocent with the shine of newness.

"I believe that we who profess the faith must be firm in our defense of it and to beat back, at every venue, those who would pervert. I also believe that we must profess with greater urgency because we are the Lord's anointed, the soldiers in His army."

Rush responded prophetically, "Thrones and kings and secular princes and usurpers must fall and perish. Their doom is fixed in the Scriptures of truth. The Messiah alone shall reign as King of Saints and Lord of the whole earth. All will end not only well, but gloriously, for those who believe and trust in his name."

I brought him up to date on the difficulties that Samuel continued to have at Rocky River and his efforts to stand firm against Universalists. But I also said I thought that Samuel had gone too far in his effort to have the religious power in the county, which was chiefly Presbyterian, control the actions of the civil government. I told him how I had once influenced the Constitution of North Carolina to block the participation of Jews and Deists in office holding.

"You were correct," Rush said. "They must be kept from too much influence. I have had an exchange with Jefferson and I have laid out my opinion in detail, and he has promised to respond in kind. I believe that we can then debate on point and I am satisfied I will be able to adjust some of his more dramatic ideas."

Rush and I went to a debate one afternoon in the Senate. It was a compliment to our friend Martin who had made the motion to have the Senate sessions open to the public. His action was hailed as a symbol of egalité, but I was aware that he simply thought that the business of the people's senators should not be done behind closed doors. Alexander had perceived that the private debate over the Jay Treaty had inspired unnecessary suspicion in the public. The Senate was its own worst enemy when secret debate merely encouraged the perception that there was something to hide.

The debate, on the day we chose to attend, concerned impeachment of one of the Senators from the new state of Tennessee, William Blount. One of the five delegates of North Carolina with Martin to the Constitutional Convention, Blount was caught up in the issue of western land frauds and Alexander had to be one to testify against him. Several times while I was in Philadelphia, I had seen young Andrew Jackson, one of the Representatives from Tennessee, who was himself very near the scandal through his brother-in-law, Stokely Donaldson. Over the course of this trip, I think I heard the name of almost every state and federal political office holder connected in some way with the land speculation frauds. I found it hard to accept that men of such stature, filling offices to which they were responsible as a trust, could become so embroiled. I could only be thankful that I was not part of that world of politics. It could be said, however, that politics, and the ministry in America, could be seen as analogous, proving that professionals are likely to divert their training to their own

386

advantage. It can only be hoped that they do not step over the very narrow line between diversion and distortion.

Since Alexander would not be returning to Philadelphia as a Senator, it seemed likely that we would not be returning for appointments with Dr. Rush. That would depend on Patsy's general condition and the difficulty of public travel. In Philadelphia, I had taken advantage of the book sellers to expand my library and to buy books for my students. I was particularly friendly with William Woodward of South Second Street and we concluded an agreement for me to act as his agent in North Carolina for the sale of books. In this way I would be able to keep advised on the latest publications and to create some income for myself. He had just published The Works of Rev. John Witherspoon in four volumes, and I thought that I would be able to make sales to many of my Presbyterian friends. I also took the opportunity to purchase a new set of Queen's ware for Rachel, and Patsy helped me choose some fabric for dresses.

CHAPTER TWENTY-THREE **1800–1810** A New Century

At Alamance, the new century began with plans for a new church building. The log church we had used for almost 40 years was far too small, so we tore it down in the spring. In the grove by the church, we set up a pulpit, and through the summer and early fall we had outdoor preaching. It was a refreshing diversion, reminiscent of our Nottingham Company ancestors who had selected this place for a church. Some of them were still with us and they passed on stories of the early settlement. There is value in reminiscence when it affirms a foundation upon which to build. Of course, when it rained the first Sunday after the log building was torn down, we had more vivid reminders of the hardships of our ancestors than we needed.

The new building measured 36' x 60', two stories, entirely frame construction. When complete, it could claim to be the largest and handsomest church building in this part of the state. Two rows of windows circled the structure providing abundant lighting to the galleries and first floor. There were two doors on the south side and a door on each end. The dark yellow of the exterior defined it in memory as the 'Old Yellow Church.' There were ornamented porticoes over each door, supported by unusual iron brackets.

The interior floor plan had the pulpit against the north wall and the main floor divided into five sections. I took particular interest in the impressive pulpit which was the defining feature of this sanctuary. It was the work of John Matthews, a carpenter from Hawfields church. A few years later, John was taken under care of Orange Presbytery and himself became a Presbyterian minister. John had earlier been one of my boys at the academy, and was one of those who had taken interest in the building of our second home. The pulpit which stood high above the congregation was built all of black walnut and profusely carved. The desk was over ten feet above the floor, and I reached my lofty station by a stairway with carved balustrade. Just above my head, and near the high ceiling was a hollowed sound board, a part of the pulpit, and similarly ornamented with an oval front of carved wood.

I stood in the pulpit, many feet above the congregation, my very placement lifting up their heads. To the left and right of the pulpit, stretched a row of pews perpendicular to me across the width of the sanctuary and then a wide aisle, also perpendicular. Then there was a center section with six pews divided in the middle, to make a dozen, with aisles and six more pews on each side against the walls; the eastern section of which was reserved for the Negroes. The balcony went down each side with five rows and across the rear with four rows and it had access by interior stairs.

In front of the pulpit was the desk occupied each Sunday by two precentors. The desk stood five feet above the floor but was still below the pulpit desk. These clerks, on alternate Sundays, lined out the hymns and led the singing. Their tasks were considered very responsible and they were offices that were held with honor. George

Donnell was a fine singer and served for years as a clerk. It was the annual rental of the pews that provided the funds for my salary.

This whole church, including gallery, could hold upwards of 1,000 people. Although at the time the congregation membership was less than 250, the church was often completely full on Sunday. Membership was not freely given, but subject to a strict examination and profession of faith before the Elders. The Presbytery and the Synod could easily have their meetings here. There was no fireplace but people stayed warm and I did my best on winter Sundays to warm them with the message.

In the yard of the church was the Session House, a small log building with a large fireplace, for the Elders to hold their meetings. It was also used as a place to warm before going into the cold church.

During our last trip to Philadelphia, it was Dr. Rush who suggested that if Patsy again needed to be trepanned, it might be possible that the Moravian doctor at Salem had experience in such surgery. He had close friends in the Moravian communities around Nazareth and was familiar with several well-prepared Moravian doctors. When we got home, I took the first opportunity to inquire, and found that Dr. Samuel Benjamin Vierling was in residence in the Salem community and was experienced in such procedures. It was reassuring to me. I now had assisted Dr. Rush on two occasions and had observed at other times, but only in an extreme emergency would I have ventured to open the skull of my own daughter.

Chapter Twenty-three 1800-1810 A New Century

Patsy did very well for several years which was a relief as we adjusted to the presence of Alexander and the pattern of existence that he required. Rush's advice on treatment had helped. At home we had been able to encourage Alexander to conduct the family prayer before meals and we were moved by the depth and sensitivity that he applied. On different occasions, particularly at Alamance, I called on him to lead in prayer, and on only one occasion did it seem to disturb him emotionally. In this process we determined the level of such pressure that he could tolerate. We were not testing him but attempting, as Rush had suggested, to help him sustain a level of normalcy for his life that he could abide.

Such a regimen we were never able to institute for Patsy. Her depressions bordered on violence. The Blue Pill and bleeding did relieve, for extensive periods, the apparent pressures that stimulated the incidents, but eventually only the trepan operation brought any substantial relief. By May of 1804, she was again at that extreme level of depression and I took her to Salem. We took rooms at the tavern, very fine accommodations for our part of the country, and on the 6th Dr. Vierling performed the operation. I found Vierling to be a very capable man and he was gracious about asking me to assist. "You have assisted before with one of the pre-eminent physicians in the country," he told me. "It would be my honor to have you beside me."

Dr. Vierling was equally as proficient in the procedure, to my mind, as I had seen with Rush. As we talked during Patsy's recovery, I found that Vierling had trained in Philadelphia and in Dresden and

391

had performed the operation more than fifteen times – only three times since coming to Salem. He was a slight man, very particular in his manner. He observed the piety typical of the Moravians, which reminded me of the struggle of faith that seemed now to possess Rush.

Of course we discussed Rush's theory about purges, and Vierling thought that bleeding was often overdone. "To my mind, there is a difference between pressure and tension related to any condition," he said. "Patients who are ill are usually tense, apprehensive. It is the nature of our response to the unknown. That can be relieved with information and a soothing manner as well as by bleeding. Pressures, built up by tumors, trauma, emotional imbalance – these are eased by bleeding but it is usually temporary if the source is not treated or removed. Over an extended period, I believe bleeding is debilitating and should be reduced in incident or it will be as harmful as the illness itself." I had heard similar arguments in Philadelphia, and although I was prone to be loyal to Rush, I favored Vierling's approach.

We spent fourteen days in Salem to allow for Patsy's complete recovery. During that time, she took particular interest in the Salem Boarding School for Girl's which was accepting students from outside the community for the first time. The Moravians too were interested in the training Patsy had in Latin and Greek, which was rarely offered to women. The school was being operated out of the Gemein Haus, but several times we observed work on the foundation for the new school building. Lessons would be conducted in subjects practical to the opportunities offered women in society. There would be no training in the classics beyond Latin grammar. Patsy was twenty-four but she appreciated the opportunity to talk with the girls who were adjusting to being students. She admitted to me that she did wish that she had enjoyed such an opportunity to attend school with other girls but knew that she had been afforded a superior education.

The entire month of May was very rainy. On several occasions the storms were severe, so we took advantage of our opportunity to learn more about the Moravian beliefs. They are very devout Christians whose roots came out of the Reformed Movement in Central Europe. I had intimate conversations with Brothers Gotthold Benjamin Reichel and Christian Lewis Benzien, two of their ministers. They were very pleased with what they heard about the new revival spirit in religion, particularly in the Presbyterian Church. I told them about the experiences at meetings at Cross Roads and Hawfields and in Randolph County, to which they expressed hearty thanksgiving. They had immediate misgivings about the shouting and falling down during services but did attribute it to the work of the Holy Spirit. We were invited to several church services and Patsy especially enjoyed the baptism of Nathaniel, the infant son of Brother and Sister Vogler.

A young man from Guilford County named John Mitchell, who was Patsy's exact age, was also at Salem for medical treatment. We had known him once very well. He suffered from cataracts and had been blind for many years. One of his eyes was completely ruined, but Dr. Vierling successfully pierced the other restoring partial sight. Mitchell told of being taken two years earlier to one of the camp meetings, more out of curiosity than any idea of salvation. He said he was actually repelled previously by such meetings. Many preachers of different denominations gave impressive testimonies, and through the spirit of God, he was led to cry out to God for grace and mercy. We all agreed to the apparent work of grace in the neighborhood.

Samuel and Abigail had their first child and asked if we could spare a slave who might be able to help with the housework and be experienced enough to care for the baby. We had enough slaves for the farm and were anxious to make this gift to them. Regrettably, as we looked over the slaves who might meet their requirements, we had no one to offer without breaking up a family. We even considered giving them an entire family unit but that would have been unfair to our other children. Rachel was particularly sensitive to the breaking up of families. Over the years, her attitude had given our slave community a degree of stability better than most. Finally, unable to ease our conundrum, we decided that Ede, a strong, healthy women in the prime of her life would be the most suitable. She had four children and they would send the youngest, a babe in arms, with Ede, which should ease the slave woman's transition. The other three children would remain with us. Ede's husband was a slave on the McQuiston Place and was a trifling Negro whom I had heard Tom indicate he intended to sell away. When we told Ede, she was distraught but I explained that slave marriages were not legal and she would probably find a better husband in Mecklenburg. Rachel was very compassionate and tried to console Ede.

The girl was so filled with grief that she seems to have immediately begun planning any way by which she might avoid the separation. The night before she was to go to Samuel's, she made up a sack of provisions and took her baby in her arms and fled to the woods. She found a hiding place a few miles from the farm in a heavy thicket some distance from the road. She made a bed of leaves sheltered by a large log and ventured a small fire. There she huddled with her child in the cold night, actually for several days and nights. It was her child who began to suffer from the cold and took a chill. Eade was terrified and saw all her attempts at tending for the baby insufficient and her food was gone. She decided to leave her hiding place and take a still greater risk for help.

I don't know how she was familiar with the Coffin family. Perhaps she only had heard that the Quakers did not hold with slavery and thought they might be kind. She made her way to their house at night and they took her in. William Coffin knew full well that the law forbid the sheltering of a known run away slave and William knew me personally and knew Ede to belong to me. The Coffin house had a reputation of voicing open support of freedom for slaves. Many said they were part of a network of Friends from North Carolina to Ohio, who aided slaves who were trying to reach freedom in the northern states. Coffin's boy, Levi, still had that passion for what he saw as the plight of the slave that he expressed a few years back at one of our 'frolics'. He yearned to hasten freedom for these people.

Because of his friendship with me, William hesitated to take Ede and the baby in but the boy and his mother said that "the child was sick and might die before morning." They would not turn her from their door. Priscilla Coffin gave Ede a comfortable resting place and did all she could for the child through the night. By morning the child was free of pain and resting well.

When Ede woke, she was overjoyed that her child had recovered but she began to weep bitterly when the Coffins began to consider what they must do with her. She pleaded that she would rather die than be separated from her family. Young Levi stepped forward and volunteered to come to me and attempt to persuade me not to send them away. It was a mature act and he hoped that he could protect his father from any penalty connected with harboring a fugitive slave.

Levi came up the road on foot dressed in his dark suit and large felt hat. His face was a grave image. He spoke to some of the boys in the yard, then came to the new house and knocked on the door. Rachel greeted him warmly and he allowed as he wished to have a word with me. When he came through the door to my library, I was hunched over my desk preparing a new syllabus and did not look up immediately. I suspect that was an uneasy moment for the boy but I did not intend it to be so. I was slow to look up because I thought it was one of the students. When I saw who it was, I stood up immediately and welcomed him.

"Young Levi, I am so pleased to see you. I am impressed with your maturity. You are a man and I am sure your parents are proud. Do you still have your strong opinions?"

"Yes sir, I do," he replied calmly. "I try not to hold too many opinions too firmly, but those I have studied out and made my own, I like to defend firmly. I think that is the duty of a man."

"Good for you and well said. Tell me about your school at New Garden. I understand that Jeremiah Hubbard is both your preacher and teacher. He is a man of considerable ability. You know, the Friends ought to pay Hubbard double price for your tuition, for I hear that he has taught his pupils the art of courting, besides the common branches of a school education. I hear that two of his pupils have made known their intentions of marriage, or 'given in meeting', as you call it. How do you suppose those young Quakers feel now that they are half married?"

I was teasing him as I did my children and students but he continued with his serious expression and replied, "Like they intended to be wholly married soon, I suppose."

I chuckled and continued, "now we Presbyterians do up such business sooner than Quakers do," — and just then Rachel came into the room. She had probably overheard me and wanted to spare the boy my extended story.

He had by now placed himself at ease and he said, "I have

come to speak to you on an important matter. Am I correct that your slave Ede has run away?"

We were startled. I said, "Indeed she ran off a few days ago to keep from going home with our son Sam, I suppose. She needs a good flogging for her foolishness — she would have a good home at his house. Do you know where she is hiding?"

"I do, sir," he said. With that he lit into the most erudite and eloquent defense of Ede's case that I might have expected from a mature barrister. He quoted a litany of Scripture then brought the matter home to us, putting us in her place as the aggrieved.

It was Rachel who first reacted saying, "Your mother has done a beautiful thing in caring for poor Ede and her sick child. I was reluctant to agree to her separation from her family but I held my counsel."

Levi resumed, "Ede said she wanted to come home if you would permit it but she would rather die than be sent away from her husband and her other children."

I had listened sympathetically to his tale but held my response.

"Do you believe my father to have done the right thing in taking Ede in?" asked Levi. "It was a violation of the law and he has laid himself liable to a heavy penalty if you are disposed to prosecute."

"Your father has done right; I shall not trouble him, and I thank your mother for her kindness to the sick child," I allowed in verdict. "As for you, you have done your part very well. Why, Mr. Coffin, you would make a pretty good preacher; if you will come to me I will give you lessons in theology without charge."

"You are kind and I appreciate your offer, but today I came on behalf of Ede who waits back at our house in suspense. What may I tell her?"

"Well, this is no doubt your first sermon, and you would be disappointed and might give up preaching if you were not successful. You may tell Ede to come home and I will not send her away."

He took his leave with some haste and Rachel laughed as she looked out the window and saw him jump into the air in delight. In the middle of the day, Ede came walking up the lane with her baby wrapped comfortably in a small blanket. We sent her to be reunited with her family.

In the last few years, we had seen less of Alexander Martin, briefly at court weeks and once we had visited him at Danbury. He had come to see the students on one occasion. He had been elected again to the North Carolina Senate, this time from Rockingham, and on his appearance was immediately placed back in the chair as President. At one point, the newly elected Governor reported it inconvenient to appear to be sworn in at the time assigned and Martin was asked to serve briefly again as Governor. That kind of experience made him bemoan the lethargy he saw in the attitude of North Carolina leadership. He feared that in the midst of what I was experiencing as a revival in personal faith, he was observing a collapse in public trust. The Glasgow Land Fraud Trial had eventually involved many of his political associates who had speculated on land in Tennessee, and that had been dispiriting.

On the 2nd of November 1807, one of the Negroes from Danbury brought word that his master had died and asking that I come. I made the ride in the bluster of a cold winter day. I mused that on a day such as this Alexander might have formerly been setting off for a meeting of the Assembly. As my horse carried me cautiously down the grade, I could see the composite of log and frame buildings that he had called Danbury. It was not a very impressive residence considering all the high offices he had held. There were buildings all around so that it appeared to be as much a village as did Martinville. The family was already gathered, the Rogers, the Hendersons, the Hunters, the Searcys, with all the several generations of Martins. My heart grieved for they had lost their linchpin. Old Mrs. Martin, the Governor's mother, still lived and she was certainly 'the matriarch.' Alex though, was the one who had brought fame to this clan. They had all basked in his light and would probably try to continue to do so. There were more nephews and nieces than I could count, all aware that Uncle Alexander had provided them patrimonies here and in Tennessee where they would prosper. They were the next generation, and most of them would turn their backs on this place and seek their fortunes elsewhere.

The Governor had planned his own funeral, but Jane Henderson, the sister who lived next door and cared for her mother for years, and James Martin of Snow Creek, Alexander's very close brother, insisted on communicating the plans to me in the presence of their mother. Since I was only eight years younger than Jane Martin, I presumed that they worried that I might not be up to the task. The Governor had expressly said that he wanted me to preach his funeral. It would be held at the house because "Mother Jane" was frail and there was no church nearby. Were they all younger, the service would have been at Buffalo, but now that was out of the question. It took only a few minutes of this conversation and Jane Martin was deep in sleep. She appeared as a little black pyramid with rounded sides, a tiny frame that snored softly. We talked over her. "His grave wrappings are being made but he will be buried in his uniform," advised his sister. "He wanted his sword and spurs to be displayed along with his Society of Cincinnati Medal, Masonic Badge, and Membership in the American Philosophical Society."

"Dr. Caldwell," began James, "we intend to use his carriage to convey the body the short distance to the vault that he had prepared over on the little bluff above the river. I think the carriage is a little pretentious but we found it could be done."

"That carriage carried me with him on two long trips to Philadelphia. I don't know why he shouldn't get to use it one more time."

James continued, "we will arrange and instruct all the dignitaries and pall bearers, so you need have no further tasks beyond the sermon and prayers. After you finish, we will place him in the vault. You know he had the vault built in imitation of Washington's burial vault at Mount Vernon. Of course it is a general copy in the style of Washington's vault.

The funeral was on Thursday morning and my family, including Rachel and Patsy and Alexander; and even Samuel and his wife from Charlotte, rode up in a train of wagons to the Dan. As we got near, the roads filled with people, horses, and wagons. Samuel helped me with the service, as I knew I would have difficulty with my voice in the cold. The crowd must have covered several acres around the house. Fortunately the sky was overcast, but there was no rain and had been none all that week. The Governor had sent a small delegation. All the lawyers and politicians for miles around were there. Alexander Strong Martin and his mother stood with the family but slightly to the side. All those who had served during the Revolution made up the honorary pall bearers. James Hunter, James Martin, Pleasant and Thomas Henderson, John May, Thomas Lacy, Peter Scales, John Morehead, all stood out just below the porch where I stood to speak. I was immediately conscious that the breeze stirred a fluffy cloud of white hair just beneath me.

"Alexander Martin was my friend," I began. "We first met at Princeton commencement in 1759, almost 50 years ago. At that time neither of us had ever been to North Carolina and we never expected in the end to settle so near to each other." I went on in this vein for some minutes concerning our long association. Then I spoke for more than an hour about his public service which I knew by heart. When I came to his contribution to the start of civil government in this country, I spoke about our debates in which Rachel had joined. "We didn't always agree, but we respected each other's opinions and I think we strongly influenced each other. That is the way it should be in life. We should all strongly influence each other because when that happens, it means that we are paying attention to each other." I talked about Alex' faith and the journey he had completed and the deep influence that his younger brother, Rev. Thomas, had on him. "Did you know that it was they who were responsible for convincing James Madison to go to Princeton, and if they hadn't, Mr. Jefferson might not have such a Secretary of State as he does today?" Although I never felt that a funeral was a place to make converts, I did press on the values of salvation. I closed with some comments about Alexander's regard for the rest of his family. It got a little tricky when I spoke of his son because it had only been the previous year that he had made a legal acknowledgment of his base-born son in open court.

When I finished, the body was loaded into that fine carriage, a physical reminder to everyone there how important this man had been. The procession itself stretched from the main house almost to the vault. Four of her grandsons carried Mrs. Martin in a chair. On a rise above a bank of dark green rhododendrons that flowed down to the fast moving brown waters of the Dan River, there was a stone and brick vault built into the side of the hill, to which I committed the body of Governor Alexander Martin.

Rachel and I enjoyed the opportunity at the banquet prepared for the mourners, to see again many people whom we had known over the years. That's what funerals are for. The living pay their respects to the dead and rejoice at their own survival. I am distressed to recognize that reality. We are present to acknowledge a progress from life, through death, to fulfillment. We cannot accompany but we can be conscious of life transforming. We put a body in the ground. We observe a soul released, translated into what it was intended to be.

Two days later, the same slave that had brought news on Monday arrived at our house from Danbury. Jane Hunter Martin had been reluctant to let her son go alone. She had died during the night.

CHAPTER TWENTY-FOUR 1797–1802 The Great Awakening

Bell's Meeting House twenty years ago had been in the center of Tory territory in Randolph County. Cornwallis had assembled his army there before proceeding to Guilford Courthouse. In January 1802, I found myself organizing a meeting at Bell's, inviting all the Presbyterian ministers west of the Yadkin River to assemble, and to bring some members from their congregations to see what the Lord was performing in their midst. Revival was awake amongst us. I was as over-awed as they by a great awakening of the spirit that was sweeping through the church. It was as if I had opened in my own congregation, a container of the Holy Spirit that I did not understand existed, and it had burst on the scene and swept beyond our midst in an epiphany. I was the shepherd ministering to my flock, preaching the word I had for 40 years, and suddenly the spirit erupted out of the everyday and transformed the church.

To explain the circumstance, I will have to go back to one of my particular students, James McGready, whose parents migrated from western Pennsylvania into Guilford during the war when James was about seventeen. He attended my academy for a few years and then his parents sent him back to Pennsylvania, where he came under the influence of Rev. John McMillan, a Princeton man, who had opened an academy. He was a good student and McMillan was a New Side man who preached the necessity of a spiritual rebirth. McGready, doubting himself because he had never experienced a saving conversion, finally had such an experience one Sabbath morning during a protracted Communion Sacrament.

In the Presbyterian strongholds in western Pennsylvania, the revival service was an outgrowth of the tradition of the Scottish Communion. We still had such communion services at Buffalo and Alamance, They would begin, often on a Friday, with services of preparation which extended to the next day. That would be a day of fasting and prayer during which candidates for communion would be examined, screened as to their worthiness, and tokens would be distributed authorizing the communicant to partake. Sunday was devoted to the sacrament itself and a follow-up Thanksgiving Service, which might be held over into Monday. Such services were inter-congregational. My two churches would combine, and Presbyterians would come from miles around. On some occasions we had outdoor preaching tents where other preachers would hold services, and frequently all night services. With few other diversions, neighbors from other churches came by the wagon load and curious observers came, often drawn into the emotion of these sacramental services. The Presbyterian service was strict and harsh and filled with judgment. To be worthy was to be among the chosen. No one came to the table without a heightened sense of emotion and Christ was present at the table. Such services represented the most important continuous tradition of the Scots Church. Over decades in new locations, it modified slowly, but in western Pennsylvania it had a close parallel in the emotional excess in revivals. It was in that atmosphere that McGready had his calling which was a part of his religious experience when he returned to North Carolina.

In Guilford, he found the sad religious conditions that Rachel and I had lamented. The turbulence of the war that tested faith, the moral breakdown, the need for things – objects, followed by the lack of religion manifest in humanism, which appealed to the ignorant as well as to the philosopher. A symptomatic example was the boisterous custom of guzzling whiskey at funerals. McGready's name first gained local attention when he was asked to deliver thanks for the refreshments at a wake. Obstinately and scathingly, he refused. Those who have imbibed too often and too frequently do not appreciate being publically scorned. By the time the furor had subsided, he had won such attention that his preaching became a sensation. He railed against stiff–necked hypocrisy and sin and preached the need of rebirth. He identified sin – named it – and charged people with being unfit to be church members until they had a saving experience and could identify the exact moment and place where it had occurred.

McGready married and bought a home between my two congregations, and I frequently asked him to preach, especially when I had to be away during the crisis with Alexander or with trips to Philadelphia. He also, at my request, came to the academy and was a great favorite with the students. James was always plainly dressed, which gave his appearance a certain gravity. He was portly, actually large, above six feet, with prominent features. He had piercing eyes that seemed to cling to another person's gaze. His voice was deep, guttural, with a tremor and his thunderous tones and gesticulations centered the attention of his listeners. He progressed with increasing tempo, volume, and enthusiasm to a blazing, fervent finish. Then with his public prayer, he would bring his audience to tears as he "wrestled with God."

McGready's interest was in the salvation of his listeners, not in creeds or covenants but he never went into the pulpit without a thoroughly prepared, organized message, usually fully written out. Typically, he spent two days in preparation, nearly memorizing his sermon. With an earnest moral seriousness, his homiletic technique was to draw the listener into an intense fear of damnation. With glowing beauty and tranquility, he would walk them into the glories of heaven, then array the horrors of hell before the wicked, imagining the fire and brimstone yawning to consume and the wrath of God thrusting them down into the abyss. Trembling and quaking, terrified listeners feared for their souls.

The only route of escape was the experience of a new birth. Only those who were dead to sin could experience this new spiritual life. Accept Christ and his salvation as set out in the Gospel and through the will of God you shall have salvation. But man has an important subsidiary roll in this sanctification process and that is to repent of his past and present sins and recognize complete obedience to God.

This relegated to irrelevance the Presbyterian interpretation of election. The role of the minister now was to arouse, startle the sinners from their security, and bring them to feel their danger and guilt. This was far removed from my mild, reasonable preaching technique. It was counter to the studied exegesis of scripture that was the standard of Buffalo and most other established Presbyterian congregations. The elect were offended. Satisfied that they were, or they had seen in others, the manifestation of the elect, their certainty was now being questioned. With no salvation experience, how could they be elect?

Anticipation of revival in religion surged through all these congregations for several years. Rachel had been meeting with a few older ladies praying for a revival in religion. Some young men in my congregation became agitated by religious concerns and did not know how to satisfy their search. I met with them more than once but was unable to focus their apprehensions. They appeared to be ardent but unable to channel their feelings. I knew with the same kind of urgency expressed by many of my students, that there was a force ready to be manifest among us but I was thinking intellectually, waiting for God to direct my actions.

McGready was the instrument of God for me, working on an old man. He came to me when I needed assistance to keep up the work in my churches and my school. He never made any kind of effort to usurp or remold the work of my life in either place. When he saw his word fall upon fertile ground, and as he saw these young people seeking nourishment for their souls, he would speak to them as individuals and his spirit connected with the yearning of their spirit. It was intellectual and emotional, not necessarily both, but his capacity was to work with both. Therefore, I never thought of him as shallow or opportunistic for himself but alive with the spirit. When he left for Kentucky in 1797, I believed a flame had been lit.

There had been verbal counter attacks against McGready's message that ultimately became physical. Pews were upset, altars were burned, and in a final effort to drive him away, a letter was written to him in blood threatening death. He answered them with a sermon based on Jesus' lament, "O Jerusalem, Jerusalem, thou that killest the prophets and stonest them which are sent unto thee, how often would I have gathered thy children together even as a hen gathereth her chickens under her wings, and ye would not. Behold, your house is left unto you desolate."

Throughout the church in North Carolina, my boys filled many of the pulpits, those who had the discipline of my classical school to mold their calling to ministry. I knew they were grounded in the faith of our denomination. These were not weak reeds blown by wild whims of emotion. These were young men I knew to be stalwart instruments in the service of their Lord. So I watched them; I paid attention to my students and the young men of my congregation. I knew that they had infinite respect for my age and my beliefs. I could turn inward on those beliefs and resurrect a contradiction to the spirit of inspiration that would confound them. I would not. My alternative was to see the spirit moving in them and rejoice; to recognize that, out of what may appear to my structured order and belief as confusion, can come the Spirit of God. Surely he who called light from darkness and order out of chaos, can bring light and order from what appears as a dark mental and moral morass such as surrounded our time.

The Communion season at Cross Roads Church in 1800 was scheduled for August. William Paisley invited me, his former teacher, along with Leonard Prather and two licentiates, my boys, E. B. Currie and Hugh Shaw. The younger men had all been part of the revivals in the west. Large crowds attended and on Monday, during the Thanksgiving service, Paisley stood to dismiss the services which had fallen into the solemn and grave traditions of similar communions. At that point the Rev. William Hodge, the former minister at Cross Roads who had followed McGready west, said in a calm and earnest voice, "Stand still and see the salvation of God." A wave of emotion swept over the congregation. Sobs, moans, and cries rose from every corner of the church. Many were struck down and thrown into a state of helplessness as on the day of Apocalypse. The congregation spent the remainder of the day in prayer, exhortation, singing, and personal conversion. It was midnight before people could be persuaded to go home.

In October, the Communion season came for Hawfields, and people came with an enhanced sense of expectation. So many people each night had been "awakened" that the pastors alone could not meet with them all, and the elders had to come forward to help. Again on

411

Monday, the people did not want an end and into the night they met. The report that I got was that multitudes were struck down and lay helpless. They recovered from hours of unconsciousness with exclamations of joy and praise to Him who had loved them and washed their sins with His own blood. This extension of the communion was referred to as a camp meeting. That was a term characterized by camp fires, fellowship with friends, and the singing of popular religious hymns.

There were many like me still struggling with the veracity of what we were seeing as truly visionary. We were no longer skeptics, but not having experienced this transformation ourselves, we wanted to satisfy the composition of what was happening once and for all.

Four ministers, whose churches lay west of the Yadkin River, came to me and asked me to summon that camp meeting at Bell's meeting-house in Randolph for the first day of the New Year, 1802. Samuel Eusebius McCorkle of Thyatira, Lewis Wilson of Concord and Fourth Creek, both my students, Joseph D. Kilpatrick of Third Creek and the venerable James Hall of Bethany met with me. They pledged they would attend, assist in leadership, and bring families from their congregation who were seeking a religious revival. I was very forthcoming with my associates. "My brothers, I have not had a revival experience. On the other hand, I do not discount the work of the Holy Spirit. The very idea of this meeting appeals to me because it will not be led by any of my brothers who have had such an experience or who have led a communion out of which such unparalleled emotional experiences have come. I will conduct the communion as I have always done so. There will be no dynamic appeals calling on the fiery image of damnation. I will not cry or pound my pulpit or flail my arms and I would ask the same of you. I do not propose a test of God, but of man. If what we are experiencing is the work of pastors eager for fame and converts, who are using the image of the spirit to inflame the emotions of unsuspecting sinners, then it shall be exposed. If we are truly seeing the intervention of the Holy Spirit in our time and in this place, we must champion that work among our flocks."

McCorkle jumped at my words as a lifeline. "I have been so prejudiced against considering these exercises as part of the work of the spirit. What you suggest, Dr. Caldwell, will help me to find answers to my prayers. I am not anxious to claim the method of these revivals, but if God wills it, I am dedicated to encourage the results."

"I am an old preacher like you," said Hall. "I do not want to become anachronistic in my faith in my late years. I have not preached the faith all this time only to wander from the pathway as my sight dims. Let us see the way of the Lord."

People arrived during the day on Friday and the evening was spent in prayer and exhortation with no effect. More people and the preachers came on Saturday until about 2000 had gathered. We heard, between the first and second sermon, that Dr. Hall and his group who had spent the night in route, had a sudden and unexpected religious experience that did not arise from oratory or sympathy which were the causes commonly assigned for this work. The second sermon was delivered and the benediction pronounced but the people seemed unwilling to leave for their encampments. A speaker rose and gave a short parting exhortation, and as if by an electric shock, a large number in every direction of men, women and children, white and black, fell on the ground crying for mercy. Others began praying for the fallen, or exhorting bystanders to repent and believe. I was with McCorkle and we viewed the scene at first with horror, and I will allow, with a degree of disgust. Could this confusion come from the Holy Spirit?

A poor black man caught my attention with his hands raised above the crowd shouting, "Glory, glory to God on high." I was moving toward him from the preaching tent when I was stopped by the image of another black man on the ground with his mother kneeling over him praying for her son. Near him was a black woman grasping the hand of her white mistress crying, "Oh, mistress you prayed for me when I wanted a heart to pray for myself. Now thank God, he has given me a heart to pray for you and everybody else."

McCorkle joined me, and we saw a white child with an angelic expression reclining in the arms of an older companion. He took her by the hand and asked her how she felt. She seemed to wake, smiled at him and fell back closing her eyes. We passed through the congregation in a circuitous route to the preaching tent, noticing one in agony of prayer; another motionless, speechless, apparently breathless; another rising in triumph, in prayer and exhortation. A young man cried out behind me and I turned. He asked me to pray for him. I attempted it. He rose with some assistance and cried out for his brothers to come forward and repent.

We felt exhausted, consumed. We had gone from camp to camp to face the same conditions. Later, McCorkle said that the little white child that we had passed, had sought him out and said to him, "I feel so happy now, I wish everyone felt as happy as I." He examined her there but found her painfully deficient in her understanding of the Shorter Catechism. He said she answered with what he called propriety, more as expressions of her present surroundings than from past education or training. The next day he was called to examine her in order for her to qualify as a communicant and he found her defective in her knowledge of doctrine and education and he persuaded her not to take communion. Later, on cooler thought, he regretted his action realizing that she possessed an experimental knowledge of salvation that is infinitely preferable to all the doctrinal, systematic knowledge in the world without it.

Afterwards I went into the woods where some had gone to seek to pray. I found them in earnest prayer with some seemingly struck down and others exercised with emotion. I viewed the whole spectacle. My mind was a great mass of sensations and I stepped back for some reflection, but I was not disturbed by what I was seeing. Certainly the disorder, the external disorder in worship, perplexed me. An awful sense of the majesty of God, a painful sense of sin, an earnest desire to be liberated from it, surrounded us. I was sure I saw a criminal element in the roving eye, and the vacant features of some who lurked on the edges. I saw it in the conversation of an intoxicated youth. I saw it in the giddy crowd running from camp to camp without any fixed object in mind. I saw it in the action of some profane persons who had overturned the communion tables and trampled the elements under their unhallowed feet. This was disorder, voluntary and bordering the criminal. But who can say this of the poor sinner moved to cry out even in such a crowd? "Please, what must I do to be saved?" Who then would stand to hold this back? I believe that the outcry is God's and the constraint is human. Surely the God of nature is a God of grace.

Natural affections begin with self and then spread around. At first, it is what shall I do to be saved? Then it extends, oh my child, my brother, or sister, 'repent and be saved.' Surely this must be the work of God and marvelous in our eyes. When I consider, it seems an astonishing way to reform mankind. It is not the way that I would do it. Then I must add, what ever is conducted as I would do it? – peace or war, plenty or famine, illness or health, life or death? No. I am left to cry, Oh God, as the heavens are higher than the earth, so are thy thoughts above our thoughts, and thy ways above our ways.

Rachel and I had many sessions on this subject. She saw with a clear eye the hand of God in her prayer for revival. She did not attempt to analyze motive or method in what she saw or heard me describe. I saw myself as tethered in some way by my position within the faith. That need not be wrong, but sometimes I ached for the liberation I saw in her response.

What we observed in North Carolina as a revival in religion, broke across the west as a wild fire. To my amazement, it was my boys who were in the lead. James McGready was soon joined by the McGee brothers, John and William. John became a Methodist, where he found their fashion of exhorting from the heart, moving to tears, and frequent shouting, to be a natural arena for revivalism, and he was a leader in this great awakening in that denomination. I recall that William was the superior student, but it was John who seemed to delight in the discovery of ideas. They were followed by John Rankin, son of George and Lydia Rankin. He was already married with a family. William Hodge left his pastorate at Hawfields to go west. Where McGready preached hell-fire, Hodge spoke appealingly of the love of God and his congregants were known to refer to him as "Son of Consolation." Finally, William McAdoo was the last of the "wild men of the Cumberland," as they came to be accounted. I remembered them all as very good students who were well prepared for the ministry. In fact, that was the only commonality that I could identify that would have drawn them together to dominate this emerging religious progression.

Another ought to be added to the list, who came by a more roundabout way to awakening. Barton Warren Stone, was Scotch-Irish but he had been raised in an Anglican parish in Virginia. His mother used the estate of Barton's late father to provide him an education. She studied his choices, and wishing him to have a classical schooling, brought him to me. I remember that he was part of the group that developed the habit of calling me "Prexy," a salutation of which I was never fond. Stone's roommate was Ben McReynolds, also from Virginia. He invited Stone to go with him to hear James McGready when he preached nearby. On that occasion, McGready had such an affect on my boys that nearly thirty professed religion. Stone was not one. He had found McGready's message both unpleasant and disturbing. It had power, and Stone saw it as a direct appeal to the sinner to act. The message took hold and overwhelmed him. For another year he struggled, then he heard McGready again at Sandy Creek. In a private session following, McGready spoke again for his concerns about the impending horrors of a Calvinist's "Hell" and left McGready without any consolation. Stone underwent intense agony of soul for weeks. His mother sent for him and his struggle moved her so much that she joined the Methodists and converted while he continued to resist. He came back to the Academy. In the spring of 1791, he attended a meeting at Alamance, where he heard young William Hodge preach. It was Hodge's appeal under God to heal the broken–hearted and bind up their wounds, that determined him to be a Presbyterian minister. At this point, it was Rachel who became influential, relating to his struggle of call. He was not certain he had a call because he had seen no miracle to convince him. Rachel brought him to the sensible view that if his ideals were pure, and if he really wanted to preach, and if the "fathers in the ministry" wanted him to preach, that was sufficient. He should go ahead.

I provided him a text for a sermon that he was to preach at the next meeting of Orange Presbytery. It would be part of his examination as a licentiate. William Hodge coached him. His subject was "The Trinity," which was indeed a complicated topic for him. He agonized with it but in the end accepted the views of Isaac Watts, then in fashion with Presbyterians. By that he saw that the human soul of Christ had been created outside the creation of the world and had been united to the Godhead (Sophia or Logos), and that the personality of the Holy Ghost was figurative, not literal. This satisfied Stone so he was not tormented further by his understanding of this contemporary theological debate. Nor was Watt, who I understand became something of a Unitarian before his death. Stone's examination was sustained.

It was McGready who suggested that Stone might acquire the pulpit at Cane Ridge, a small meeting-house in Bourbon County in central Kentucky. Stone followed the suggestion, became their permanent minister and was ordained. He was in this post in August 1801, when I have heard it claimed that better than 10,000 people, some estimated as many as 20,000, attended a communal service on the grounds. Cane Ridge became the defining experience of what we broadly call the Great Awakening. Perhaps 2,500 Presbyterians were present, and people came from great distances to participate. There was such noise and disorder that few heard the full content of any single sermon. Virtual anarchy meant that people were confronted with something primordial, certainly visceral, and their reason and self-control were at least momentarily overwhelmed. At any one time perhaps 300 people were exhorting simultaneously. Stone estimated in a letter to me that 1,000 people were converted. I knew Barton never grasped the finer tenets of Calvinism, which he saw as too rigid to allow for an all-embracing unity of the Christian faith. He continued to struggle with what he interpreted as constrictive in the Presbyterian Church.

The Great Awakening had come to define the Church equipped to serve the population of an expanding nation. It had been initiated by an emotional revival that is hard for me to evaluate as other than a rebirth of the spirit. I was not called on to alter my message or my pulpit presence to serve my congregations that were no longer frontier people. I had nothing to fear from the action of the revivalists who were preaching to people who, living a subsistence life in an unyielding, sometimes hostile wilderness, craved the emotional moment when they could see glory.

What do you give to an old man who has everything? The University of North Carolina decided in 1810 that one of the first of three honorary doctorates they would bestow might be appropriate. So Buffalo became Bubulus and Alamance became correctly Allemance, the original name brought from Germany, and as Davidem Caldwell, I became Doctor of Divinity (D.D.). It was an honor that I warmly received because the university was a progression of my classical academy in my heart. I was often praised in my lifetime for the importance to the history of North Carolina of my little school, but until the opening of the university, I really was not sure that my labors might take any more permanent root. My son, Rev. Samuel Craighead Caldwell, was awarded a Master of Arts degree at the same commencement and we stood robed together, to Rachel's great pride.

The rain last night had built a full rush in the creek, and I had told Tom and Cecil to plan to do some flour milling today. Two of the Negro families had said they were low on flour and Rachel said she could use some herself. I took my walk down by the mill each morning whether we were operating or not. This was the place where I was reminded most of Lancaster in my youth. I had modeled our gristmill after the one I had helped my father and brothers build many years ago. That was where I first began my training as a carpenter. It had reassured me to hear that our Lord had trained as a carpenter and I had the feeling I was close to Him in this way.

It was late in the year 1811. My bearskin cape was wet around the bottom from brushing against wet grass and branches. Regularly I wore a hat outdoors but now, with the colder weather, I had on my worsted wool cap and I walked with my gold handled cane, finding myself gradually more dependent upon it for support. It was difficult for me to straighten my back and I guess I walked with quite a hunch because I had to stop and straighten up every now and then to get a broader look around. As I looked back up toward the house, I saw a gentlemen and young boy approaching me. "Good day to you, Dr. Caldwell," the man said and I recognized John Morehead, whom I had known since the time of the battle at Guilford.

"Oh, hello John. How are you, my friend, and who have you brought with you to see this old man?"

"This is my oldest son, John Motley. You have met him before a few years back."

"You mean he is that scrawny pup you had with you at the last court day at Martinville? Why he was so small, a person could trip over him, and look what a fine boy now. Hello, young Mr. Morehead. It is a pleasure to see you again."

"I am pleased to see you again, Dr. Caldwell. I hope you are well."

We began walking back up toward the house - at my pace.

"You see now that well is one of those relative words, my boy, particularly when you get to my age. I figure that if I can take my walk in the morning, I am well. Some days the Lord eases the aches more than others."

Morehead proceeded right to the point of his visit. "I don't see many students around the place. Have you abandoned your school?"

"Yes, several terms back. My son, Robert, still takes a few students using the building, and I have one or two who are sent to me to prepare for entrance to the university. I am afraid the days of the classical academy are over."

"Well, you must remember the promise you made to me on several occasions that you would teach my eldest son when he was old enough. On that promise, I have brought the boy to you and I swear that only you can educate him."

"John, did you think my promise was to live forever? If you wanted me to educate him, you should have presented him long since."

"You sir, are an institution and there is no end to an institution," he said.

I laughed, then in my broadest Scottish accent I said, "Weel, mon, we must try and see what we can do with the lad." Then, I turned to the boy. "But mon, have ye an appetite for reading?"

"I am not very hungry for it," he said, then his face reddened as he studied his words.

As we entered the house, it was Rachel who came to the

423

hallway to greet us. "Mr. Morehead, what a fine surprise, and this must be Obedience's son."

"You mark him rightly, mum, for he is my oldest boy, John Motley."

"Welcome, John Motley. We are particularly partial to well-mannered young men like you."

Rachel prepared some hot tea and we all sat in my library and discussed the young man's future. He had already studied the rudiments of Latin under Thomas Settle, a young neighbor who had several months' study in Caswell. "It isn't much training sir. I am afraid I am little more than still a beginner," the boy admitted, anxious that I not expect too much of him.

I liked the boy. He wasn't afraid of his elders but gave them a natural respect. He seemed to be immediately at ease in our home, which confirmed what I knew to have been his own loving family life. Morehead had already arranged for the young man to board with the Donnells nearby, and the plan agreed upon was that he would come to me daily. I had presented myself as the weary old man, but in truth I had little new to interest me these days and I missed teaching. I might even add a few others so that I might have a small class, just to keep the benches in the school house dusted.

The next week when we began, John Motley arrived at eight o'clock, as agreed, soon after I had completed my morning walk. That first day I didn't assume any prior training, so that with what he had absorbed from Settle, he might feel comfortable with the subject.

When we formed our routine, the boy would recite from four to six hours a day. I was an easy taskmaster, but we never passed over any subject until I considered that he knew it accurately and thoroughly. Having to go back later to review something from a past lesson annoyed me and I considered it a waste of time. He caught on to that reaction right away and tried very hard to understand the first time. I think his method, when stumbling over something he should have already learned, was to study it again at night on his own, then recover the next day. I liked that initiative. It demonstrated to me that he took the responsibility on himself. As we progressed into the rules of Prosody and Syntax in Greek and Syntax in Latin, there were times when rules I knew as well as I did the alphabet hid somewhere in my mind, and I groped to bring them forward. I had to apologize to the lad, afraid he might cork me. He was always gracious, as respectful of my feelings as I was of his. More than once he caught me in the morning reviewing his lesson so that I might be alert to the content. On one occasion, I had asked him a rule that he could not give, and struggle as I might, the phraseology was lost to me. I admitted it was like a tangled skein and I could not find the end. "Don't worry, sir. I have helped my mother with such a tangle many times," he said with an encouraging smile. There were times when a rule in English failed me, but reciting the same in Latin rolled from my tongue. The boy treated these lapses as if he were observing an eastern mystic seer, drawing an image from the aether, with awe and respect. It was therapeutic salve to an old man's ego that I always appreciated.

By his second year, I had taken on four more students – one in medicine. The boy added Hebrew to his Latin and Greek, and responding to his eagerness, I included him in the scientific study. That was the year when my eyesight nearly failed me completely. I even tried two sets of spectacles – if that wasn't a laugh. But as suddenly as it had gone, sight returned so completely that I could read the finest print in Greek without glasses at all. I even accused God, in prayer, of teasing me.

My voice was failing and I knew I would soon have to give up my pulpits, but I would rather have my voice give out while I was teaching these boys. I figured if I hadn't gotten God's message across to those families at Alamance and Buffalo after nearly 60 years, it probably wasn't going to be. My message to my boys was still new, and for me, it was like watering a garden.

We went to war with England again but it is difficult for people to draw out support when the fighting is so distant. Civil patriotism is easy. Name the enemy and call him the devil. Wave some flags and make some speeches and you can get people worked up. Trying to get their sons to leave home is a little more difficult. In 1814, war came closer and we anticipated that the British would land troops at Norfolk and try again to split the coastal chain of states. The militia captains were having difficulty raising their quotas, so General Samuel Martin asked me to speak one Saturday at a rally to be held at the new court house in Greensborough. There were fewer of us left who had been around for Guilford Court House, and I guess my exploits, mostly keeping myself from being caught by Cornwallis, had been repeated enough as to be legend. I agreed and had Tom take me over in the carriage. Rachel insisted on going to keep an eye on me but I forbade my students from coming, lest they be caught up in the moment themselves and join up.

It was an especially fine day and when we arrived we were cheered raucously. As soon as the energetic young man in uniform who was speaking completed his harangue, the General stepped up and introduced me like I had single-handedly routed the whole invading army myself in '81. They were using the court room and all the windows were open so the overflow crowd could hear the speeches. Using my cane, I got up the steps but almost had to crawl up onto the judge's bench to speak. People were hushed by the scene of my struggle, but once I was mounted, they roared out in the most thunderous hurrahs. I knew I could not speak long, for my voice would just not hold out and I had to speak loud enough for all to hear, or what good was my message.

"My friends," I began. "It was 43 years ago that I stood in my pulpit at Buffalo and cautioned my congregation about armed conflict as a course to resolve disputes. Many of those people took up arms against Governor Tryon and fought, and some died, in battle at Alamance Creek. [Applause] I was already 46 years old then, and although I advised them of their rights, I also advised them that they were not prepared for battle. Five years later, I looked into the faces of some of those same people, and I declared that a man had a right to break his covenant with a King who no longer honored his contract with his citizens, and I urged them that it was time to throw off the burden of colonialism and declare their independence. I warned them then that they were going to have to fight for that independence. [Applause] Five years more, and I had to tell them that as free men, it was time to defend their liberty and we fought a great battle not more than a few miles west of this place. [Applause] Since those speeches which seem to me so long ago, North Carolina has become one of the original states of a great and expanding country, the United States of America, with a form of government envied by every other country in the world. [Applause]

"Now, as citizens of that great country, it would appear that the same British who abused our freedom, and fought against our independence, and tried to beat us up at Guilford Court House, are at it again. They want to invade Virginia and take us back. [Cries of shame and Boo! Boo!] How well I remember that when the great General Nathanael Greene was assembling his army and preparing the selection of the terrain to do battle with General Cornwallis, he maneuvered his army in a race to cross the Dan River into Virginia. There he pled with boys and young men to come to his aid. They responded in such number that they made up much of his second line of defense at the battle in your neighborhood. Now Virginia calls you back, asking you to remember what they once did in response to your hour of need. You can but answer – 'Yes we will. Here we come!'[Rousing cries.]

"You all know me as a preacher, and no preacher worth his salt can end without turning to the Bible for a text. I turn you to the Gospel of Luke, the twenty-second chapter, verse 36– 'And he said unto them, But now, he that hath a purse, let him take it, and likewise a wallet; and he that hath none, let him sell his cloak, and buy a sword.' " I made that final exertion, "and buy a sword," from the depths of my soul and that crowd just exploded in cheers as I scrambled down. I am told that it saved the day. The recruiting tables were immediately filled and over-subscribed. So moved was a young Quaker boy, Isaac White, that without concern for the disfavor of his church and family, he signed up. I was relieved that at the end of the war, he returned home safely and was forgiven and returned to good order.

On the ride home, Rachel said, "what memories today has aroused. All those young faces hung on your every word. It must have had special meaning for you as well."

"I did feel that I was fulfilling something that had begun a long time ago. I have been considering of late why God has left us to live so long on this earth. As for you, I understand that God was enamored by your special patience and intelligence and He knew that I needed more than usual governance."

"Do I see yet that streak of Irish blarney that cavorts through your veins?"

"Perhaps, a bit." I laughed. We rode further and I continued,

" I had trouble, however, defining why I should be similarly singled out for such long life. I concluded that God gave me a very late start and to make up for that, He left me around an extra score or two. With further consideration, I think that God meant for me to understand, by observation, something of His plan for humankind. When I was younger, I spoke with the liberation of ignorance about 'God's will' and 'working out God's purpose.' Now, in my old age, I can look over the several formats within my life and see a pattern. Today, I spoke about the moments of history which I did not seek, but found myself a catalyst in, and they connect. As a doctor, I pursued an inquisitive interest, and when special tragedies affected the lives of three of our children, I had the best available knowledge to be able to deal with them. I was called by God to the ministry, and I was able to guide two congregations for nearly 60 years and be an organizer in the administration of my denomination. I believed that I knew the will and way of God and I could find my proof in Biblical text, but God showed me that His ways were not always my ways. God burst forth, right in front of me, with a most unexpected voice and moved the hearts of poor people whom the church was leaving out. I was a natural teacher and I have seen several generations of my boys, exposed to learning before me, become instruments of leadership in ministry, law, medicine and government. Near the end, I am given one final young man to mold so that I can nourish one last bloom with a special touch. I see God's will as the exercise of the human spirit within the nurture of the Holy Spirit. I'm just stubborn enough to think that God did not leave me around just long enough to get it wrong."

The day came in late January 1815, when a dusty rider galloped into our yard and John Morehead burst in our front door, something he had never done, screaming, "He won! He won! Andy Jackson beat 'em at New Orleans!" The rider it turned out was Alexander Strong Martin, the late Governor's son, and he strode in moments later to confirm that Andrew Jackson had indeed defeated the British at the Battle of New Orleans. "It is victory for sure," he proclaimed. Some people might say there was some irony here, but you know, irony can be lost on young people. Rachel smiled at me. We rejoiced. As we celebrated the victory, we remembered a lanky young lawyer ready to go west to make a name for himself. When we hugged the young rider, we remembered an eager politician, who confessed that his near neighbor was going to have his baby and his mama was having trouble adjusting to it.

For the four years that he was my student, John Motley Morehead would go home after each semester and tutor his younger brother, James Turner, and his five sisters in the subjects that he had just completed. His sly old daddy, Scotsman that he was, got the education of seven for the price of one.

I believed that I had done the boy all that I could and that he should finish his education at the university. His father was reluctant as the University of North Carolina had a good reputation for learning, but a poor reputation for discipline. I was perfectly confidant that the boy was too mature to be caught up in youthful pranks and was serious about his education. He was examined in reading, spelling, Webster's Grammar, Arithmetic to the Rule of Three, Latin Grammar, Aesop's Fables, and Eutropius, Erasmus, Selectae de Profanis and Vocables, Caesar, Latin Introduction, Sallust, Ovid and Virgil's Eclogues, French grammar, French Fables, Telemachus, Gil Blas, Voltaire and Racine, and credited with sufficient preparatory work.

Then he was examined on Virgil, Latin Introduction, Greek Testament, Dialogues of Lucian, and the Odes of Horace, to be credited with his Freshmen year. He was further examined in Cicero, Geography, Arithmetic, Webster's Grammar, Syntax and Lowth's Grammar, the Satires, Epistles and Horace's Art of Poetry for credit for his Sophomore year. Finally, he was examined on Ewing's Synopsis, Algebra and Ferguson's Astronomy, Euclid, Trigonometry, Heights and Distances, Navigation and Logarithms. so that he was accepted into the Junior Class.

On the day he left for the university, the boy came early enough to join me on my walk. He was profuse in his appreciation for the efforts that I had made to instruct him. I told him how proud Rachel and I were at his impressive results in the entrance examinations. Of course, I gave him some advice about the snares of youth. At the mill, we went inside and watched the wheels turn and the flour being ground. As we stared at the lumbering, inexorable grind of the stones together, there was a natural analogy not lost on either of us. At the end of the walk, we went inside and Rachel had breakfast waiting. She hugged the boy repeatedly, stroked his head, and generally fussed over him unashamedly. Finally, he mounted his horse and just as he turned, I said, "do ya steal hav' a hunger fur readin' lad?"

"I'm starved," he responded and went on his way.

Postscript

Reverend David Caldwell died August 25, 1824 at his home. Rachel Craighead Caldwell died June 3, 1825. They were buried side by side in Buffalo Presbyterian Churchyard, immediately behind the sanctuary. Reminiscent of their Scottish ancestry, a rock wall later enclosed their graves and those of other members of the family.

They survived their three "unfortunate children" so Caldwell's will charged son David with the care of Martha "Patsy." John Washington and Robert Craighead Caldwell were directed to care for James Edmund and Rev. Alexander Caldwell. David Caldwell left $4,000 to be divided among David, John and Robert for caring for their siblings. Patsy lived only until January 27, 1826. James Edmund lived until 1836, and Rev. Alexander Caldwell lived until October 2, 1841. All of these are believed buried at Buffalo with their parents, although the graves of Patsy and Edmund are not marked, or their stones have been lost.

Of the children, Samuel Craighead and Alexander became ministers and are dealt with in the novel. Andrew also became a minister and teacher. One of the twins, David, became a doctor and took over his father's medical practice. The other twin, Thomas, became a merchant and businessman in Greensboro and Clerk of the Superior Court of Guilford County. John Washington succeeded his father at the Academy beginning in 1807 and later served in the North Carolina Senate. Robert C., the youngest, was left the home house and meadow. He later moved the home house and built another home on the original site for himself.

The Academy does not seem to have survived long after the death of Rev. Caldwell. During its existence of about fifty years, the format shifted focus as times demanded, but it was always preparing students for more advanced education and toward learned professions. Primarily it produced ministers, mostly for the Presbyterian Church. Many future lawyers matriculated, including Governors Isreal Pickens, John Murphy, and Gabriel Moore of Alabama; Governor Newton Cannon of Tennessee; Governor John Motley Morehead of North Carolina. Under Caldwell and his son, David, many were prepared as doctors.

No list of the academy students has survived but a partial list has been reconstructed with the help of Gary N. Brown:

STUDENT LIST
David Caldwell Academy 1765-1820

ANDERSON, Isaac (H) (J)

ANDERSON, John,(1768-1840) Doctor of Divinity, son of William and Anne Denny Anderson. (B) (E) (H) (J) (O)

BALCH, Hezekiah, Minister (H) (J)

BALCH, Stephen B. (H) (J)

BARR, David Minister (H) (J) (O)

BORROWS, William (H) (J)

BROWN, Duncan DD Minister in TN. (C) (H) (J)

BROWN, John (H) (J)

BROWN, Matthew (H) (J)

BROWN, William (H) (J)

CALDWELL Alexander (1769-1841) Son of David Caldwell, Minister (H) (J)

CALDWELL, Andrew (1771-1845) Son of David Caldwell, Minister, Princeton 1794 (H) (J)

CALDWELL, David (1777-1857) Son of David Caldwell. Doctor

CALDWELL, James Edmund (1772-1836) Son of David and Rachel Craighead Caldwell. Injured head as a youth and considered insane.

CALDWELL, John Washington (1780-1844) Son of David and Rachel Craighead Caldwell

CALDWELL, Martha (Patsy) (1775-1829) Daughter of David and Rachel Craighead Caldwell. Lost her mind about 1795.

CALDWELL, Robert Craighead (1786-1878) Son of David and Rachel Craighead Caldwell

CALDWELL, Samuel Son of Alexander Caldwell and nephew of David Caldwell

CALDWELL, Samuel Craighead (1767-1826) Son of David Caldwell. Presbyterian minister. (H) (J)

CALDWELL, Thomas (1777-1859) Son of David and Rachel Craighead Caldwell

CALDWELL Thomas Son of Alexander Caldwell and nephew of David Caldwell.(N)

CANNON, Newton grandson of Richard Thompson (Regulator), Governor of Tennessee (1835-1839) Son of James Cannon. (G) (H) (J) (O)

COALSTON, Henry (H) (J)

CRAIGHEAD, Samuel L. (H) (J)

CRAIGHEAD, Thomas B. Princeton 1775 (H) (J)

CUMMINS, Francis Minister, son of Francis Cummins (H) (J) (O)

CURRIE, Ezekiel C. Presbyterian minister Orange Presbytery (B)(C)(H)(J)

CUSICK, William (H) (J)

DICK, Thomas (H) (J)

DONNELL, George son of George Donnell (1759-), grandson of Thomas Donnell (1712-1795), in 1804 moved with family to Wilson County, TN, became renowned Cumberland Presbyterian minister. (O)

DONNELL, Samuel (1760-) son of Robert and Mary Donnell. Minister of

Spring Creek Presbyterian Church in TN.(H) (J) (O)

DONNELL, Thomas (1754-   ) Presbyterian minister, son of Robert Donnell, Sr.(H) (J)(O)

DONNELL, Thomas, son of Thomas Donnell (1712-1795), became a physician and located in Mecklenburg County, NC. (O)

DONNELL, Washington (F)

FLINN, Andrew (H) (J)

GILLESPIE, John, son of Daniel Gillespie, Orange Presbytery Licentiate, Presiding Professor of University of North Carolina (E) (H) (J) (K) (O)

GOOSE, Jacob (H) (J)

GORRELL, David, (1770-1848), son of Ralph Gorrell, Jr. Of Alamance Presbyterian (A)

HALL, Robert, brother of Rev. James Hall (B)

HATCHes, The brothers (H) (J)

HENDERSON, John Minister (H) (J)

HICKS, John (H) (J)

HODGE, William (1747/50-1819/20) Alamance County. Student ca 1780. Son of John and Agness Hodge. Protogee and student of Caldwell and McGready. Ordained Presbyterian minister 1792 in Orange Presbytery. Pastor at Hawfields and Cross Roads. Moved Sumner County TN in 1798. One of Six Wild men of the Cumberland. Part of Great Revival in West.
(H) (J)

HOOGAN, Rodeny (H) (J)

HUNTER, Charles (H) (J)

IRWIN, Alecxander (H) (J)

JACKSON, Andrew (Speculative student) Through John McNairy he certainly knew Caldwell and may have taken some classes but there is no record that either Caldwell or Caruthers claimed him as a student. President of the US.

JOYCE, Alexander (H) (J)

KROMEs, The brothers (H) (J)

MACAY, Spruce (ca1755-1808) Davidson County, son of James Macay. Student ca 1773 then graduate of Princeton in 1775. Lawyer, judge, law tutor of Andrew Jackson. (A) (B) (H) (J)

McADEN, John eldest son of Rev. Hugh McAden of Red House, Caswell County. He says he spent much of his youth at Caldwell's and was summoned home a few days before the death of his father on January 20, 1781.(C) (H) (J)

McADOO, Samuel Orange Presbytery Licentiate (E) (H) (J)

McADOO, William Moved to Logan County TN in 1800. One of Six Wild Men of Cumberland

McCORKLE, Samuel Eusebius Presbyterian Tyatira, Princeton 1772. Professor of Moral and Political Philosophy at University of North Carolina (B) (C) (H) (J) (K)

McCUISTON, Thomas (H) (J)

McGEE, John Student ca 1790. Brother of William McGee. Became Methodist preacher. One of Six Wild Men of the Cumberland.

McGEE, William (1768-1814) Student and colleague of James McGready ca 1790. One of the "Six Wild Men of the Cumberland" in the Great Revival of 1800 in the West. Brother of John McGee. (H) (J)

McGOWEN, James (H) (J)

McGREADY, James (1763-1817) Born Pennsylvania. Student from Guilford County ca 1778. . Son of James and Jean McGready. Presbyterian minister 1790. Moved West in 1796. One of the Six Wild Men of the Cumberland. Called "Son of Thunder", father of the Great Revival in West (D) (H) (J)

McMILLAN, Murdock Minister Orange Presbytery (C) (H) (J)

McMURRAY,Robert (H) (J)

McNAIR, Malcolm Minister, Orange Presbytery (C) (H) (J)

McNAIRY, John, (1762-1837) Guilford County, student ca 1778. Judge of Mero District, TN, friend and mentor of Andrew Jackson. (B) (O)

McREYNOLDS, Benjamin Student ca 1790 from Virginia. Roommate of Barton W. Stone (H) (J)

McWHORTER, George (H) (J)

MATTHEWS, John (1801-1848) DD Minister in New Albany IN. (C) (F) (H) (J)

MECKLIN, Hugh, Jr. Minister in Cumberland Presbyterian, son of Hugh Mecklin, married Agnes Anderson, daughter of William Anderson, Jr. (O)

MECKLIN, Robert minister, ordained Orange Presbytery in 1783, may have been another son of Hugh, Sr. (O)

MOORE, Gabriel (1785-1844) Stokes County, NC. Son of Matthew and Letitia Dalton Moore. Student ca 1800. Graduate University of North Carolina. Governor of Alabama 1829-1831, U. S Senator 1831-1836 (G) (H) (J)

MOREHEAD, James Turner Congressman (H) (J)

MOREHEAD, John Motley (1796-1866) Guilford County. Son of John and Obedience Motley Morehead. Student November, 1811 - Fall 1815 then went to the University of North Carolina. Governor of North Carolina 1840-1844. (H) (J)

MURPHEY, Archibald Dubow (1777?-1832) Born Caswell County son of Archibald and Jane DuBow Murphey. Student ca 1793 then entered University of North Carolina in 1796.Attorney, legislator, jurist.(A) (H) (J)

MURPHY, John (1785-1841) Born Robeson County NC son of Neil Murphy. Student . Governor of Alabama 1825-1829. (G) (H) (J)

MURPHY, Murdock Minister Orange Presbytery (C) (H) (J)

PAISLEY, Samuel Orange Presbytery Licentiate, minister (E) (H) (J)

PAISLEY, William Denny, Orange Presbytery Licentiate, minister (D) (H) (J)

PICKENS, Israel (1780-1827) Born Cabarras County son of Capt. Samuel and Jane Carringan Pickens. Student ca 1798 (speculative). Governor of Alabama 1821-1825, US Senator 1826. (G) (H) (J)

RANKIN Jesse (1802-1876) Minister (H) (J)

RANKIN, John 1796 moved to Sumner County, TN with McGees. One of Six Wild Men of the Cumberland. In 1801 he brought all the enthusiasm of the Revival back to North Carolina. In 1810 after conflict with Cumberland Presbytery he joined the Shakers. (M)

SHAW, Hugh Presbyterian minister Orange Presbytery (C) (H) (J)

SMYLE, James (H) (J)

SPRAGINS, Thomas L. (H) (J)

STEWART, James (H) (J)

STONE, Barton Warren (1772-1844) Born Port Tobacco, MD. Student from Pittsylvania County, VA ca 1790 - 1793. Son of John and Mary Warren Stone. Ordained Orange Presbytery 1796 and moved West. Founder of the Christian (Disciples) Church with Alexander Campbell. (H) (J)

THACKER, David Ordained 1779 (B)

THACKER, Daniel One of students who helped Caldwell discourage the Tories.

Van HOOK, Lloyd (H) (J)

WHITEFIELDs, The brothers, ministers (H) (J)

WIGGINS, Nathan (H) (J)

WILLIAMS, Lewis (B) (H) (J)

WILLIAMS, Robert (ca 1770-1836) Possible student. Rockingham County, NC. Territorial Governor of Mississippi Territory 1805-1809.

WILSON, Joseph (H) (J)

PROBABLE STUDENT LIST

DICK, John McClintock, son of James and Isabella (1768-1818) McClintock Dick. He became a judge. (O)

GILLESPIE, James Smiley Martinville, NC, son of John Gillespie, was Professor of Natural Philosophy at University of North Carolina (K)

LINDSEY, Harper Brown, (1806 -   ) Greensboro, Student at UNC 1822-25 (P)

LINDSEY, Robert Goodloe (1816 -   ) Greensboro, Student at UNC 1832-36 (P)

MARTIN, Alexander (1779 -   ) son of James Martin, Stokes County, student at UNC 1799 (P)

MARTIN, Alexander Strong (1787 -   ) Illegitimate son of Governor Alexander Martin.

MARTIN, Henry Alexander (1802-   ) Stokes County, son of James Martin, student UNC 1820 (P)

MARTIN, James Franklin Stokes County, student at UNC 1820, physician (P)

MARTIN, Joseph Stokes County, student at UNC 1813 (P)

MARTIN, Samuel Stokes County, student at UNC 1819 (P)

MARTIN, Samuel A. Stokes County, student at UNC 1801 (P)

McNAIRY, Boyd, Guilford County, student at UNC 1824-26 (P)

McNAIRY, Nathaniel A., Tennessee, student at UNC 1801 (P)

McNAIRY, Samuel A. Tennessee, student at UNC 1801 (P)

MEBANE, James (1774-1857) Orange County, student UNC 1795, NC House of Representatives and Senate (P)

MEBANE, John Briggs Greensboro, student UNC 1809, NC General Assembly (P)

MOORE, Benjamin Tyson Stokes County, student UNC 1823, physician (P)

MOORE, Gabriel Stokes County, nephew of Gov. Gabriel Moore of AL, student UNC 1822-25, NC General Assembly (P)

MOORE, Gideon E. Stokes County, nephew of Gov. Gabriel Moore of AL, student UNC 1822 (P)

MOORE, Matthew Redd Stokes County, brother of Gov. Gabriel Moore of AL, student at UNC 1815, NC Senate (P)

ROGERS, Alexander Martin Rockingham County, student UNC 1803 (P)

WILLIAMS, Alexander Surry County, student at UNC 1813, physician (P)

WILLIAMS, Robert Surry County, student at UNC 1809 (P)

WILLIAMS, Thomas Lanier (1786-1856) Surry County, student at UNC 1808-1812, General Assembly TN (P)

SOURCES:

(A) **Dictionary of North Carolina Biography**, William S. Powell, ed.
(B) Eli Caruthers, **Life of David Caldwell**
(C) Rev. William Henry Foote, **Sketches of North Carolina**
(D) Barton W. Stone
(E) Robert Hamlin Stone, **History of Orange Presbytery**
(F) Greensboro Historical Museum Archives
(G) Mark F. Miller study mid-1970s
(H) Mark Francis Miller, **David Caldwell: The Forming of the Southern Educator**

(J) Gary H. Brown

(K) Kemp P. Battle, **"History of University of North Carolina"**

(L) Charles C. Ware-**"Barton Warren Stone"** - Chapter 3

(M) Paul K. Conklin, **Cane Creek**

(N) Paul Conklin, **What Caldwell's Boys Did In the Cumberland**

(O) Rev. S. M. Rankin, **History of Buffalo Presbyterian**

(P) Student list for University of North Carolina

Caldwell-Craighead

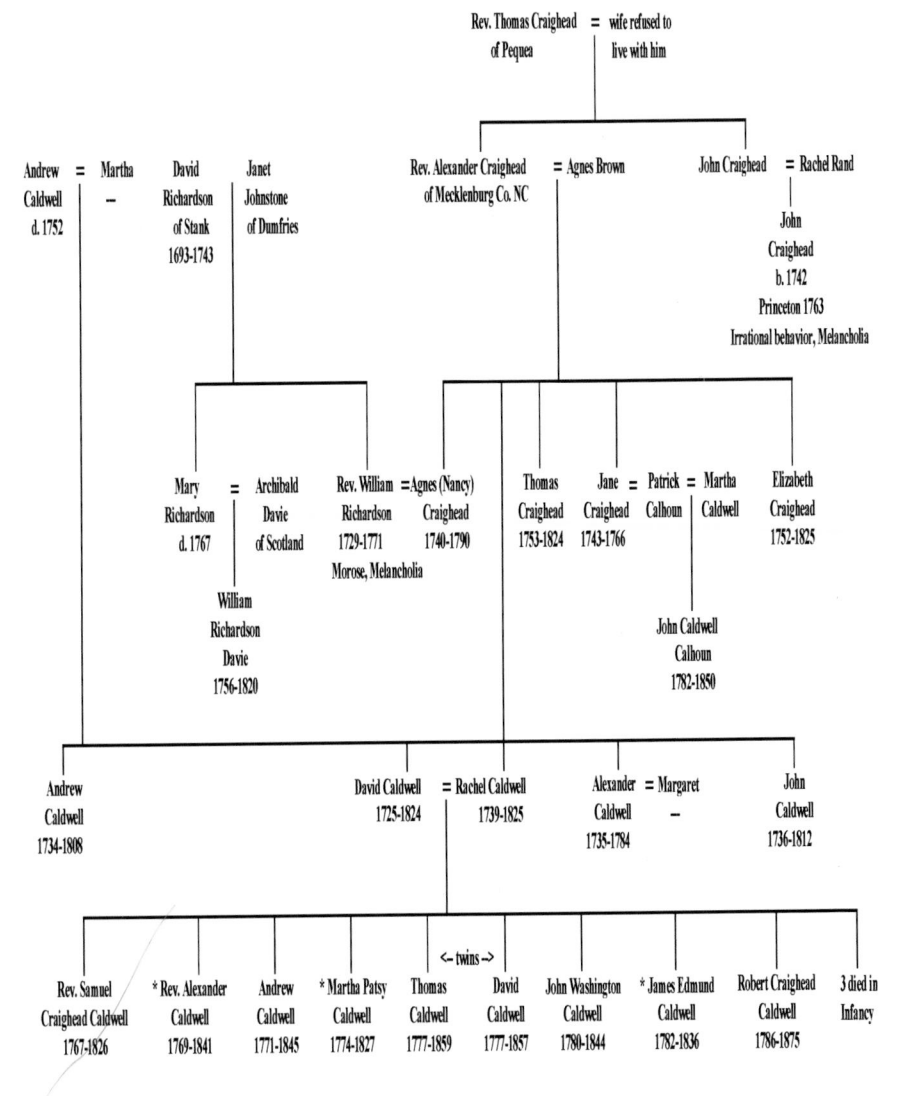

Rev. Thomas Craighead = wife refused to
of Pequea   live with him

Andrew = Martha   David   Janet   Rev. Alexander Craighead = Agnes Brown   John Craighead = Rachel Rand
Caldwell   –   Richardson   Johnstone   of Mecklenburg Co. NC
d. 1752   of Stank   of Dumfries   John
                1693-1743   Craighead
                                                            b. 1742
                                                         Princeton 1763
                                          Irrational behavior, Melancholia

Mary = Archibald   Rev. William = Agnes (Nancy)   Thomas   Jane = Patrick = Martha   Elizabeth
Richardson   Davie   Richardson   Craighead   Craighead   Craighead   Calhoun   Caldwell   Craighead
d. 1767   of Scotland   1729-1771   1740-1790   1753-1824   1743-1766   1752-1825
                          Morose, Melancholia

William
Richardson
Davie
1756-1820

John Caldwell
Calhoun
1782-1850

Andrew   David Caldwell = Rachel Caldwell   Alexander = Margaret   John
Caldwell   1725-1824   1739-1825   Caldwell   –   Caldwell
1734-1808   1735-1784   1736-1812

<- twins ->

Rev. Samuel   * Rev. Alexander   Andrew   * Martha Patsy   Thomas   David   John Washington   * James Edmund   Robert Craighead   3 died in
Craighead Caldwell   Caldwell   Caldwell   Caldwell   Caldwell   Caldwell   Caldwell   Caldwell   Caldwell   Infancy
1767-1826   1769-1841   1771-1845   1774-1827   1777-1859   1777-1857   1780-1844   1782-1836   1786-1875

* "my helpless children"

MELANCHOLIA
The CRAIGHEAD CONNECTION

Note: This chart is not based upon medical diagnosis but is constructed from a mixture of reports that have survived.

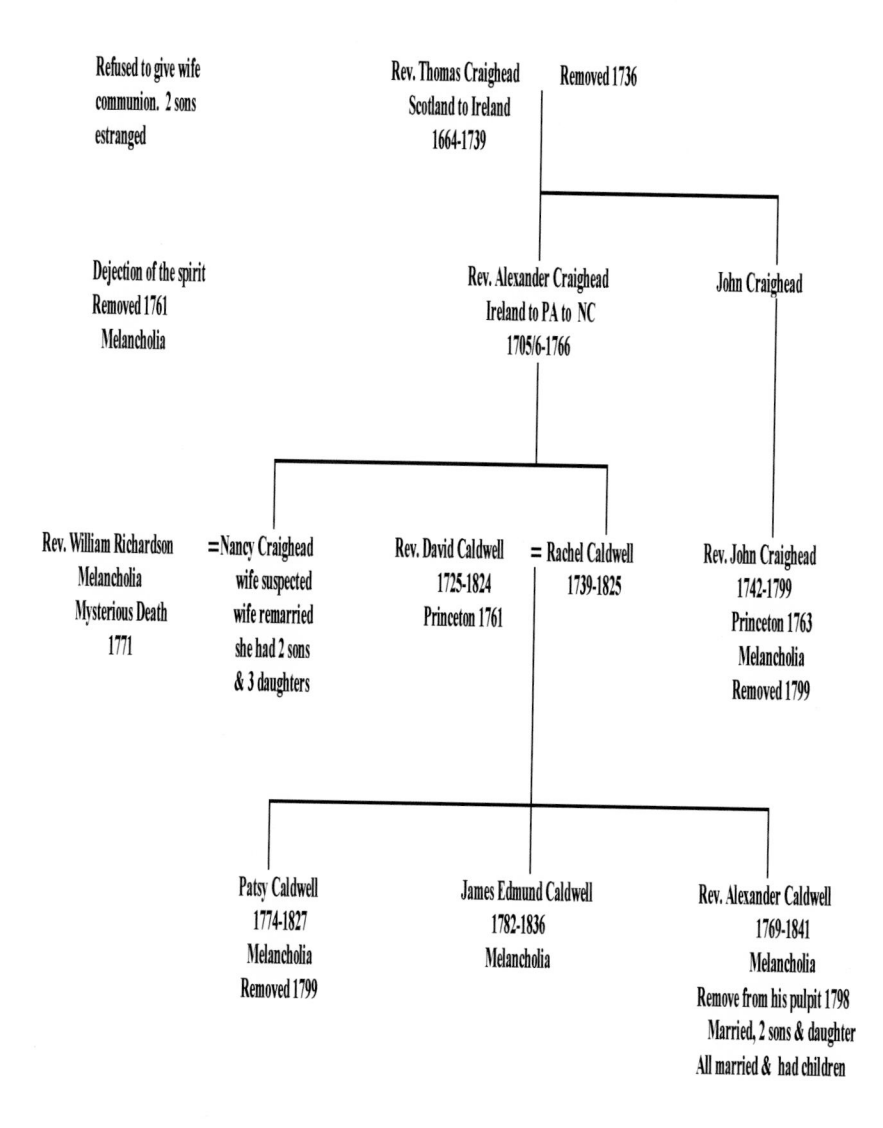

Refused to give wife
communion. 2 sons
estranged

Rev. Thomas Craighead
Scotland to Ireland
1664-1739

Removed 1736

Dejection of the spirit
Removed 1761
Melancholia

Rev. Alexander Craighead
Ireland to PA to NC
1705/6-1766

John Craighead

Rev. William Richardson
Melancholia
Mysterious Death
1771

=Nancy Craighead
wife suspected
wife remarried
she had 2 sons
& 3 daughters

Rev. David Caldwell
1725-1824
Princeton 1761

= Rachel Caldwell
1739-1825

Rev. John Craighead
1742-1799
Princeton 1763
Melancholia
Removed 1799

Patsy Caldwell
1774-1827
Melancholia
Removed 1799

James Edmund Caldwell
1782-1836
Melancholia

Rev. Alexander Caldwell
1769-1841
Melancholia
Remove from his pulpit 1798
Married, 2 sons & daughter
All married & had children

BIBLIOGRAPHY

MANUSCRIPT SOURCES

Chapel Hill, North Carolina
  University of North Carolina
  Southern Historical Collection
    David Caldwell Collection
    Calvin Wiley Collection

Durham, North Carolina
  Duke University Library
  Perkins Library
    Caldwell Collection

Greensboro, North Carolina
  Greensboro Historical Museum /Archives
    David Caldwell Papers
    Miller Supportive Documents (Site Research)
    Donnell Family Papers
    Gillespie Family Papers
    A. E. Weatherly Papers

Montreat, North Carolina
  PCUSA/South Archives

Philadelphia, Pennsylvania
  The Pennsylvania Historical Society

Princeton, New Jersey
  Princeton University
  Mudd Library
    David Caldwell Papers

Raleigh, North Carolina
  Office of Archives and History, Department of Cultural Resources
    Mecklenburg Co., Wills
    Mecklenburg County Estate Records.
    David Caldwell Collection

West Chester, Pennsylvania
  Chester County Archives
    Wills and Administrations

BOOKS AND ARTICLES

Aaron, Larry G. *The Race for the Dan, The Retreat that Rescued the American Revolution.*, Halifax, VA: Halifax Historical Society, 2003.

Addis, George, "The Blue Bills," Edinburgh, 2002

Agniel, Lucien, *The American Revolution in the South, 1780-1781*, Riverside, CN: The Chatham Press, 1972.

Allen, Dr. Roscoe J. And Anna Mae Allen (compilers), "Alamance Presbyterian Church Cemetery, Guilford County, NC," *The Guilford Genealogist,* vol. 4, no. 2, Spring 1977.

Arnett, Ethel Stephens, *Greensboro North Carolina, The County Seat of Guilford*, Chapel Hill: The University of North Carolina Press, 1955.

　　- *David Caldwell*, Greensboro:Media, Inc., 1976

Babits, Lawrence E. and Howard, Joshua B., *Long, Obstinate, and Bloody,* Chapel Hill: The University of North Carolina, 2009.

Baker, Thomas E., *Another Such Victory,* New York, Eastern Acorn Press, 1981.

Baroody, John C. *Archaeological Investigations at the Site of David Caldwell's Log College,* 1980.

Battle, Kemp P. *History of the University of North Carolina, 1789-1868,* Raleigh: Edwards & Broughton, 1907.

Bell, Whitfield J. Jr., *The Colonial Physician and Other Essays,* New York: Science History Publications, 1975.

Best, J. A. "The Adoption of the Federal Constitution by North Carolina from Historical Papers," Trinity: Historical Society of Trinity College, 1905

Binger, Carl, *Revolutionary Doctor, Benjamin Rush, 1746-1813,* New York: W. W. Norton & Company, 1966.

Boles, H. Lee., *Biographical Sketches of Gospel Preachers,* (Barton Warren Stones), 1932.

Boles, John B. *The Great Revival 1787-1805, The Origins of the Southern Evangelical Mind,* The University Press of Kentucky, 1972.

Booraem, Hendrick, *Young Hickory, The Making of Andrew Jackson,* Dallas: Taylor Trade Publishing, 2001.

Bowen, Catherine Drinker, *Miracle at Philadelphia,* Boston: Little, Brown and Company 1966.

Brodsky, Alyn, *Benjamin Rush, Patriot and Physician,* New York: Truman Talley Books, 2004.

Brown, Gary N. *"Dedication Address,"* David Caldwell Interpretive Center, 2007.

　　- "Participatory Archaeology at the site of the 'Log College'." David Caldwell Historic

Park, 2007.

Buchanan, John, *The Road to Guilford Courthouse, The American Revolution in the Carolinas,* New York: John Wiley & Sons, 1997.

Butler, Lindley S. *North Carolina and the Cdoming of the Revolution 1763-1776,* Raleigh: Department of Cultural Resources, 1976.

Caldwell, David A. *A Light in the Wilderness, Biography of Rev. David Caldwell (1725-1824),* San Jose, CA: DAC Press, 2002.

Caldwell, Finis Jay, *Dr. David Ca ldwell, An 18th Century Flame for Christ, 1725-1824,* Lubbock, TX., Mumbo   Jumbo Multimedia, 2008.

Calhoon, Robert M., *Religion and the American Revolution in North Carolina,* Raleigh: Department of Cultural Resources, 1976.

Caruthers, Rev. Eli W., *Sketches of the Life and Character of Rev. David Caldwell*
    - *The Old North State in 1776,* 2 vols. Greensboro: The Guilford County Genealogical Society, 1985.

Cavanagh, John C., *Decision at Fayetteville, The North Carolina Ratification Convention and General Assembly of 1789,* Raleigh: Division of Archives and History, 1989.

Cheney, John L., Jr., ed., *North Carolina Government 1585-1974,* Raleigh: North Carolina Department of the Secretary of State, 1975.

Coffin, Levi, *Reminiscences of Levi Coffin,* Cincinnati: Robert Clarke & Co, 1880.

Collier, Christopher, Collier, James Lincoln, *Decision in Philadelphia, The Constitutional Convention of 1787,*New York: Ballentine Books, 1986.

Concise Medical=Booklet, for People and Animals, Containing CXXVIII. Selected Recipes, with a prognostication Table, Vienna, 1791.

Conkin, Paul K. *Cane Ridge, America's Pentecost,* Madison, WI, The University of Wisconsin Press, 1990.
    - *What Caldwell's Boys Did in the Cumberland,* Nashville: Vanderbilt University, 1995.

Conner, R. D. W., *A Documentary History of the University of North Carolina 1770-1799,* 2 vols, Chapel Hill: The University of North Carolina Press, 1953

Coon, Charles L., *North Carolina Schools and Academies 1790-1840,* Raleigh: Edwards & Broughton, 1915.

Corbitt, David Leroy, *The Formation of the North Carolina Counties 1663-1943,* Raleigh, State Department of Archives and History, 1950.

Craig, Burton, *The Federal Convention of 1787, North Carolina in the Great Crisis,* Richmond: Expert Graphics, 1987

"'Doctor' Lewis' Thunderclappers," *Smithsonian Magazine*, June 2004. Donnell,
Raymond Dudau, (Compiled by) *Buffalo Presbyterian Church and* Cemetery,
Greensboro, North Carolina, Greensboro: Guilford County Genealogical Society, 1994.

Duncan, Louise C., *Medical Men in the American Revolution 1775-1783,* Carlisle Barracks, PA:
Army Medical Field Service, 1931.

Edgar, Walter, *Partisan & Redcoats, The Southern Conflict That Turned the Tide of the American
Revolution,* New York: Harper Collins Publisher, 2003.

Elliot, Jonathan, *The Debates in the Several State Conventions of the Adoption of the Federal
Constitution as Recommended by the General Convention at Philadelphia in 1787,*
Philadelphia: J. B. Lippincott & Co., 1863, volume 1.

Fischer, David Hackett, *Albion's Seed, Four British Folkways in America,* New York: Oxford
University Press, 1989.

Fisher, Sydney G., *The Quaker Colonies,* New Haven: Yale University Press, 1919.

Foote, Rev. William Henry, *Sketches of North Carolina,* Dudley, Harold James, ed., New York:
Robert Carter, 1846, 1965 revision

Ford, Henry Jones, *The Scotch-Irish in America*

Fries, Adelaide L., ed., *Records of the Moravians in North Carolina,* 12 vol., Raleigh: State
Department of Archives and History.

Ganyard, Robert L., *The Emergence of North Carolina's Revolutionary Government,* Raleigh:
Department of Cultural Resources, 1978.

Gilpatrick, Delbert Harold, *Jeffersonian Democracy in North Carolina 1789-1816,* New York:
Octagon Books, Inc., 1967.

Glasgow, W. M.,ed, . , *Renewal of the Covenants, National & Solemn League; A Confession of
Sins; An Engagement to Duties; and a Testimony, Octorara, PA, 1743,* Beaver Falls,
PA, 1895.

Guilford Courthouse, *Administrative History,* Greensboro, Guilford National Battleground Park,
2003.

Hairr, John, *Guilford Courthouse, Nathanael Greene's Victory in Defeat, March 15, 1781.*Da
Capo Press, 2002.

Hatch, Charles, Jr., *Guilford Courthouse National Military Park, Guilford Courthouse and its
Environs,* Greensboro: Greensboro Public Library, 1970.

Hawke, David Freeman, *Benjamin Rush, Revolutionary Gadfly* ,Indianapolis: The Bobbs-Merrill
Company, 1977.

Headspeth, W. Carroll & Compton, Spurgeon, *The Race to the Dan,* South Boston, VA, South

Boston News, 1974.

Henderson, Archibald, *Washington's Southern Tour 1791,* Boston: Houghton Mifflin Company
1923.

- *The Conquest of the Old Southwest,* New York: The Century Company, 1920.

Hicks, George W. *Colonial Wars and the Southern Frontier, Defining a New People,* Baltimore:
Publish American, 2003.

Hill, Jane Smith (transcribed by), *Guilford County, North Carolina Court Minutes, August Term of
Court 1781 to May Term 1788,* Greensboro: The Guilford County Genealogical Society,
1999.

Hooker, Richard J., ed., *Charles Woodmason, The Carolina Backcountry on the Eve o9f
Revolution,* Chapel Hill: The University of North Carolina Press, 1953.

Hoyt, William Henry, *The Mecklenburg Declaration of Independence,* New York: Da Capo Press,
1972.

Hughes, Fred, *Guilford County, NC, a Map Supplement,* Jamestown, NC: The Custom House,
1988.

James, Marquis, *Andrew Jackson, The Border Captain,* Indianapolis: Bobbs Merrill, 1933.

Johnson, Guion Griffis, *Anti-Bellum North Carolina, A Social History,* Chapel Hill: The University
of North Carolina Press, 1937

Kennedy, Billy, *The Scotch-Irish in the Carolinas,* Belfast: Causeway Press, 1999.

Konkle, Burton Alva, *John Motley Morehead and the Development of North Carolina 1796-1866,*
Philadelphia: William J. Campbell, 1922.

Lambert, Paul F., "Benjamin Rush and American Independence," Pennsylvania History, volume
XXXIX, no. 4, October 1972.

Lee, Tommy, "Presbyterians and Revivalism, The New Side/Old Side Division which Lasted from
1741 until 1758," *Theologia,* 1997.

Lee, Wayne E., *Crowds and Soldiers in Revolutionary North Carolina, The Culture of Violence in
Riot and War, Gainsville: University Press of Florida, 2001.*

Lefler, Hugh Talmage, Newsome, Albert Ray, *The History of a Southern State - North Carolina,*
Chapel Hill: The University of North Carolina Press, 1954.

Leyburn, James G., *The Scotch-Irish, A Social History,* Chapel Hill, The University of North
Carolina Press, 1962.

Long, Kimberly Bracken, "The Communion Sermons of James McGreedy: Sacramental Theology
and Scots-Irish Piety on the Kentucky Frontier," *The Journal Of Presbyterian History,*
volume 80, number 1, Spring 2002.

Madison, James (reported by), *Notes on Debates in the Federal Constitution of 1787,*New York: W. W. Norton & Company, 1987.

Massengill, Stephen E., *North Carolina Votes on the Constitution*, Raleigh: Division of Archives and History, 1988.

Masterson, William H., *William Blount,* New York: Greenwood Press.

McLachlin, James, *Princetonians 1748-1768*, Princeton: Princeton University Press, 1976.

McClellan, James & Bradford, M. E., eds., *Elliot's Debates, Debates in the Federal Convention of 1787, vol. 3, Richmond: James River Press, 1989.*

Meyer, Duane, *The Highland Scots of North Carolina, 1752-1776,* Chapel Hill: The University Press of North   Carolina, 1957.

Morris, Richard B., *The Forging of the Union 1781-1789,* New York: Harper & Row, 1987.

Murray, Rev. E. C., *A History of Alamance Church 1762-1918,* Greensboro: private printing, 1918.

Newlin, Algie I. *The Battle of New Garden*, Greensboro, The North Carolina Friends Historical Society, 1977.

North, Robert L. "Benjamin Rush, MD: Assassin or Beloved Healer," *Baylor University Medical Center Proceedings, Dallas, TX, 200.*

O'Kelly, Patrick, *Nothing but Blood and Slaughter, The Revolutionary War in the Carolinas,* volume three, 178, Blue House Tavern Press, 2005.

Paine, Thomas, *Common Sense and Other Writings,* New York: The Modern Library 2003, Gordon S. Wood, ed.

Pancake, John S., *This Destructive War, The British Campaign in the Carolinas, 1780-1782,* Tuscaloosa: University of Alabama Press, 2003.

"Pedigree of Alexander Craighead 1705/6-1766," http://www.concentric.net/~pvb/GEN/ac.html.

Phillips, Kevin, *The Cousins' War, Religion, Politics, & the Triumph of Anglo-America,* New York: Basic Books, 1999.*

Pilcher, George William, *Samuel Davies, Apostle of Dissent in Colonial Virginia*, Knoxville: Tennessee Press, 1971.

Poe, Clarence H., "Indians, Slaves, and Tories: Our 18th Century Legislation Regarding Them." *The North Carolina Booklet,* volume IX, No. 1, July 1909.

Poquette, Nancy, "History of the Guilford Militia: Winter 1781, *The Guilford Genealogist, Vol. 35, no 1, Issue 120, Spring 2008.*

Powell, J. H., *Bring Out Your Dead,* New York, Time Inc., 1949.

Powell, William S., Huhta, James K., Farnham, Thomas J., eds., *The Regulators in North Carolina*, Raleigh:State Department of Archives and History, 1971.

Presbyterian History Homepage, "Early American Presbyterians, C,"
http://mal.net/EarlyPresbyterians/presbioc.htm.

Preyer, Norris W., *Hezekiah Alexander and the Revolution in the Backcountry,* Charlotte: Heritage
Printers, 1997.

Ramsey, Robert W., *Carolina Cradle, Settlement of the Northwest Carolina Frontier, 1747-1762,*
Chapel Hill: University of North Carolina Press, 1964.

Rankin, Hugh F., *Greene and Cornwallis: The Campaign in the Carolinas,* Raleigh: Department of
Cultural Resources, 1976.

Rankin, Rev. S. M., *History of Buffalo Presbyterian Church and Her People Greensboro, N. C.,*
Greensboro: Joseph J. Stone & Co.

Ray, Worth S., *The Mecklenburg Signers and Their Neighbors,* Baltimore: Genealogical Publishing
Company, 1966.

Reiss, Oscar, *Medicine and the American Revolution,* West Jefferson: McFarland Publishing, 1998.

Remini, Robert V. *Andrew Jackson and the Course of American Empire, 1767-1821,* New York:
Harper and Row, 1977.

Robinson, Blackwell P. & Stoesen, Alexander R., *The History of Guilford County, North Carolina,
U.S.A.to 1980,* Greensboro: The Guilford County Bicentennial Commission, 1971.

Rodenbough, Charles D., *Governor Alexander Martin, Biography of a North Carolina
Revolutionary War Statesman,,* West Jefferson, NC, McFarland Publishing, 2004.
"James Hunter Remembers Andy Jackson," *The Guilford Genealogist, vol. 35, no. 4,
Womter 2008, issue no. 123.*

Rossiter, Clinton, *1787 The Grand Convention,* New York: The McMillan Company, 1966.

Russell, Phillips, *North Carolina in the Revolutionary War,* Charlotte: Heritage Printers, 1965.

Salley, A. S., Jr., "The Mecklenburg Declaration of Independence," *The North Carolina Booklet,
volume VIII, no. 3, January 1909.*

Simpson, Donald R. "Pennsylvania Records of Some Early Guilford Settlers," *The Guilford
Genealogist,* vol. 26, no 1, Winter 1999, Issue no. 84.

Smith, Charles Lee, "Schools and Education in Colonial Times," *The North Carolina Booklet,
volume VIII, no. 4, April 1909.*

Smylie, James H. *"American Presbyterians: A Pictorial History," Journal of Presbyterian History,*
Volume 63, Numbers 1 & 2, Summer/Spring 1985.
- Ed., "Presbyterians and the American Revolution, A Documentary Account," *Journal
of Presbyterian History, volume 52, Number 4, Winter 1974.*
- Ed., "Presbyterian and the American Revolution, An Interpretive Account," *Journal of*

Presbyterian History, volume 54, number 1, Spring 1976.

Sosin, Jack M. *The Revolutionary Frontier, 1763-1783,* New York: Holt, Rinehart and Winston, 1967.

Stevenson, David, *Scottish Covenanters & Irish Confederates,* Belfast: Ulster Historical Foundation, 2003 reprint.

Stockard, Sallie W., *The History of Guilford County, North Carolina,* Greensboro: The Gui8lford County Genealogical Society, 1983.

Stone, Robert Hamlin, *A History of Orange Presbytery 1770-1970;* Heritage Press, 1970

Thane, Elswyth, *The Fighting Quaker: Nathanael Greene,* New York: Hawthorn Books, 1972

The Debates on the Constitution, two parts, New York: Library of Americas, 1993.

"The Scottish Covenanting Struggle, Alexander Craighead, and the Mecklenburg Declaration," http://members.aol.com/letterman2/craig.html.

Thompson, Ernest Trice, *Presbyterians in the South, 1607-1861,* 3 vols., Richmond: John Knox Press, 1963.

Thompson, Ruth F. and Hartgrove, Louise J. (Compiled by), *Abstracts of Marriage Bonds and Additional Data Guilford County, North Carolina 1771-1840,* Greensboro: The Guilford County Genealogical *Society, 2001.*

Troxler, Carole Watterson, *The Loyalists Experience in North Carolina,* Raleigh: Department of Cultural Resources, 1976.

Turner, Herbert Snipes, *Church in the Old Fields, Chapel Hill: The University of North Carolina Press, 1962.*

     - The Dreamer, Archibald DeBow Murphey, 1777-1832, Verona, VA: McClure Press, 1971.

Van Doren, Carl, *The Great Rehearsal,* New York: The Viking Press, 1948

Wagstaff, H. M. "States Rights in North Carolina through Half a Century.," *The North Carolina Booklet,* vol. IX, no. 2, October 1909.

Wenster, Irene, B., (compiled by) *Guilford County, North Carolina Will Abstracts, 1771-1843,* privately printed, 1979.

Wertenbaker, Thomas Jefferson, *Princeton 1746-1896,* Princeton: Princeton University Press, 1946.

Westerkamp, Marilyn, "Division, Dissension, and Compromise: The Presbyterian Church During the Great Awakening," The Journal of Presbyterian History, Spring 2002.

Wheeler, John H. *Reminiscences and Memories of North Carolina and Eminent North Carolinians,* Baltimore: Genealogical Publishing, 1966..

Witherspoon, Rev. John, *The Works of John Witherspoon,* 9 vol., Edinburgh, 1804

Yates, Robert, *Secret Proceedings and Debates of the Convention Assembled at Philadelphia, in the Year 1787,* Albany, 1821, Bicentennial Edition, 1987